TOO HEAVY A LOAD

ALSO BY DEBORAH GRAY WHITE

Ar'n't I a Woman?
Female Slaves in the Plantation South

Let My People Go
African Americans 1804–1860

TOO HEAVY
A LOAD

Black Women in Defense of Themselves

1894–1994

DEBORAH GRAY WHITE

W. W. Norton & Company   New York | London

For information about permission to reproduce selections from this book,
write to Permissions, W. W. Norton & Company, Inc., 500 Fifth Avenue,
New York, NY 10110.

The text of this book is composed in Perpetua
with the display set in Chevalier Open
Desktop composition by Gina Webster
Manufacturing by the Maple-Vail Book Manufacturing Group
Book design by Chris Welch

Library of Congress Cataloging-in-Publication Data
White, Deborah G. (Deborah Gray), 1949–
Too heavy a load : Black women in defense of themselves, 1894–1994
/ by Deborah Gray White.
p. cm.
Includes bibliographical references (p.   ) and index.
ISBN 0-393-04667-2
1. Afro-American women—Civil rights—History—20th century.
2. Afro-American women—Societies and clubs—History—20th century.
3. Afro-American women—Social conditions. I. Title.
E185.86.W43875 1998
305.48'896073'006—dc21   98-6518
CIP

W. W. Norton & Company, Inc., 500 Fifth Avenue, New York, N.Y. 10110
http://www.wwnorton.com

W. W. Norton & Company Ltd., 10 Coptic Street, London CW1A 1PU

1 2 3 4 5 6 7 8 9 0

For
Maya Anneke
and
Asha Shani

CONTENTS

ILLUSTRATIONS

ACKNOWLEDGMENTS

This book took much longer to write than I thought it would. At times it was "too heavy a load." But like the women whose experiences unfold here, I learned a lot about perseverance.

I did not, however, persevere without help. I am deeply indebted to my friends and colleagues for the pressure they put on me to finish. As in the past Anne Firor Scott was a guiding light. She read several drafts, and her perfectionism and keen insight forced me to continually sharpen its focus and refine its thesis. Nancy Hewitt and Dorothy Sue Cobble also read drafts and offered valuable suggestions. Dorothy Sue Cobble and Alice Kessler-Harris helped me understand the relevant issues surrounding gender and labor organizing, and conversations with Linda Gordon and Guida West helped me with welfare issues. I also benefitted from the critical analysis of my Fall 1996 graduate class in African-American history. I thank Kirsten Brunkow, Sarah Buck, Dana Capell, Sara Dubow, Tiffany Gill, Baerbel Hafner, Justin Hart, Michael James, Daniel Katz,

Samantha Muccini, Khalil Muhammad, Amrita Myers, and Kay Tanaka.

Inspiration came from many others in the academic community. I am indebted to Mia Elisabeth Bay and Carolyn Anderson Brown for joining the Rutgers faculty just in time to give me emotional support; to Nell Irvin Painter for caring and for gloating only a little bit when she won our bet; to Lora Dee Garrison and Wesley Brown for being the family I chose; to Bonnie Smith for always having an encouraging word; to Evelyn Brooks Higginbotham for sharing; and to Darlene Clark Hine for her compassion and gentle nudging ("only 'one' book?").

People outside the academic community also kept me going during the long research and writing period. Charlene Griffin-Jordan, Delores Johnson, Ellen Leshe, and Joann Schram all treated this book as such a "fait accompli" that I could hardly let them down. Laura Fuerstein seemed to know the meaning of the book's title before I did. I am indebted to them all.

Hopefully I have succeeded in making this history of black women accessible to a lay audience. If I have even made it clear to academics, it is because of Ed Barber's black editorial pen, and because Jacqueline Brown-Harvest, Rita Butler Holliday, Cynthia Ann Lewis, Deborah C. Lyons, E. Sandy O'Reilly, Renee Ralph, Nancy Robertson, and Jean A. Williams, members of my book club, gave it a patient reading.

Support came from a variety of other sources as well. The assistance of archivists Esme Bahn, Susan McElrath, Anthony Toussaint, Donna M. Wells, and Daniel T. Williams was indispensable. So was the last minute help of graduate assistants, Khalil Muhammad and Yasmin Rahman. I also thank the American Association of University Women, the American Council of Learned Societies, and the Ford Foundation for the financial assistance they provided.

Introduction

✦

DIVIDED AGAINST MYSELF

In October 1991 I sat alone for days watching the Clarence Thomas Supreme Court confirmation hearings. The more I watched the more anxious I became. I opposed Thomas because of his positions on affirmative action and reproductive freedom. His description of his sister as a welfare queen seemed slanderous to me. No better were the Republicans, playing their cynical game on black people by replacing the renowned liberal jurist, Thurgood Marshall, with a mediocre conservative. Still, as much as I disapproved of Thomas, as the hearing progressed, I found myself in sympathy with him.

As the questions moved from his politics and professional qualifications to his sexual preferences, and charges of sexual harassment, there was, I realized, something very familiar about it all. Once again, a black person was being reduced to the sensual and the sexual. It had been that way since the beginning of American history. Slavery had been justified as a way to tame the savage, sexual nature of Africans, who, some thought, sank so low as to mate with orangutans.[1] The terms routinely used to describe black men and women—buck, wench, brute beast—supported the animalistic and sensual conception of blacks. These perceptions had historically been used by Europeans to dominate Africans and to separate them from whites. They justified the rape of black women by white men, the lynching of black men by white men and women, and the segregation and degradation of all black people.[2] These reflections made it hard to watch the Senate hearings.

Even more wrenching was the testimony of law professor Anita Hill, which led me to reflect on the black woman's history. As I watched this articulate woman speak forthrightly about Thomas's sexual harassment, I thought about the black woman's history of sexual exploitation by white and black men, the backbreaking toil that was considered too hard and dirty for white women, the stereotypes of promiscuity and impurity, and the emasculating images of Mammy and Sapphire. I saw Hill walking in the footsteps of women who had survived stereotypes, slavery, sharecropping, and domestic work; who had improved themselves and their communities, and generally triumphed against the odds. As proud as I was of Hill, who, like so many black women before her, had silently borne sexual assault and harassment, I was disturbed that her story unfolded only in the context of harassment in the workplace, and not in a way that revealed the black woman's historical fight against sexual exploitation and stereotypes.

My anxiety only deepened as I heard Hill vilified as a traitor to her race. I had originally sympathized with Thomas for the same reasons most black people did—the historic memory of white on black violence. Although I thought it outrageous when Thomas labeled the hearing a "high tech lynching," I understood that by evoking images of white justice meted out on the burning body of the black male, Thomas had elicited sympathy. This history black people knew. Hill's experiences had no such familiar context. Rather than evoke sympathy, Hill's testimony—and her support from white feminists and Senate Democrats—seemed to confirm the sentiment that black

women do not support black men, that they conspire with white men to defeat the black man and keep him down.[3]

Each time I confronted this attitude I became angrier, more tortured. The way the issues were put, the way the debate spun out, forced me to take sides against myself, to choose between my blackness and my womanhood. How could I side with one part of my identity without denying the other? How could I side with either Thomas or Hill when I deplored the position both were put in, when both their situations provoked thoughts of white privilege? And then another question began to gnaw at me. Where were black women's voices? Where were *my* advocates? Where were the people who were supposed to explain to the country who *I* was, to explain why *I* felt as I did, to deal with *my* conflicts? Why were they silent?

I had begun to think about black women's organized voices years before 1991, but the hearings crystallized the questions I wanted answered. Were there others who felt divided against themselves? Did black women who sided with Thomas have *any* empathy for Hill? Did income and status make a difference in determining how individual black women felt? If black women did come to Hill's defense would they say what I wanted said? Had black women in the past been so similarly excoriated, and, if so, had other black women come to their defense? When did white women start defending black women, and how far back did the animus between black men and black women go? Had black women ever organized in defense of themselves? Would they now?

The last question achieved a relatively quick answer when I was asked to sign and help pay for an advertisement in the *New York Times* on November 17, 1991. Under the banner "African American Women in Defense of Ourselves" several hundred African-American women deplored the seating of Thomas on the Supreme Court, and protested the racist and sexist treatment of Professor Anita Hill. The statement reminded Americans of the black woman's history of sexual exploitation and of the legal obstacles and accepted stereotypes that historically kept the black woman from combating her victim-

ization. It deplored Thomas's manipulation of the legacy of lynching to shelter himself from Hill's allegations, and it defined sexual harassment not as a race or gender issue, but as both. In noting that the seating of Thomas endangered the rights of all women, of the poor and working class, and of elderly people, African-American women showed how their concerns were linked to those of other groups. In stating "we cannot tolerate this type of dismissal of any one Black woman's experience or this attack upon our collective character without protest, outrage, and resistance," black women spoke for themselves. As a historian I certainly understood the last line of the statement was as close to historical truth as one could get: "No one will speak for us but ourselves."[4]

Indeed, in writing about black women's national association history this last line emerged as a basic truism, and it is presented here as an underlying theme of this book. Black women who signed the *New York Times* statement placed themselves within a long tradition, for in American history, black women have had few defenders as steadfast as themselves, whether in slavery, sharecropping, migration, urbanization, or civil rights. This book begins with the club organizing of the 1890s that led to the formation of the National Association of Colored Women, and ends with a black woman's conference held in 1994. In between it explores the history of five national black woman's organizations and shows how black women persistently spoke on their own behalf on issues of race leadership, negative stereotypes, woman's suffrage and woman's rights, and civil rights and civil liberties.

This book also demonstrates how hard that undertaking was, why it was often "too heavy a load." Had African-American women been perfectly united they would possibly have better fought their adversaries. However, black women were never a monolithic group. Race and gender united them as often as class, religion, sexuality, and ideology pitted them against each other. Black women's association history is, therefore, not a story of harmonious sisterhood, nor one about women selflessly sacrificing themselves for the good of the

group. It is about women with missions that varied and often clashed, about women who aimed for progress and unity, but who sometimes fell short, about women who sometimes found the job of representing and fighting for themselves burdensome.

It is also about women who found themselves caught in the middle of race and gender conflicts. At the turn of the century they stood excluded from white women's organizations and they were at odds with black men who, they felt, were not doing their duty to black women or to the race. By the end of the century another conflict arose—black women were caught in a widening conflict between feminism and black nationalism. During the century they charted a course that made sense to them but that proved how difficult it was to hold their race, gender, and class (and sometimes sexual) identity in workable balance when events pushed them to value one part of themselves over the other. Throughout the twentieth century black women were confronted with race, gender, and class issues that were sometimes in conflict, and were asked to pick a side. So it was with woman's suffrage, woman's leadership, black employment, black patriarchy. Black women weathered the storms created by these and other issues but not without injury to their organizations, and not without identity crises.

In balancing the different variables of their identity, certain approaches were consistently chosen by black women's national organizations. Seldom did African-American women organize across class lines. Poor, working-class, middle-class women all organized nationally but mostly within their own groups. Although it cannot be said that black women always chose race over other aspects of their identity, it can be said that race, *along with* gender and class were variables *always* factored into whatever national organizations did. Sometimes organizations functioned so that they served black women while they served the race. At other times, it was assumed that the race was served when black women were, or that class interests were met when race and gender issues were addressed. Although the century saw subtle and strong shifts in perspective,

always there was an attempt, sometimes conscious and sometimes unconscious, to put the variables in reasonable order so that no part of the black woman's identity was denied.

This book will chart the shifts and show how they affected organization members, relationships between women of different classes, between black men and women, and between black and white women. It is designed to demonstrate the changes in black women's thinking and outlook in the twentieth century. As such it is not a study of national organizations per se but the ideological bases for them. The organizations considered here—the National Association of Colored Women, the National Council of Negro Women, the Ladies Auxiliary of the Brotherhood of Sleeping Car Porters, the National Welfare Rights Organization, and the National Black Feminist Organization—provide a way of traveling through the twentieth century with African-American women.

TOO HEAVY A LOAD

❖

Chapter 1

❁

THE FIRST STEP
IN NATION-MAKING

That organization is the first step in nation-making, and that a nation can rise in the scale no higher than its womanhood, are principles which have come to be looked upon by sociologist and all students of the development of humanity as self-evident truth. . . .

—JOSEPHINE SILONE YATES

On a sticky hot night in 1916, Charleston's black women met at Mt. Zion A.M.E. Church to hear Mary Church Terrell speak on "The Modern Woman." As recalled by Mamie Garvin Fields, perspiration dripped from the women, and in the sweltering heat, their dresses clung to them. So many packed the sultry chapel that their hats touched and they were unable to move their pasteboard fans any further than a few inches from side to side without elbowing each other. It mattered little, for all were eager to hear what this preeminent educator and first president of the National Association of Colored Women had to say.

Terrell did not disappoint them. According to Fields, Terrell spoke not only about the modern woman, but in her pink evening dress and long white gloves, with her hair beautifully done, "she *was* that Modern Woman." Fields marveled at Terrell's graceful walk to the platform and the way she projected her voice out across the huge crowd. "We have our own lives to lead," she told them. "We are

MARY CHURCH TERRELL. *Photo courtesy of Photographs and Prints Division, Schomburg Center for Research in Black Culture, The New York Public Library, Astor, Lenox and Tilden Foundations.*

daughters, sisters, mothers, and wives. We must care for ourselves and rear our families, like all women." Going on, she spoke of the special mission of the educated black woman. "We have to do more than other women. Those of us fortunate enough to have education must share it with the less fortunate of our race. We must go into our communities and improve them; we must go out into the nation and change it. Above all, we must organize ourselves as Negro women and work together." Terrell went on to tell them about how representatives of different clubs had organized the National Association of Colored Women in 1896 when they met to formally protest

an insulting letter written by James Jacks, the white president of the
Missouri Press Association. She told them how Jacks had attempted
to silence the effective antilynching campaign of club leader Ida B.
Wells by labeling all black women prostitutes and thieves, and she
asked them to turn their numbers "to face that white man and call
him a liar." At the word "LIAR," Terrell's voice resonated so wonder-
fully that Fields all but felt it on her skin. In fact, everything Terrell
did that night made an indelible impression. As Terrell spoke, she
paced back and forth across the podium, extending her gloved hand,
so regal, intelligent, and powerful, that to Fields's mind, Terrell did
not walk, "she *strode.*" And when she asked them "and who were the
Negro women who knew how to carry their burden in the heat of
the day?" they sat riveted, without flicking a fan. By the time she fin-
ished heralding Harriet Tubman, Sojourner Truth, and so many other
women who had worked for the race, all in the audience were ready
to rise and follow in the footsteps of their great foremothers. Before
she ended, she asked, "WHO OF YOU KNOW HOW TO CARRY
YOUR BURDEN IN THE HEAT OF THE DAY?" Giving Fields, and
every woman present, a chance to ask themselves "Do I?" she
paused, and then said a quiet "Good evening."[1]

This speech, and many others delivered by Terrell and club leaders across the country, had the desired effect. Fields, a South Carolina teacher already active in community work, could hardly wait
until morning to get going. As she put it, "everywhere you might
look, there was something to do." She joined the Charleston City
Federation of Women's Clubs, and with twenty other women established the Modern Priscilla Club, which specialized in homemaking,
making clothes for the disadvantaged, and raising funds to support
the Wilkinson Home, a refuge for wayward black girls. With other
women, Fields worked tirelessly to get the city to fill a dangerous
ditch that more than one black child had died in. The Priscilla Club
surveyed the most impoverished black areas and urged the city to
erect new housing. With the outbreak of World War I they helped set
up a United Service Organization for black soldiers, and when the

war ended they worked with the NAACP, pushing city officials to hire black teachers in black schools.[2]

This was what Terrell had meant, what it meant to carry one's burden in the heat of the day. All over the country, especially in urban areas, black women took up their burdens. They were doing it before James Jacks's letter, but by tying the progress of the race to the morality of its women, Jacks's insulting letter ignited a new fire under them.[3] Race work became the means wherein black women could change their image, and from their point of view, the uplift of women was the means of uplifting the race. This was the call to arms of the National Association of Colored Women. As put by one of its most articulate members, Anna J. Cooper, it was time for action, a time for women, in particular, to step forth to "help shape, mold, and direct the thought" of their age, a time for organized female resistance.[4]

In short, the National Association of Colored Women became the black woman's primary vehicle for race leadership. Its members saw a set of interlocking problems involving race, gender, and poverty, no one of which could be dealt with independently. They believed that if they worked for the poor, they worked for black women, and if they worked for black women they worked for the race. Since, in their minds, "a race could rise no higher than its women," they felt that when they improved the condition of black women, they necessarily improved the condition of the race. When they spoke in defense of black women, they automatically spoke in defense of all black people. They talked about their work as "race work," and their problem as the "race problem." In their minds, though, the problems of the race revolved around the problems of its women.[5]

A STORY IN the *Richmond Daily Enquirer*, reported sixteen years before Terrell made her rousing Charleston speech, illustrates why this period in African-American history is known as the nadir. The story told of a twelve-year-old black boy who, in March 1890, narrowly escaped being lynched by a mob of white youths, none older than thirteen years. Richmond's newspapers, both black and white, lamented the sad state of affairs that had children attempting to lynch other children. But as the editor of the *Richmond Planet,* a black weekly, courageously noted, children learned by example, and as long as white adults did such dastardly deeds, their children would do the same. "Lynching," the editor concluded, "was demoralizing to young and old."[6]

No doubt the temper of the times prevented the *Richmond Planet* editor from being more critical, for his comment was surely an understatement. As the centerpiece in the South's post–Civil War reign of terror on black people, lynching and mob violence was more than demoralizing, it was the most savage and barbaric manifestation of white on black violence since slavery. Between 1880 and 1930 there were at least 2,018 separate incidents of lynching, in which some 2,362 African-American men, women, and children were murdered.[7] These lynchings often became ritualistic affairs, where victims were mutilated and burned at the stake in a carnival-like atmosphere. At the same time, the practice of whitecapping was spreading, wherein black landowners and sharecroppers were subjected to such prolonged intimidation and violence that they fled their land, making way for white tenants and owners.[8] Northern and Southern urban areas provided some refuge, but a series of riots— Wilmington, North Carolina, in 1898, Atlanta in 1906, Springfield, Illinois in 1908, Chicago and East St. Louis in 1919—saw white rioters, with the sanction and even assistance of law enforcement officials, beat blacks indiscriminately, destroy their businesses, and force them to leave their homes and abandon their possessions.

Unprosecuted white lawlessness was but one manifestation of the African American's loss of civil liberties. Everywhere one turned black rights were trampled. Laws regarding vagrancy, work contracts, and crop liens were written so that black people were kept either tied to the land in perpetual debt or in prison. State after state disfranchised blacks by use of poll taxes, literacy laws, property qualifications, and "grandfather clauses," which waived voting requirements for those whose fathers and grandfathers were qualified to vote in 1860 (thereby disqualifying most blacks from easy access to the polls). By 1880 blacks were separated on trains, in depots, and on wharves. After the Supreme Court declared the Civil Rights Act of 1875 unconstitutional in 1883, blacks were banned from public and private establishments, including hotels, restaurants, theaters, parks, and libraries. By 1885 most states required separate schools, and eleven years later, in its infamous *Plessy v. Ferguson* decision, the Supreme Court legalized Jim Crow, or racial separation, by declaring that states could use their police power to separate blacks from whites as long as facilities provided for the two races were equal.

Black people dealt with the assault by turning inward. Locked out of most arenas of American life, they accommodated racism by retreating to their own institutions. Before 1880 most black businesses catered to a white market. However, as racial exclusion forced black businesses out of the mainstream into a strictly African-American market, the number of black retail merchants, undertakers, bankers, newspaper owners, beauticians, and craftsmen increased. As blacks turned to use the products and services of their own businessmen they also made black institutions central to their social, economic, and political life. The church, in particular, thrived. Outside of the family, it was the means by which communities were organized, and the channel through which members received fellowship and status. For men especially, the church became the political arena where they vied for leadership and exercised dominance.

Mutual aid, beneficial, and fraternal societies were sometimes connected with churches, and with the spread of Jim Crow, they too increased in importance as centers of black social, political, and economic life. For example, the Odd Fellows, the largest of the black male secret orders, grew from some eighty-nine lodges and four thousand members in 1868 to over four hundred lodges and four hundred thousand members by 1904.[9] Like the Masons, the Order of the Eastern Star, and the Independent Order of Saint Luke, they offered members aid in times of illness, organized savings and burial associations, and became the vehicle whereby members gave help to the community's unemployed, orphaned, aged, or otherwise disabled.

The clubs of the National Association of Colored Women rose to prominence during this period of retrenchment. Well before any national organization existed, local groups had coalesced throughout the country. The Colored Women's League of Washington, D.C., was among the first of the clubs that would later form the NACW. Organized in 1892 by Mary Church Terrell, Anna Julia Cooper, and Mary Jane Patterson, the Colored Women's League called on a united black womanhood to solve the race's problems. The Women's League soon branched out into the South and as far west as Kansas City, Missouri. A few months after the founding of the League, the Woman's Loyal Union, under the leadership of journalist Victoria Matthews, brought together seventy women from Brooklyn and Manhattan in support of Wells's antilynching crusade. The New York-based Union formed sister clubs in Charleston, Memphis, and Philadelphia. Not long afterward, community activist Josephine Ruffin founded the New Era Club in Boston, which provided the prototype for similar clubs in other areas of New England. In Illinois, the Chicago Women's Club organized in late 1893 after Wells appealed to black women to support suffrage and fight lynching. Thereafter, the number of clubs multiplied so rapidly that by the time the National Association of Colored Women pulled them together it was hard to keep count.[10]

While some regional peculiarities existed, the guiding principle behind all the clubs was racial uplift through self-help.[11] Black clubwomen believed they could help solve the race's problems through intensive social service focused on improving home life and educating mothers. Some programs aimed at increasing the skills and intellectual ability of club members, while others sent members into local neighborhoods to assist poor blacks, particularly women and children. Most clubs did both.

The Colored Women's League of Washington, D.C., and the Tuskegee Woman's Club exemplified the spirit and work of black Woman's clubs. With seventy-four members in 1905, the Tuskegee club was larger than average. It was also exclusive. Only female faculty members of Tuskegee College or wives or other female relatives of male faculty could join. Activity went forward on many fronts. In 1905 members made thirty visits to the black men and boys in the town jail, taking food and clean clothing on each visit. In the poor section of town called Thompson's Quarters the club members conducted a Sunday school, ran picnics and parties for the children, assisted in paying the funeral expenses of one child, and helped find new homes for four children. The club sponsored public and private lectures on the virtue of temperance, and organized the senior girls at Tuskegee into a club that taught them the necessity of community service and the basics of how to do it. Younger girls at Tuskegee were likewise organized, and in 1905 they "adopted" an elderly woman, helped her buy a Christmas dinner and basic necessities. Throughout the year the clubwomen assisted a community worker by conducting cooking and sewing classes at the E. A. Russell Settlement House, which club members founded and supported. By 1913, when the Tuskegee club had 102 members it assumed responsibility for a night school that was initially established by Tuskegee College. The club also established a reading room for young boys. Although woman's suffrage fell outside the rubric of community service, Tuskegee women stayed abreast of national developments on the issue and made literature on the subject available to interested members.[12]

The Colored Woman's League of Washington did similar kinds of service work. In 1898 it founded a Kindergarten Normal Training Class for young women, as well as a free kindergarten for some of the capital's black youth. The club held regular sewing and mending classes for black girls, and held regular mothers' meetings for the mothers of the kindergarten children.[13]

In both North and South, mothers' clubs were among the most popular type of club to affiliate with the National Association. Both the Tuskegee Woman's Club and the Woman's League held mothers' meetings at which community women discussed and received instruction in all subjects relating to the care and upbringing of children. The definition of "mother's" responsibilities was wide ranging. The Tuskegee club taught women how to buy land and build houses. In Savannah, members of a mothers' club set up a community watch program. They wore badges so they could be recognized by police and community residents. The black clubwomen of Kingsville, Texas, were likewise organized, and were successful at closing down a gambling house they thought was bad for their neighborhood.[14]

Patrolling their communities, teaching children to read, improving homemaking skills—there were few things that black women's clubs did not do. Everywhere the Phyllis [sic] Wheatley Club of Buffalo, New York, turned they found a task. Early in the century the club forced the Buffalo police to focus on crimes of vice in Buffalo's black neighborhoods. Mary Talbert, a future president of the NACW, and her club were so demanding that Talbert was invited to join the city-wide committee that monitored police enforcement. Through her, the club lobbied for police protection in black neighborhoods. Along with other women's clubs in the city, it established girls' clubs where delicate subjects like personal hygiene and moral improvement were addressed. In the 1920s the Phyllis Wheatley Club helped form a junior YWCA and a Buffalo chapter of the National Association for the Advancement of Colored People. They donated books by black authors to the city's public library, conducted community seminars on the power of the black female vote, and organized political clubs to get the vote out. Like clubs in other parts of the country, Buffalo women regularly visited jails, established kindergartens, and supported homes for aged adults or wayward girls.[15]

Activities like those in Buffalo occurred all over the country.

Women's clubs that were part of the Texas Federation of Colored Women's Clubs bought land on which they erected parks and playgrounds. Similarly, the Woman's Musical and Literary Club in Springfield, Missouri, helped raise money for a hospital. The Semper Fidelis Club of Birmingham, Alabama, a literary society, gave out scholarships to local high-school students and donated money and clothing to the Old Folks and Orphan Home of the city.[16] While the Phyllis [sic] Wheatley Club of New Orleans established a nurse-training program and raised money to build a hospital, women in Vicksburg, Mississippi, bought a house and established it as a nursing home and orphanage. Following the example of their counterparts across the United States, black women in Indianapolis turned their club into a kind of employment agency, securing work for migrant black women in the canning factories of the city.

Helping rural black women establish themselves in urban areas had special significance for black women's clubs because so many members had made the lonely and dangerous migration themselves. Jane Edna Hunter, for example, was not prepared for the Northern brand of racism that she encountered when she reached Cleveland in 1905. Fresh from her nurse-training courses at Hampton Institute, she fully expected her skills to support her. She found, however, that unlike Southerners, who preferred blacks to take care of them, Northerners preferred white nurses. One doctor said as much to her face, advising her to go back to the South because "white doctors did not employ nigger nurses." Unable to secure work as a surgical nurse—her training—Hunter got work in private homes, but only after working at cleaning jobs in office buildings. Finding employment proved as hard as finding decent housing. When Hunter first arrived in Cleveland, she found a room in a boardinghouse that turned out to be a house of prostitution. She despaired as she fearfully walked "up one dingy street and down another." Alone in the city, Hunter had no place to turn. The YWCA residence accepted only white women, boardinghouses often charged extra for laundry, gas, and use of bathtubs, and their owners preferred male over female boarders. Middle-class black families did not rent to strangers, and most women, even those who were professionals, were compelled to stay in districts filled with gambling houses, dives, and brothels. Forced to settle for the least desirable room, where she paid what was for that time a considerable amount of money, Hunter found the loneliness of the city unbearable. At one point she went looking for peer companionship only to inadvertently find herself in a club that was a recruiting ground for prostitutes.

After this thoroughly alienating and frightening experience, Hunter resolved to remedy the housing problem confronting black women. Six years after arriving in Cleveland she met with seven other black women and together they discussed the indignity of living in boardinghouses where they had to turn lights out at 10 P.M., had no place to entertain friends, and had no access to kitchen facilities. With no social agency to provide or refer services to black women, they resolved that they alone had to initiate the change. After electing Hunter president of the new Working Girls' Home Association, they each pledged to raise a nickel per week and to gather as many new members as they could to increase their funds. From this inauspicious beginning came the Phillis Wheatley Association, a settlement house that provided rooms, recreation, and employment referrals to black women.[17]

Similar stories could be told of other homes founded by black women. Both the Harriet Tubman Club of Boston and the New Century Club in Providence, Rhode Island, founded homes for working women. In New York, in 1897, Victoria Earle Matthews became the guiding spirit of the White Rose Mission Home, and in Buffalo, New York, clubwomen helped found the Friendship Home for Girls. Like the Phillis Wheatley Association, these homes provided affordable housing, social activities, and employment referrals. Some offered educational courses. The Friendship Home, for instance, offered enrichment classes in first aid, sewing, music, and English.[18]

As the clubs, and the institutions that they built, grew, so did local federations and the national body they affiliated with. Local federations encouraged coordinated service work and allowed clubs to undertake projects too expensive for a single organization. For example, the Tuskegee Woman's Club had persistently lobbied state officials to provide separate facilities for juvenile delinquents to keep them from coming under the influence of hard-core adult criminals. It was not, however, until the better-financed Alabama State Federation of Colored Women's Clubs took matters into its own hands— by establishing the Mt. Meigs Reformatory for Juvenile Negro Law-Breakers, and later the Mt. Meigs Rescue Home for Girls— that the Tuskegee club's aims were achieved. While the Meigs Reformatory eventually became a state institution, Alabama clubwomen

THE MT. MEIGS INSTITUTE WAS ESTABLISHED BY THE ALABAMA STATE FEDERA-
TION OF COLORED WOMEN'S CLUBS. HERE THEY EXHIBIT CLOTHING AND
LINEN MADE BY THE GIRLS IN THE HOME. *Photo courtesy of the Library of Congress.*

CLUBS OF THE NACW ESTABLISHED NURSERIES LIKE THIS ONE IN NEWPORT, RHODE ISLAND. *Photo courtesy of the Library of Congress.*

assumed financial responsibility for the Rescue Home. Similarly, the thirty clubs that composed the Empire State (New York) Federation of Women's Clubs adopted the financially troubled White Rose Mission Home in 1924.[19]

As time passed, and more and more clubs affiliated with the National Association of Colored Women, the structure of the organization became more complex, and the projects undertaken or supported by clubs more sophisticated. In 1896 the NACW reported a membership of two hundred clubs. By the 1916 national convention there were fifteen hundred affiliates. Over this period, the NACW structure changed to meet women's varied interests. In 1901 the departments of organizational work included kindergartens, mothers' meetings, domestic science, rescue work, religion, and temper-

THE EXECUTIVE BOARD OF THE WOMAN'S LEAGUE OF NEWPORT, RHODE
ISLAND, SUPERVISED THE IMPLEMENTATION OF SEVERAL COMMUNITY SERVICE
PROJECTS. *Photo courtesy of the Library of Congress.*

THIS KINDERGARTEN CLASS AT TUSKEGEE INSTITUTE WAS TYPICAL OF THOSE
ESTABLISHED BY CLUBS OF THE NACW. *Photo courtesy of the Library of Congress.*

THE BUFFALO WOMAN'S CLUB. *Photo courtesy of the Library of Congress.*

ance. In 1904, five new departments were added, including art, literature, professional women, businesswomen, and social science. Business and the professions were combined into one department in 1908, the religion department was dissolved, and the departments of parliamentary law, forestry, and humane interest were added. Since the hands-on work of the NACW was done by local clubs, these departments helped the National Association of Colored Women define the needs, set the goals, and voice the concerns of black women. Coordinated activity also came through the process of city, state, and regional federations. By 1909, there were twenty state federations of black woman's clubs, including regional federations in the North, North Central, Northwest, and South.[20]

The philosophy of the black woman's clubs equalled in importance their specific projects. Philosophy, in fact, glued the disparate parts together and impelled the women to take action. Local clubs had, of course, functioned before 1896 and could do so after 1896, effectively carrying forward their community based self-help, racial uplift programs. The NACW, however, was established to say to the nation what black women were saying to their communities. What it said, the philosophy it expounded, was unprecedentedly "feminist" in that NACW leaders insisted that only black women could save the black race.[21] To NACW women, the national organization was not just another narrowly focused woman's organization, but as one of its early presidents, Josephine Silone Yates, claimed, it was "the first step in nationmaking."[22]

Yates's sentiment was echoed by other club leaders. According to Gertrude Culvert, a president of the Iowa State Federation of Colored Women's Clubs, "it is to the Afro-American women that the world looks for the solution of the race problem." The "first step has been the banding of ourselves together . . . putting our heads together, taking counsel of one another."[23] Culvert was joined by Fannie Williams of Chicago, and Virginia-born Addie Hunton. Williams, who belonged to both the white and black women's clubs in Chicago, was also the first black woman to serve on Chicago's Library Board. She believed that black women were showing the race the way to meet the challenges of the era. In Williams's words, "the Negro is learning that the things that our women are doing come first in the lessons of citizenship."[24] Hunton agreed. As the NACW national organizer from 1906 to 1910, she boasted that "the Negro woman has been the motive power in whatever has been accomplished by the race."[25]

At the heart of these feelings lay a sad loss of confidence in the ability of most black men to deal effectively with the race problem. Disfranchisement, Jim Crowism, lynching, and race riots seemed to be spreading unchecked. Clubwomen wanted something done, but black men had, as an editorial in the *Woman's Era* claimed, failed "to strengthen the belittling weaknesses which so hinder and retract us in the fight for existence." The editorial called for "timid men and ignorant men" to stand aside.[26] Indeed, Williams ridiculed male attempts to tackle the race problem when she quipped that the black male's "innumerable conventions, councils and conferences during the last twenty-five years have all begun with talk and ended with talk."[27] Similarly, Anna Cooper thought black men were more a part of the problem than the solution. She claimed that Southern black men, in particular, had sold their vote "for a mess of pottage," something the black woman would never do, being ever "orthodox on questions affecting the well-being of her race."[28]

If black men could make little headway against the race problem, leaders like Cooper believed that black women would prevail. In this they had plenty of support. Like late-nineteenth-century white male and female reformers, Association leaders endorsed the popular belief that women were more nurturing, moral, and altruistic. Women were better suited than men for social welfare work because man's nature was belligerent, aggressive, and selfish. Frances Ellen Watkins Harper, a mid-nineteenth-century black suffragist, frequently lectured clubwomen on their duty to the race, and the advantages of womanhood. She insisted that women had to be "the companions of man, must be a sharer in the social and moral development of the human race." Yet she criticized men for their "greed for gold" and "lust for power," for being destructive warmongers. Woman's work she deemed "grandly constructive." Harper proclaimed the latter part of the nineteenth century to be the "woman's era," a sentiment endorsed by one of the earliest black clubwomen, Josephine St. Pierre Ruffin. Founder of the Boston-based New Era Club, and later a founding member of the National Association of Colored Women, Ruffin published the first black woman's newspaper and appropriately titled it *Woman's Era*.[29] Anna Julia Cooper also saw possibilities for women in the period. In 1892, she claimed it was up to women to mold "the strength, the wit, the statesmanship, the morality, all the psychic force, the social and economic intercourse" of the era. It was the "colored woman's office to stamp weal or woe on the history of her people."[30]

Cooper's confidence in her ability to tackle race problems was nourished by her sense of equality with black men. Black women, like black men, had endured incredible hardships during slavery; neither sex had gained any advantage in the nearly two and a half centuries of enslavement. "In our development as a race," argued Fannie Williams, "the colored woman and the colored man started even." She continued:

> The man cannot say that he is better educated and has had a wider sphere, for they both began school at the same time. They have suffered the same misfortunes. The limitations put upon their ambitions have been identical. The colored man can scarcely say to his wife "I am better and stronger than you are," and from the present outlook, I do not think there is any danger of the man getting very far ahead.[31]

Cooper sounded a similar chord when she argued that gender equality grew from the denial of the franchise to the race. Cooper observed that neither black men nor women had the vote. The black man had been driven from the polls by repression, and the black woman had never been given the franchise. Cooper was dismayed but not discouraged by the harsh and exclusionary politics of late-nineteenth-century white America. She thought it might be God's way of preparing the race for something nobler than what white Americans had wrought. Like Williams, she evoked the image of a new and equal beginning for men and women, declaring that "the race is young and full of elasticity and hopefulness of youth, all its achievements are before it."[32]

For Williams, Cooper, and the many women who proclaimed the "woman's era," the fact that black men functioned in a wider arena than black women was clearly inconsequential. Racism severely limited the life chances of black men, but some black men voted, particularly those in the North, and a few held political positions. Black men also dominated the black church, and most, although not all business people, were male.[33] Of course, clubwomen could have

pointed to their steadier employment, a few very successful businesswomen, and a host of school founders and educators.

Yet women like Cooper and Williams did not add and then compare the things that black men and women were doing. Their bottom
line was the eradication of racism. The economic successes of individual black men, and/or the positions of power a few held in black
and white society, mattered less than the ineffectiveness of black
men as a group when it came to the race problem. If club leaders
considered anything it was the endurance of black women during
slavery, their belief in the more humane sensibilities of women, and
their acknowledgment of the debilities of black men in white society. For the women who proclaimed the "woman's era," the sum of
their equation was the superiority of women in matters concerning
the moral welfare of black people, and the equality of black men and
women in everything else.

This sense of real equality with black men made the black
woman's club movement different from its white counterpart of the
period. Some scholars have argued that, essentially, black clubwomen worked for their race, and white clubwomen worked primarily for improvement of the gender, and only occasionally for
their communities.[34] Yet, white women's clubs created makeshift
libraries, worked for better schools, and medical care of children,
lobbied for improved streetcars, sewage, and garbage collection.
They, too, argued that women brought a greater sense of humanity
to the public sphere than did men, and they established a national
organization—the General Federation of Women's Clubs—to coordinate their activities.[35] But because the context of black and white
women's efforts was different, so were the implications of their
respective movements, even when they pursued similar goals and
used similar rhetoric. At the end of the nineteenth century black
people were not only responding to the new industrial environment
but to racial repression as well. The period was remarkable for black
peonage, lynchings, disfranchisement, white primaries, race riots,
and a white supremacist ideology, which on the national level sup-

ported imperialistic expansionist policies. The race was under assault from all sides. Black men were especially challenged because disfranchisement was aimed at them, and they were, by and large, the direct victims of the convict lease system and lynch mobs. It was during what has been called the nadir in the black experience that black clubwomen, with full knowledge of the ravages being wrought, proclaimed the advent of the "woman's era," and came forth with a plan that made black women the primary leaders of the race, a plan based on the premise of equality between black men and women. Clearly their burden was different—indeed many times heavier than that borne by white women.

In their view, too, white women, like black men, were part of the problem. Having been denigrated as immoral, black clubwomen now insisted that their white counterparts accept them as equals. White women, they thought, could play a pivotal role in ending lynching and racism, and reversing its effects. Black membership in national women's organizations would give black women recognition of their role in national progress and an institutional voice in affairs regarding all women.[36] They were bitterly disappointed, therefore, when so many white women's groups endorsed the same malicious stereotypes as their men. When white women set themselves apart, they became part of the burden black women had to carry.

Although a few white organizations, most notably the National Council of Women, made an effort to include black women, most of the major women's associations, especially those anchored in the South or with a large Southern membership, were openly antiblack. Thus, the only way many black women, including Adella Hunt Logan, an Alabama clubwoman, got to attend conventions of the National American Woman Suffrage Association (NAWSA) was to pass for white. When black women were allowed to speak at conventions they repeatedly urged their white audiences to support black women. Michigan clubwoman Lottie Wilson Jackson asked the 1899 convention to publicly oppose the treatment of black women in Jim

Crow railway cars. In 1904, at the Washington, D.C., convention, Mary Church Terrell urged them to have the same concern for African Americans as they had for children and animals. Turning a deaf ear, NAWSA ignored these requests, and in 1903 it voted to fight for woman's suffrage, not so that all women could vote and use the ballot to express their individual and collective will, but as a "medium through which to retain supremacy of the white race over the African."[37]

The all-white General Federation of Women's Clubs (GFWC) and its state federations were similarly hostile. In 1900, for example, the newsletter of the GFWC carried a mean-spirited story that spoke to the perceived danger of integration. The story, entitled "The Rushing in of Fools," told of a wealthy do-gooder white woman who invited her similarly wealthy, well-bred, and almost-white neighbor to join her club. As their friendship grew so did the relationship between their children. The light-skinned black woman's son was an educated and cultured physician, and like his mother had only an "invisible drop" of black blood. With the consent of their parents, and in spite of the social taboo against interracial marriages, the two children wed and set up housekeeping in another town. About a year later the white clubwoman's daughter died a sudden death. According to the story, the daughter gave birth but when the baby was presented to her, and she saw that it was jet black, she died of shock.[38]

This offensive story was more than a warning against admitting black women into white women's clubs.[39] It was a slap in the face of the mostly mulatto leaders of the black women's club movement. It was a way of bringing the likes of Mary Church Terrell, Anna J. Cooper, Fannie Barrier Williams, Josephine Ruffin, and many more, down a notch or two. Indirectly, it spoke to Terrell and the many others who spoke two and three languages and were educated at the best schools in America and Europe. It told them that even though they were well traveled, could play musical instruments, and were accomplished journalists, lawyers, artists, and lecturers, the "invisible drop" of black blood that coursed through their veins would always be a mark of inferiority. It would always separate them from white women.

This message was apparent when Josephine Ruffin arrived at the GFWC fifth biennial convention in 1900. Ruffin was the lone black member of the New England Federation of Women's Clubs, but at this convention she was sent as a delegate of both the New England group and the New Era Club, a black club organized in Boston. When she arrived, turmoil erupted as the white women objected to seating a black woman. They realized too late that they had approved the application of the New Era Club without noting that it was a black club. To pacify the white delegates, some of whom threatened to resign if membership were not restricted to white women, Ruffin was seated, but only as a member of the New England club. That way, the convention circumvented recognition of the black club. It was able to keep the General Federation of Women's Clubs all white by subsequently instructing state federations not to approve applications from black clubs. Since application to the national body was made through state federations this policy proved an effective means of separation.

Black women did not let the actions of the white women's organizations deter them. Alone, they took on the burden of racial uplift. Behind Josephine Yates's insistence that the NACW was the first step in nation-making was the belief that the progress of women marked the progress of the race. According to Yates, "that a nation can rise in the scale no higher than its womanhood, are principles which have come to be looked upon by the sociologist and all students of the development of humanity as self-evident truth."[40] Anna Jones, a University of Michigan alumna, wrote the same thing: "the status of its womanhood is the measure of the progress of the race."[41]

The most eloquent explanation of this concept came from Oberlin graduate Anna Cooper. In *A Voice from the South*, she argued that "no man can represent the race." Even someone as great as the black nationalist Martin Delany could not, in Cooper's view, speak for black people, because he knew nothing about the lives of "the rank

and file of horny handed toiling men and women of the South. . . . "
Women, however, were in a position to know because women were
at the center, the heart of the family and the community. Black
women were also doubly oppressed: as women and as blacks. Therefore, when black women spoke, they spoke for all the masses. Only
when black women were totally free would the black race be free.
This was the meaning behind one of the most memorable passages in
A Voice from the South:

> Only the Black Woman can say "when and where I enter, in the
> quiet, undisputed dignity of my womanhood, without violence
> and without suing or special patronage, then and there the whole
> Negro race enters with me."[42]

Not only black clubwomen but many black men also subscribed
to the notion that "a race can rise no higher than its women." Dr.
Monroe Majors, a Texas physician, made his feelings clear in the title
page of his 1893 book on the achievements of black women:

> A race, no less than a nation, is prosperous in proportion to the
> intelligence of its women.
>
> The criterion for Negro civilization is the intelligence, purity and
> high motives of its women.
>
> The highest mark of our prosperity, and the strongest proofs of
> Negro capacity to master the sciences and fine arts, are evinced
> by the advanced positions to which Negro women have attained.[43]

The book, *Noted Negro Women*, was written not only to put the
accomplishments of black women before the world, but to demonstrate how far black people had progressed since slavery. Since the
progress of the race was measured by the progress of its women,
Majors's purpose in presenting almost four hundred pages of text

was to show how worthy of respect the race was. As Majors put it in his preface, the book was written as a "signification of Negro progress."

Of course, the issue of progress was not so clear cut. As the previous quotations from Majors and others suggest, progress, including the progress of women, meant different things to different people, and not all black women, let alone black men, measured it the same way. While most clubwomen and black men shared the idea that the race would rise as women did, and while most clubwomen believed that the torch of leadership had been passed to them, just how leadership should be exercised was a subject of debate. Not all believed that women ought to exercise leadership by speaking publicly for the race, or by bargaining and mediating with public officials. One of the most fundamental ideological discussions among clubwomen, and one that sometimes put them at odds with each other, was the way that women would lead the race.

Among the leaders it came down to a discussion of a woman's "place." Many believed that a woman exercised her greatest influence on behalf of the race in her role as wife, mother, and teacher. This did not imply notions of woman's inferiority to man. On the contrary, like Alice White, a clubwoman from Montgomery, Alabama, they agreed that "woman is man's equal intellectually." But inasmuch as they also believed in the superiority of women in the sphere of morality they insisted that women did their best work in the home, school, and church. For White, as long as the home was a place of peace, it was woman's source of power.[44] Ursula Wade of Mississippi envisioned pious and morally pure black women instilling confidence and strength in family members. She reasoned that "from pure womanhood must necessarily follow pure homes and from pure homes will spring a people strong in intellect, morals and religion."[45] It seemed crucial to women of this bent that blacks, who had for so long under slavery been denied the right and power to establish stable homes, should develop this foundation. They could agree with Yates that the National Association of Colored Women was the first step in nation-making because the NACW did so much in the name of family and community. To build the black home was to build the black nation. At the center of it all was the woman. Because hers was the hand that rocked the cradle, she would mold the nation.[46] As Margaret Murray Washington, Booker T. Washington's third wife and a preeminent exponent of this position, believed, black women would be the "deliverer, for through her will come the earnest, faithful service for the highest development of home and family that will result in the solution of the so-called race problem."[47]

For others the solution to the race problem lay in black women assuming more wide-ranging roles. They had no quarrel with the argument that the home was the first battleground, or that the NACW did important work in making the home and community

FANNIE WILLIAMS. *Photo courtesy of the Photographer, Collection, Moorland-Spingarn Research Center, Howard University.*

ADDIE HUNTON. *Photo courtesy of the Photographer, Collection, Moorland-Spingarn Research Center, Howard University.*

strong. They just did not believe that a woman's work ended there, or that the Association's role should be confined to coordinating club activity to this end. Nellie Francis, for instance, wrote eloquently about the home as the central source of uplift. She agreed that "neither society nor state can exist without its well-being." She did not, however, believe that a woman's sphere should be confined to the home. Like many white female reformers she believed that the family was best served by women who were involved in politics and public lobbying efforts. Women, in her view, had a responsibility to help improve pure food laws, to shape laws that curbed the high cost of living, and to use the ballot as a way of improving society.[48] Fannie Williams agreed. Women, including black women, would be the corrective force in the public arena. Women should promote temperance, municipal reform, and better education.[49] Addie Dickerson, a Philadelphia clubwoman and leader in the Northeastern Federation, added her voice to those of Francis and Williams. Like her conservative counterparts, she

MARGARET MURRAY WASHINGTON. *Photo courtesy of the Photographer, Collection, Moorland-Spingarn Research Center, Howard University.*

believed that women reached their highest function as mother and director of the home. She believed that in "civilized" nations the home was the basis of the state. Without a stable home there could be no state, and consequently no foundation for "civilized" culture. Yet Dickerson also believed that women had to fight vigorously against Jim Crow and join with progressives of both races to improve the economic opportunities of black women who worked outside the home.[50]

JOSEPHINE BRUCE. *Photo courtesy of the Photographer, Collection, Moorland-Spingarn Research Center, Howard University.*

Clubwomen who wanted to expand the black woman's role beyond the traditional spheres were militant supporters of woman's suffrage. Unlike Margaret Murray Washington, who felt that suffrage did not warrant the full attention of black women, women like Francis, Williams, and Dickerson insisted that black women needed the vote to do the political work that would bring about reform. Speaking of the political rights that black people had lost as a result of widespread disfranchisement, Dickerson was certain that when women got the vote, black women "will have an opportunity to make right that wrong."[51] An anonymous editorial in the *Woman's Era* agreed. "A woman's place is where she is needed and where she fit in." One could no more return women to the confines of the home and traditional "womanliness" than "turn back the hands of time."[52]

Once again, Anna Cooper's voice most fully expressed the sentiment of activist clubwomen. A supporter of woman's suffrage, Cooper at once believed that the family, with the woman as its guiding force, would be the salvation of the race, and that women had to have the same opportunities as men to develop intellectually in order to "help men tug at the great questions of the world." Intellectual development translated into self-reliance and the "capacity for earning a livelihood." It made women less likely "to look to sexual love as the one sensation capable of giving tone and relish, movement and vim to the life she leads." Education and intellectual development were necessary for all women but they were essential for black women. They could not afford to just "look pretty and appear well in society." Black girls had to learn that "there is a race with special needs which they and only they can help; that the world needs and is already asking for their trained and efficient forces." Like her conservative counterparts, Cooper argued that black women did essential race work in the home as wives and mothers, but she also insisted that the time had come for woman's "personal independence, for intellectual and moral development, for physical culture, for political activity, and for a voice in the arrangement of her own affairs, both domestic and national."[53]

These philosophical alliances mirrored those that formed around the philosophies of race leaders Booker T. Washington and W. E. B. Du Bois. Thus, it should come as no surprise that the debate between Washington and Du Bois influenced the ideological discussion taking place among club leaders. Washington, like conservative women, discouraged political activity and civil disobedience as a means of achieving civil rights. He argued that progress and uplift began in the home and community with the individual who was dedicated to hard work and economic success. All clubwomen subscribed to this agenda for all believed that women had to make their homes the foundation of race progress. But most of those who reached for

more, who endorsed suffrage and activism, were less comfortable
with Washington, and naturally more in tune with Du Bois, who
argued that black people had a duty to use all means to bring about
political and civil equality, and that the most talented and fortunate
blacks had to assume this responsibility. The divisive debate between
Washington and Du Bois only intensified the differences that already
existed among clubwomen.[54]

·These differences were set forth in letters written to Margaret
Washington by Josephine Silone Yates. Like her husband, Washington
generally believed that quiet, persistent, and diligent work would
accomplish self-help racial uplift. Since this work began in the home
and community, and these were relatively private spheres, clubwomen did not have to issue public pronouncements or agitate in
the political arena. Yates agreed. Writing to Margaret Washington she
expressed her belief that the National Association had to create a
positive image of black womanhood, but that it was counterproduc-
tive to "go into the market place crying out 'I am virtuous, I am virtuous.'" Clubs of the Association made their greatest contribution by
finding ways to "work, work, work" for the race. Just as she urged
black women to demonstrate their worthiness quietly, she urged all
blacks to stop "continually clamoring for more and crying prejudice,
discrimination." Sounding very much like Booker T. Washington,
Yates wrote:

> If colored people generally speaking were to live up to the oppor-
> tunities we now have in place . . . we would soon be in a position
> where opportunity would seek us, but we want the automobile,
> before we have a wheel barrow. . . .[55]

Of course, Cooper disagreed with Yates. She had made her feel-
ings clear long before the public debate between Washington and Du
Bois. Her activist feminism made her an unhesitant ally of Du Bois.
In 1892, twelve years before the public debate between Du Bois and
Washington, she penned this rather Du Boisian statement:

Nature has made up her mind that what cannot defend itself, shall not be defended. Complaining never so loud and with never so much reason, is of no use. What cannot stand must fall; and the measure of our sincerity and therefore of the respect of men is the amount of health and wealth we will hazard in the defense of our right.[56]

As different as were the opinions of Cooper and Yates, we must not infer that club leaders were hopelessly divided into ideological camps. They were divided, but they had every reason to hope that their common ground would make their differences insignificant. To begin with, they all suffered humiliating experiences under Jim Crow. They all resented the exclusionary membership policies of white women's clubs. Most were well educated, making their outcast status all the more difficult to accept. Moreover, all believed that it was the "woman's era," that black women could and would solve the race problem.

They thought this possible only if they avoided divisive issues as well as partisan politics. Yates warned the National Association to stick to the purposes for which it was founded. The "moment it goes after crosscuts and by-paths, it is doomed to the same death that has beset so many national bodies." One of those bypaths that Yates wanted the Association to have no part of was the contemporary debate over whether blacks should be called "Colored Americans" or "Afro-Americans." To her mind this issue—among others—served no purpose except to tear a national organization apart.[57]

The kind of politics that led to partisanship and bossism was also disruptive. Many club leaders felt that black men had been ineffective in dealing with race issues because they had been sidetracked by the activities of the Democratic and Republican parties. Black women would stay above party politics. "Must we begin our political duties with no better or higher conceptions of our citizenship than shown by our men when they were first enfranchised," asked Fannie Williams. "Are we to bring any refinement of individuality to the ballot box? Shall we learn our politics from spoilsmen and bigoted partisans or shall we learn it from the school of patriotism and an enlightened self-interest?"[58]

For Mary Church Terrell, the National Association's first president, the worst thing black women could do was to bring the practices of corrupt politicians into the Association. To be a "corrective force" in American society, black women had to religiously eschew party politics. Nonetheless, Terrell thought it essential that black women protest against the system that deprived them of their legal rights. Terrell admired clubwomen who had petitioned the legislatures of Louisiana and Tennessee to end segregation on railroad cars, and women who were waging what she called a ceaseless war against the convict labor system.[59] Yet, she and all clubwomen were suspicious of any sign of what they called "bossism." Equal to the meanness and the usurpation of other people's power that characterized the political "boss" would be a political "mistress in a woman's organization," wrote Williams.[60] One way to avoid the "mistress" was for clubs to have as few officers as possible. This was Margaret Murray Washington's advice in a lecture in 1910 on how to organize a woman's club. A club, she suggested, needed only a president and a secretary. Since communities generally united behind their teachers, and since unity made clubs effective, in Washington's view, teachers were the best organizers.[61]

As we will see, unity did not come naturally, but NACW women made their best effort when they stuck to issues on which they all agreed. The defense of black womanhood united them as did no other single cause. Both conservatives and activists believed that black women were beset with both a race problem and a woman problem. In their view, this made black women so unique among Americans that only they could voice their concerns and needs. No one else cared as much and no other group had so much at stake. What hurt most were the charges assailing black women's morals. To club leaders it seemed that all the shortcomings of the race were being traced to the black woman's alleged failures—failure to be pure, pious, submissive, and domestic, the failure to raise future generations of blacks to be good citizens, and the failure marked by continued sexual connections with white men. Clubwomen wanted the world to know that all the allegations impugning the black woman's character were false, that black women had gone for hundreds of years able to "cry for protection to no living man."[62] They celebrated black mothers for their "painful, patient, and silent toil . . . to gain a fee simple title to the bodies of their daughters," their heroic struggles "against fearful and overwhelming odds that often ended in death." Through the travail of slavery, "the Afro-American woman," Cooper argued, "maintained the ideals of womanhood unshamed by any conceived."[63] She had subsequently made tremendous progress in education, and in homemaking. It was the black woman, clubwomen so often reiterated, who was responsible for all the forward strides taken by the race.

In making their case they realized differences. Not all black women could meet their standards. Such faults could be traced back to slavery when their natural ethics had been destroyed by whites who gave them backbreaking work, broke up black families, and rewarded black women for promiscuous behavior. If some black women needed lessons in homemaking, if some had not achieved the moral ideal, or had not taught their children to distinguish between right and wrong, it was only to be expected since the effects of over two centuries of slavery could not be wiped out overnight. Furthermore, club leaders argued, no race of people were all good or all bad. Whites had their immoral class, their criminals and prostitutes. Why, they asked, did whites insist on judging the black race by its bad element; why were all black women judged by the actions of the least cultured and educated?

Clubwomen wanted racial progress to be measured by their own success. In their estimation they were their own best argument against discrimination. Their temperance, intelligence, and moral rectitude reflected positively on the race and proved James Jacks's slander wrong. With the words, "now with an army of organized women standing for purity and mental worth, we in ourselves deny the charges . . . not by noisy protestations of what we are not but by a dignified showing of what we are," they created the National Association of Colored Women.[64] The NACW motto, "Lifting As We Climb," meant that they pledged to help others as they helped themselves. Their very existence meant that black people had taken the first step in nation-making. It also meant that black women would always have a defender as well as a national voice. While they might dispute the usefulness of woman's suffrage, or argue over "a woman's place" or the best tactic to achieve equal rights, on this one point they agreed unanimously. The National Association of Colored Women was their watchdog, and their defender across the nation.[65]

In many ways, the clubwomen's record was impressive. At the turn of the century, the National Association of Colored Women presented an unprecedented and bold program. It integrated the unique concerns of black women into a program that addressed the problems of race and poverty. In a period when white women were often compelled to choose between a career and marriage, activist clubwomen insisted that black women could both save the race and build model homes; they could do all that a man could do and all that a woman should. Unlike future generations of black feminists they did not fear that their feminism would split the race movement into conflicting camps, nor did they feel torn between their race and gender identity. On the contrary, convinced that black female issues and race issues were identical, they spoke publicly in opposition to black men and openly revealed their disillusionment with black male leadership. In their minds it was not dirty laundry they were airing, it was just cold hard truth.

Just as they saw only congruity in their race and gender outlook, they saw only wisdom in their approach to black poverty. Both conservatives and activists embraced Du Bois's talented-tenth philosophy even before he penned the term. Clubwomen codified their duty by making "Lifting As We Climb" the Association motto. Again, unlike black women leaders of a more modern era, who were tentative about speaking for the lower classes, they did not hesitate to represent poor black women, few of whom belonged to their organization. Proud of their work on behalf of their less fortunate sisters, they felt it a duty to speak for them.

Yet, for all NACW women had to be proud of, and confident about, there was reason for apprehension. Ideological differences threatened their unity. They could not forever avoid issues that divided them, for some issues were obviously pivotal to the future of blacks and women. Moreover, for women who functioned in such a constricted public arena, the potential for "mistrissism" was ever present. So was the danger that black people, and especially black men, would see the female leadership that came with club activity as a usurpation of male roles and as inherently unfeminine. Clubwomen could not expect black men to silently accept their increasingly bitter characterizations, nor the black masses to always take marching orders from women who could at times appear obsessed with morality. There was always the danger that the clubwoman's zeal might undermine her goal to change the black woman's image.

Most dangerous of all was endorsement of the idea that a race could rise no higher than its women. It was risky business to buy into an ideology that had so much potential to be their own undoing. What would happen if the race did not rise, if whites rejected the Association's program, or if all the self-help projects sponsored by the clubs made no difference in the status of black women? This ideology could justify black female activism and equal educational opportunities, but it also left black women vulnerable to blame for the condition of the race, especially in 1896 when so much hardship beset blacks.

As the twentieth century progressed, the NACW would be challenged on many fronts. Some challenges it would successfully meet while others would prove its undoing. But in 1896 club leaders were sure that they could lead the race out of its nadir.

❖

Chapter 2

THE DILEMMAS OF
NATION-MAKING

> . . . for a long time, it has been a question in my mind as to whether we
> are really and truly living up to our standard—"Lifting as we climb."
> And are we as helpful and useful in the community where we live as we
> should be?
>
> —KATHERINE MACARTHY

Atlanta clubwomen must have been thrilled when John Hope accepted the invitation to speak to their club. A graduate of prestigious Brown University, Hope came to Atlanta in 1898 as a classics professor and bookkeeper for Atlanta Baptist College, and became its first black president in 1906. Like clubwomen, Hope believed in self-help uplift. At the Fourth Atlanta University Conference in 1898 he urged African Americans to set up their own businesses as a way to avoid the racist employment practices of whites. A close friend and ally of W. E. B. Du Bois, Hope opposed Booker T. Washington's accommodation to racism, and vigorously denounced any program that called for less than full black rights for African Americans. In fact, at a time when it was dangerous to broadcast thoughts about racial justice and equality, Hope rose before a Nashville audience commemorating George Washington's birthday and boldly proclaimed, "I want equality. Nothing less." He told his stunned audience of faculty and students at Roger Williams University in Nashville, "if we are not striving for equality, in heaven's name for what are we living. . . . If we cannot do what other freemen do, then we are not free."[1]

Hope chose a different subject for his address before the Atlanta clubwomen, but he was just as outspoken. This time his target was not racism or black accommodation. His subject was club work and clubwomen, and he was anything but approving. His first words set a contentious tone:

> The world has been ruled too long by men. It is a women's time to take a hand. And I as one among millions of men welcome [sic] into the broadest and highest activity. But I welcome you *as women.*[2]

Reminding the clubwomen of the "caustic remarks" they had previously made about men, Hope chastised them for their "brow-beating spirit" and accused them of being "more masculine than feminine." Although many men had applauded clubwomen for fighting racism more vigorously than black men, Hope was not among them. Black people, he insisted, "are in need of men," and "it [is] a great calamity for our women to act as substitutes." African Americans needed men to act like men, and to Hope's mind "the surest way for our men to become more manly is for our women to become more womanly." Women, thus, had to take less initiative, had to support their men as helpmates. To be more than that was to be emasculating. Rather than behave like Queen Elizabeth or Joan of Arc, who, in his opinion, "did not appear to have been an improvement ov[er] men," Hope suggested clubwomen model themselves after Florence Nightingale or Jane Addams, whom he commended for being "distinctively feminine."[3]

Hope went on to detail every weakness he had observed in the clubs, and without any acknowledgment of their contributions, he wished for a more productive future. According to Hope, clubwomen were too concerned with the religious denomination of their members, and paid more attention to social status than to community work. He felt that clubwomen had not done enough for the poor children and homeless women of Atlanta, and that clubwomen were self-indulgent. Borrowing a page from club leaders' attacks on men, he claimed that they passed too many resolutions followed by no action, and they were too concerned about running for club office. Although he concluded with the statement that Negro men and women, "acting as leaders," could produce a change in the degraded status of black people, there appeared to be little room for women's leadership when he predicted the future. That future would "be replete with honorable, heroic thoughts and acts by whites and blacks filled with such *manliness*," that "all will be vindicated."[4] [italics added]

If Hope's denunciation caught Atlanta's clubwomen off guard, it was because too many were oblivious to the tension that club ideology had spawned, and the pressure clubwomen had put themselves under. The speech itself was evidence that black men and women were in conflict, and its substance suggested that the conflict extended across both gender and class lines. Moreover, Hope had plumbed some inherent weaknesses in the clubwomen's logic. If woman's status was the measure of progress, and if that status did not show remarkable improvement, how could black women claim they could lead the race better than men had done? What if the large numbers of female agricultural and domestic workers did not accept the leadership of clubwomen, or worse yet, suppose clubwomen succumbed to the kind of political maneuvering and ideological bickering they criticized the men for? As the century progressed the claims for women's superiority succumbed to all these misfortunes. Time proved that while race, class, and gender issues could be worked out as part of a single problem in a philosophical construct, in practice it was not so easy.

HOPE'S SPEECH CAME at a time when black men and women clashed over the most effective response to the unchecked violence and discrimination that beset them. As rape, lynching, disfranchisement, and other horrors of the period continued unabated, so too did the debate between men and women over the most effective response. Caught in their gender struggle, neither black male nor female leaders seemed aware that their fight against racism had turned as much inward on themselves as outward toward whites.

Although NACW leaders did not deliberately mount a malevolent campaign against black men, their rhetoric and that of their supporters juxtaposed the abilities of black men and women in such a way as to generate tension between them. Comments like those quoted earlier by Anna Cooper and Fannie Williams were far too common for black men to ignore. For instance, in 1894, Victoria Earle Matthews, a founder of the New York Woman's Loyal Union and an editor for the black woman's newspaper, *Woman's Era*, described the tremendous praise that had been heaped on that newspaper. In her editorial column she quoted a gentleman whose comments were clearly challenging to black men. About the paper, the man allegedly said:

> For my part, I am ready to say that if the women can do such things as that, the men ought to sell out, transfer their books, etc., over to the women, and a great change would come over us. Why, the excellence of this edition . . . will stir the men to either shut up shop, or do better generally than they have done for the past twenty years.[5]

A similar comment was made by the male editorial board of the *Voice of the Negro*, an early-twentieth-century race periodical. In 1904, the *Voice* advised the Association to "set their faces like a flint against the political methods of our men." They added:

> Eschew 'Resolutions,' 'Petitions' and 'Memorials' to congress, governors or anybody else. The men in the religious, political, social and educational conferences and conventions have filled up

the Book of Resolutions. There is not a single page left. But the Book of Acts has not had the first page or character written in it. Women of the Negro Race!! Write a Book of Acts for the race.[6]

By the 1920s many Association women were working harmoniously with black men in the National Association for the Advancement of Colored People (NAACP), an organization some clubwomen had helped to found and shape. Even so, the underlying gender tension would not abate. In fact, a new crop of club leaders joined the open criticism of black men. For example, at the fourteenth annual convention of the Empire State Federation in 1922, the president of a Brooklyn club, a Mrs. Fayerweather, urged her sister clubwomen to join the fight for equal rights. She told them to "Stand up! Stand up! for the Cause of Humanity, demanding our rights. The Negro man has tried for half a century with but little results."[7] In 1927, when the noted educator and race leader Mary McLeod Bethune was president of the Association, an article in *National Association Notes* claimed that "the Negro Woman has practically carried her own man on her back, her children by the hand, while she fought off the men of other races. . . ."[8]

The last part of that comment raised an issue that had long been a sore spot in the relationship between black men and women, namely the black man's alleged failure to support and protect black women. In 1892, Cooper wrote of being hampered and shamed by black men who would not admit that women could influence anything. Twenty-three years later when the Texas Federation of Women's Clubs submitted its annual report, it said, "our men have never given us the support and encouragement we so well deserve."[9]

The call for black men to show support for black women also came from the celebrated journalist and club activist, Ida B. Wells. In 1891, four years *before* her antilynching crusade prompted the white editor James Jacks to write that all black women were liars and prostitutes, a *black* minister in Vicksburg, Mississippi, made an *identical claim* about Wells and all Southern black women. The minister boasted that he had married a Northern woman because they were more virtuous and more desirable as wives. When some of Wells's admirers held her up as an example of virtuous Southern black womanhood, he countered that Wells's dismissal from her teaching position in Memphis was proof of her promiscuity. Wells, who had committed no impropriety but had lost her position by criticizing the school system for its substandard provisions for black children, was livid. Having already left Vicksburg when she heard of the charge, she made a special trip back to confront the minister. In a room full of male witnesses she challenged the preacher to repeat the derogatory remarks to her face. When he apologized she gave him a stern lecture on how Southern black women had courageously fought off would-be white rapists, how they had died rather than submit, and how they were still keeping themselves spotless and morally clean. She then made him sign a statement that he agreed to read before his congregation, testifying that his remarks on the character of Ida B. Wells were false and that he was recanting them in deference to her "as a lady."[10]

This minister's slight was only one of many made by black men against black women. In a 1904 article entitled "Negro Womanhood Defended," Addie Hunton upbraided a black man, William Hannibal Thomas, for his outrageous charge that "not only are fully ninety per cent of the negro women of America lascivious by instinct and in bondage to physical pleasure, but . . . the social degradation of our freedwomen is without parallel in modern civilization." Hunton called Thomas a "Judas Iscariot," and warned against what she perceived as a tendency to blame women "for every weakness of the race."[11] While Hunton insisted that black women needed protection, Fannie Williams issued perhaps the most direct challenge to black men. According to Williams, black women had to rely on themselves for their own defense because there were "too many colored men who hold the degrading opinions of ignorant white men, that all colored girls are alike . . . How rare are the reported instances of colored men resenting any slur or insult upon their own women."

Williams challenged black men: "Is the colored man brave enough to stand out and say to all the world, 'Thus far and no farther in your attempt to insult and degrade our women?'"[12]

Clubwomen were not alone in their concern for the treatment and protection of black women. Not only the *Voice,* but other black periodicals carried editorials urging black men to be more respectful to black women. An 1899 *Savannah Tribune* editorial found it painful to admit that many black men had little respect for black women, and added that black men had to understand that "the greatness of the Caucasians was attained on account of their regard for their women, and their readiness to defend their homes." Eight years later the *Tribune* suggested that a black man who defended a black woman against a white assailant could serve as a model for all black men. W. Calvin Chase, editor of the *Washington Bee*, also criticized the treatment of black women by black men. He felt that black men in the nation's capital took sexual advantage of black women because they lacked respect for the black woman's morality.[13] Chase's editorial appeared in 1893; thirty-two years later E. L. Park, the dean of men at Howard University, asked Mary Church Terrell to speak to students on "How the College Young Men of the Negro Race Should Treat the Women of the Race." Park claimed that young black men showed "a lack of thoughtful respect for the personality of the young women," and needed instruction on how to treat and think about them. In his view women had "taken their place by the side of men" in economic and political development. Only when they respected each other would black men and women "advance together in the highest and noblest development."[14]

While some, like Chase and Park, chastised black men for their less than chivalrous behavior toward black women, others, like William Hannibal Thomas, blamed black women themselves. Thomas had turned the ideology that a "race can rise no higher than its women" on its head and used it against its proponents. When he claimed that ninety percent of black women were lascivious by instinct, he was doing more than just endorsing a white stereotype:

He was defending black men while he attacked the ideology that was at the heart of the black clubwoman's movement. If a race could rise no higher than its women, and if the race found itself at its nadir, then the logic of the initial argument led Thomas to conclude that the women of the race had not progressed very far. Even while Addie Hunton defended black women against Thomas's attack, she understood the potency of Thomas's argument, for in her defense of black women she noted a growing tendency to blame black women for every weakness of the race.[15]

Thomas's voice was one among many. Along with its criticism of men, the *Savannah Tribune* published admonitions to black women. Of some significance was the fact that the *Tribune* not only was a black newspaper serving Savannah's black community, but it was also the official organ of the Masonic Grand Lodge of the State of Georgia, and thus the mouthpiece of a large black male organization in that state. As the various editorials suggest, the *Tribune* was even-handed in this debate. It also took seriously the notion that "a race could rise no higher than its women." The boomerang effect of that ideology is clearly revealed in one editorial that insisted "if certain ones of our female [sic] knew that they are important factors in the development of the moral status of our race, they may be constrained to act better." In another editorial, after reminding black women that "the standard of our race is measured by them," the writer accused black women of being disloyal to their men. In yet another piece, the persistence of Jim Crow in theaters was indirectly blamed on black women. The tremendous burden that clubwomen had accepted was revealed in this editorial, which held them accountable for the progress of the race:

> The Tribune deplores the fact that so many of our young ladies of respectability, stultify their womanhood by climbing up the winding steps into the peanut gallery of the theatre. And upon them too, we are depending to solve whatever there may be of the race problem.[16]

W. J. Gaines, a bishop in the African Methodist Episcopal Church, also laid the degradation of the race at the feet of black women. In 1897, Gaines's book, *The Negro and the White Man,* assessed the status of the race and prescribed a program for its advancement. Although he held both black men and women responsible for the negative status of black people, he reserved for black women his harshest criticism. "It is often the case," he claimed, "that by failing to be a 'keeper at home,' and to preserve herself chaste and pure, she forfeits the love and respect of her husband, and this renders his marriage distasteful and repulsive." Black women also bore the brunt of his attack against miscegenation. While he noted that they went unprotected into white homes to do domestic work and that white men were unscrupulous in their methods of debauchery, he never called for more protection for black women, but faulted them for their ignorance and lack of chastity. "Colored girls in the South," he claimed, "often prefer to be the mothers of white children."[17]

If Addie Hunton was furious with Hannibal Thomas, Gaines's comments could only have exacerbated her fear that black women were being blamed for all the race's problems. She and others, however, seemed not to understand the gendered dynamics racism had spawned. When club leaders criticized and ridiculed the political methods of black men, and vowed that black women would not sell votes, make deals with party bosses, pass endless resolutions that resulted in no action, or use intrigue to gain office in black organizations, they laid the groundwork for new criticism from men, criticism that could only mount if clubwomen failed to live up to their own expectations. The moment any sign appeared of rivalry for an organization office, or the day they passed a resolution on a subject over which they had no control, in fact, any day when they were less than perfect, black women were doomed to suffer the same criticism they so often meted out.

That day came soon enough. In the 1899 election for president of the National Association of Colored Women, Terrell won a third term as president, even though the organization's constitution limited the presidency to two terms. Terrell's supporters argued that since the nonretroactive constitution went into effect after Terrell's first term, she was still eligible for the office. Terrell's main opponent was Josephine Ruffin, the founder of the New Era Club of Boston and preeminent Northeastern club leader. Her supporters charged Terrell with "mistrissism." They claimed that Terrell had moved the National Association convention from Indianapolis to Chicago so that she could control the election. Terrell was further accused of handpicking Josephine Bruce of Mississippi to be her successor, and with manipulating delegates so as to exclude Ida B. Wells-Barnett (who had married Ferdinand Barnett in 1895) from the convention. The conflict was so bitter and so divisive that Ruffin, Wells-Barnett, and Anna J. Cooper stayed away from national meetings for many years.[18]

Such contention also gave black men ammunition they could use against Association women. In both the *New York Age* and the *Colored American*, Association leaders were accused of participating in an "unseemly scramble for office. . . . " Both Bruce and Terrell denied the charges, and Terrell in characteristic stinging language accused the reporter from the *Colored American* of representing suspicious and misinformed black men. She maintained that the women of the NACW were "the best women of his race," and demanded that the reporter see the error of his ways, and refrain from "mean insinuations and deliberate falsehoods which mischief makers and defamers of character whisper in his ear."[19]

Terrell might well have brushed aside such a young reporter's criticism as brash, but since disapproval came also from such eminent men as John Hope, the indictment of black woman's clubs could not be easily dismissed. Terrell and others clearly did not realize that underneath male attacks on club work and the black woman's character lay a struggle over the meaning of black masculinity and femininity. When club leaders attacked black male political tactics and ridiculed their leadership, endorsed the advent of the woman's era, insisted on protection for black women, and organized

activity on everything from kindergartens to antilynching, they challenged the black man's authority and masculinity. Predictably, Hope
and others rebutted by questioning the clubwoman's propriety and
femininity. Clubwomen were, thus, unwittingly caught in a Catch
22: To accomplish their goals they had to act in ways that most contemporary Americans, including black men, considered unfeminine,
yet one of those goals was to be judged moral, chaste, and virtuous,
indeed *feminine*. Clearly, lectures on "the modern woman," such as
the one Terrell gave in Charleston, were meant to broaden the definition of femininity, as were the very broad range of activities undertaken by mothers' clubs. Ironically, however, the African-American
woman's image as immoral forced clubs to emphasize a definition of
femininity that they knew to be narrow. That Hope and others used
this narrow definition to define the limits of the club woman's
activism is not surprising. For a long time efforts to silence women's
rights advocates had included accusations of unfeminine behavior.
The difference here was that the argument was potentially more
effective when employed against black women. Not only was the
status of the race alleged to be at stake, but clubwomen were particularly vulnerable to this line of attack because so much of their
defense of black womanhood was based on their own insistence that
black women were as feminine and as worthy of respect as white
women.

John Hope certainly thought them equal to white women, but he
also had typically set notions about a woman's place. He believed
that a wife's role was to serve her husband. His wife, Lugenia Burns
Hope, was a social worker and institution builder. In addition to her
membership in several Atlanta organizations, including the YWCA,
the NAACP, and the Southeastern Federation of Colored Women's
Clubs, Lugenia eventually founded and became president of
Atlanta's Neighborhood Union. This network of clubs offered voca-
tional classes for black children, established health clinics, and operated an extensive vaccination and anti-tuberculosis program. Among
its many achievements were the extra schools it had the city build

for black youth, including its first black high school in 1924. This work, as Lugenia Hope's biographer tells us, gave Lugenia "a chance to express her views on woman suffrage, racial oppression, and sexual discrimination (both intraracial and interracial); it brought her international solidarity with women of color; and it opened the opportunity to share strategies on organizing and reforming." In short, it gave her status "as a woman, not as a wife, mother, or first lady [as the wife of John Hope who was president of Atlanta Baptist College]."[20]

John struggled with this status. When he and Lugenia were engaged he assured Lugenia, who wanted a marriage based on mutual respect, that "we are to control our little realm 'mutually' [;] neither of us is to be the servant, yet both of us gladly serve each other in love and patience." But John obviously was not committed to equality. Even though Lugenia was involved in social work when he first met her in Chicago in 1893, he saw her service with various agencies as work, not a career. Upon marriage he expected her to give up her work and make a career out of nurturing and supporting his needs and desires. John was pleased, for example, when Lugenia agreed to move to Atlanta. It showed him that she was interested in "his affairs," and he wrote her that "that is what you were born to do." In another letter, written just prior to his return from a European tour, he wrote of how he missed and dreamed of her. Although his work took him away from home more than did hers he put the burden of their relationship on her when he wrote: ". . . when I return you will be so busy that you will have no time to listen to me. Your work as mine takes me from you. You blame me, yet you are too busy for small talk. However, we have been a long time apart and 'you' must be more with me." John also saw Lugenia as the primary caregiver to their son, Edward. Obviously concerned that Lugenia's work was taking her away from him and Edward, John, again writing from Europe, "charged" *her* to get to know Edward's cares and feelings.[21]

Early in his public career even W. E. B. Du Bois, like Hope, put femininity above feminism. Du Bois was a genuine supporter of black women and feminism. However, during the same period that he publicly challenged Washington's accommodationist strategy by urging blacks to be more militant in their quest for civil rights and suffrage, he told the black women of Spelman College that in civilized cultures men were breadwinners and women were physical and spiritual mothers.[22] With no mention of the "woman's era," or any defense of black womanhood, themes that molded even the most conservative clubwoman's thoughts on homemaking, motherhood, and the race, Du Bois cautioned young Spelman women against avoiding their physical duty to have children for the race. Sounding a note that would haunt black feminists, particularly during the Black Power movement of the late 1960s, Du Bois warned:

> Unless the Negro women of today are prepared to assume the responsibility of healthy families, of two or three children, . . . we are not going to keep progress with the virile races of the world.[23]

Du Bois's comment highlighted the gulf separating leading middle- and upper-class men and women. For club leaders, race and women's rights were one issue. Their feminist and race consciousness were so inseparable that their race work was done in the context of their ideas about a "woman's age" and the innate abilities of women to lead. All of the community work that they did, the condemnation of black men—all the work that enhanced their status as independent women—was done in the name of race advancement. Black men, however, saw things differently. Taking clubwomen at their word, many were inclined to believe that the race was not rising because its women were deficient in the qualities of womanhood. Other men saw club activity undermining woman's *place*. For them, the connection that club leaders drew between race work and gender roles was lost. When their masculinity was threatened they struck back. Behind it all was the racism that both black men and women were responding to, racism that would drive intraracial gender tension throughout the century.

Class conflict was another source of intraracial tension created by the programs and ideas of club leaders. A sense of class privilege permeated every aspect of club-leader thinking about race and gender. For instance, when Fannie Williams challenged black men to protect black women, she also challenged them to recognize differences, implying that some black women were more worthy of protection than others.[24] Hunton said almost the same thing. In her defense of Negro womanhood, she was upset not only because Thomas had joined forces with the white race to insult black womanhood, but because "those who write most about the moral degradation of the Negro woman know little or nothing of that best element of our women. . . . "[25] Such distinctions were made all too frequently by club leaders. Sylvanie Williams of New Orleans found the white person's blanket condemnation of all black women to be the "darkest shadow and deepest wound." She wanted whites to recognize class differences: "We could not, nor would not feel aggrieved, if in citing the immorality of the Negro, the accusation was limited to the pauperized and brutalized members of the race."[26]

The entire issue of sexual exploitation, then, spoke to the issue of class. As noted earlier, clubwomen correctly believed that the sexual exploitation of black women originated during the slavery era, when white men used black women to increase the slave population. When whites forbade legal slave marriages, separated families, and took sexual advantage of female slaves, they further debased them. Clubwomen believed they could overcome their history, indeed that it was a prerequisite to race progress. One aspect of their plan of action was to lecture to anyone who would listen on the unbridled lust of white men, the complicity of white females, and the helplessness of black women. Mostly, though, their program was directed inward. Notwithstanding the service nature of the clubs, the goal of many was to teach social and cultural improvement. Above all they aimed to teach black women how to lead moral lives and make their homes bulwarks in the defense of black womanhood. The motto of the NACW, "Lifting As We Climb," expressed this bond between the middle and lower classes. The duty of the middle-class clubwoman was to provide not just social services for the poor but services that in one way or another educated blacks, particularly black women, on the means and benefits of achieving the moral life.[27] In the club leaders' thinking, moral purity was the key to social and cultural improvement. Social and cultural improvement included everything from music appreciation to civic responsibility, but the first step was chastity. Chastity would liberate black women from their "blighted past." Fending off the advances of white men would, according to Sylvanie Williams, preserve race integrity.[28]

Thus, chastity became the litmus test of middle-class respectability. As a group, black people could not rise in the traditional economic and political ways. At least through the first quarter of the twentieth century, middle-class status in black society was associated as much with "style of life" as with income. Adoption of a particular "style" qualified one for the middle class. Manners, morality, a particular mode of consumption, race work—these criteria were as important as economics for middle-class status.[29] For clubwomen, chastity topped the list of qualitative criteria. It could be nowhere else in rank, for only by giving it highest priority could the Association fulfill its pledge to protect black women against slander. If all black women were chaste, then clearly all of the onus, either for exploiting black women, or failing to protect them, was on men. Furthermore, since clubwomen like Fannie Williams believed that "there will never be an unchallenged vote, a respected political power, or an unquestioned claim to position of influence and importance" among Negroes, "until the present stigma is removed from the home and the women of its race," chastity had to be the preeminent goal of the Association, the organization that its members claimed represented the first step in nation-making.

Yet in keying on chastity, clubwomen established an orthodoxy bound to drive a wedge between themselves and the masses of black women. Unwittingly, NACW women placed the burden of sexual exploitation and social improvement on the shoulders of the victim.

They might sympathize and empathize with their poorer sisters. They might call on white men to stop taking advantage of black women, and chastise black men for not defending them, but the educational programs of most clubs set out to reform the very persons on whose behalf they spoke. Their race and gender ideology left them little room to do anything else. Since they could not control white men, the source of most of their woes, and since they believed that a race could rise no higher than its women, they had to begin that elevation with the women themselves.

A few clubwomen spoke bluntly about the need for elevation. Anna Jones declared that some women of the race had refined their social life but that few black women had followed their example. She regretted the disgrace that came from the "crimes of the lower millions," and claimed that the moral standards of most blacks were lower than that of whites.[30] Less belittling than Jones was Adella Hunt Logan, a member of the Tuskegee Woman's Club. She thought that even the minority of blacks who were "incompetent menials" were too many.[31]

Most clubwomen were not so directly negative, but their continuous stream of advice made clear their feeling that the masses of black women did not measure up to middle-class standards. Believing that slavery had left blacks deficient in moral, social, and hygienic values, clubwomen counseled black women to keep themselves and their homes clean, bathe their children regularly, and provide them with music, games, and books to keep them usefully occupied. Women had to stop sitting on stoops and talking and laughing loudly in public. Girls should stick close to home, and boys be kept from wandering. Families had to live within their means, domestic workers had to stop buying clothes they could not afford. Women should choose their husbands more carefully, save money, and buy homes. Alcohol was strictly verboten, and, above all, women had to lead, and teach their daughters to lead, virtuous lives.[32]

Much club work aimed at disseminating these values. In the club kindergartens children learned the fundamentals of moral living, as did the working women who sought refuge in settlements and missions. The gospel was taught to boys and girls in their rescue homes and reformatories and in libraries. Mothers' clubs were also effective at spreading the message, for they focused on everything from homemaking skills and land buying, to patrolling the community.

Sometimes patrols resembled moral crusades, as did the Investigation Committee of the Neighborhood Union in Atlanta. Like many of the mothers' clubs of the NACW, this Committee, established in 1908, set out to report "everything that seems to be a menace to our neighborhood," and to remove people of unsavory character. Women divided black neighborhoods into districts. When a member found disreputable people, or houses of illicit activities, they told the woman who was district head. She, in turn, solicited signatures on a petition that identified the person or activity and presented it to the mayor, directing him to act swiftly to remove the undesirables. In 1911, the committee got rid of two families who, they claimed, "indulged in doing such things that were immoral such as breaking the Sabbath and gambling." In 1912, the minutes reported that "the Holy Rollers were made to move on the grounds of disorderly conduct."[33]

The removal of the "Holy Rollers" was quite in keeping with most clubwomen's disapproval of black religious practices. Clubs wanted intellectual development and cultural refinement, not the emotionally charged religious services of most black churches. In 1892, Anna J. Cooper found the emotionalism of black worshippers "ludicrous," and in 1936, Terrell confessed to her diary that she found it "discouraging and shocking to see how some of the women shout, holler and dance during services." Alice Dunbar-Nelson frequently derided such worship as "very monkey," behavior that only reinforced the pervasive negative images of black women.[34] Cooper, in particular, found the Protestant Episcopal Church more to her liking, praising "its quiet, chaste dignity and decorous solemnity," as infinitely more proper than the "semi-civilized religionism" of most black churches.[35] Fannie

Williams attacked black religion on other grounds. For her, it had not caught up with the age of science and reason. Although encouraged by the slow but sure acceptance among black women of the many different religious doctrines "from the Catholic creed to the no-creed of Emerson," Williams regretted that black women adapted only slowly to "the growing rationalism in the Christian creeds."[36]

Besides class differences, a crucial gender issue was raised by club leaders' religious practices and beliefs. To their concern over image and reason, they added a fear that most black ministers retarded race progress. Preachers preached the "new day" sermon but, unlike clubwomen, did little to usher it in. Instead of initiating self-help programs and executing plans to eliminate race prejudice, they avoided hard work while living off the contributions of the more industrious. By choosing emotion over reason, ministers both hindered the progress of the black masses and proved an embarrassment to the race. This made them, in the club leaders' view, part of the race problem, part of the ineffective male leadership.

Few NACW leaders had good things to say about preachers, especially rural itinerants. Ida B. Wells described black preachers as "corrupt" and "ignorant."[37] Fannie Williams felt that the race was "more hindered by a large part of the ministry intrusted with leadership than by any other single cause."[38] Of Quaker background, Margaret Murray Washington shared her husband's belief that most black ministers were self-aggrandizing opportunists. Suggesting that black women could use their time more profitably she cautioned them against spending too much time in church.[39]

Mamie Garvin Fields's firsthand encounters with the preachers and elders of St. Johns Island, off the coast of South Carolina, led her to the same conclusion. Unlike Terrell, Williams, Wells, and Cooper, all part of the urban black elite, Fields lived among the people in this rural community. She, too, however, thought that the church often "held the people back." In her view, preachers drank too much corn liquor, got girls pregnant, and often only came to the island to make money off the rural residents. She noticed, for example, that children sometimes skipped school for long periods at a time. When she asked why, she was told that church elders kept them out "to seek." On further inquiry she discovered that "seeking" was a ritual that children had to "come through" to find God before they could join the church. The "coming through" process took children to the woods where they stayed until they had a visitation from angels through dreams. To Fields's dismay, she found that the only dreams thought to be real visitations from God were those that had white people in them. White was the symbol of the Spirit come to free one from sin, any black was thought to be the devil bringing and spreading evil. Children who had these unfortunate dreams would have to remain in the woods, or wear their clothes inside out, until they dreamed of something or someone white. To Fields, it was a double disgrace to keep children out of school to teach them that blackness represented evil. Even worse, while in the woods some church elders took advantage of the girls so that "some real babies came out of that process."[40]

If Fields and others could have remade black people, they would have purged much black behavior they perceived as "common." Many clubwomen, for example, complained that black people did not read the right books. "Reading common books is like associating with common people," said Mrs. H. E. Thomas in a 1912 *National Association Notes* article. Both dulled the "finer perceptions" and lowered the "social standard." Thomas preferred historical stories to "stories with lots of social life and deeply laid love scenes."[41] Charlotte Hawkins Brown, president of the North Carolina Federation of Women's Clubs from 1915 to 1936, complained about the books black people read as well as their lack of appreciation for art and music. "What kind of pictures do we select for our homes, for our children to look upon? . . . Are there many Negroes to whom a real symphony would be a treat?" she asked. "Do we care to listen to Bach, Shubert, Beethoven?" In Brown's view, blacks clearly lacked "culture," and unless the situation was remedied blacks would forever be judged "awkward" and remain "embarrassed" by "truly cul-

CHARLOTTE HAWKINS BROWN. *Photo courtesy of Photographer, Collection, Moorland-Spingarn Research Center, Howard University.*

tured people."[42] The art, music, and literary departments that were staples of the NACW, and the hundreds of "culture" clubs that affiliated with the Association, are testimony to the pervasiveness of Brown's ideas.[43]

One such club, the Book Lovers' Club of Kansas City, gives us a feeling for how these clubs functioned—and for how removed they were from the masses of black people. Founded in 1903, records for this club exist from 1921 through 1945. During that period the club met once every two weeks and maintained a membership of approximately twenty-five women, most of them married. Their subjects were varied. They studied the work of such great philosophers as Confucius, Socrates, Christ, and Mohammed. They studied the architecture of different periods, the history of Russia, the novel as an art form, and they kept abreast of trends in art, music, drama, and education. Although they read black authors and poets, including Langston Hughes, Zora Neale Hurston, Du Bois, and Richard Wright, most of their reading was by Western white authors. Even had they read more black authors it seems doubtful that working-class black women could have kept pace or would have felt comfortable with the social sessions that the club held at least twice a year, or the "fashionette promenades" that occasionally spiced their agenda.[44]

Indeed, few black women, including clubwomen, could keep up with the fashion demands of club life. In Chicago, conspicuous consumption was a must at some of the clubs' annual charity dances. At one particular event in 1908, women's dresses were reported to cost as much as five hundred dollars.[45] If clothes did not "make" the clubwoman, it was surely a mark of her social status. Unkind gossip would follow a wardrobe that fell short of expectations. One hopes, for example, that Alice Dunbar-Nelson told only her diary that Philadelphian Addie Dickerson, a clubwoman and head of the Republican Council of Colored Women at the time, "looked tattered, unmended, and ungroomed."[46] Josephine Bruce staved off gossip by skipping the 1904 NACW biennial. Claiming that she did not have enough clothes, she wrote to Margaret Murray Washington asking her to go in her stead. To Washington she confided, "I have nothing but a traveling dress to wear. And one must be prepared for social functions on an occasion like this meeting. . . . Clothes are an important part of a woman after all."

That clothes could keep Bruce, then chairwoman of the NACW executive committee, away from the biennial demonstrates how important clothes were to the clubwoman's self-image and status. Bruce was a wealthy woman. The widow of Blanche K. Bruce, the black senator from Mississippi from 1874 to 1880, she owned choice real estate in Washington, D.C., and plantations in Mississippi. What her letter makes clear is not that she had no clothes to wear but she had none that her club sisters had not already seen or were not going to see when she, along with some other wealthy clubwomen, attended the 1904 International Congress of Women in Berlin. As a former resident of Indianapolis, Bruce cared about her appearance among the elite in that city. It is clear that she wanted to go, but her residence, at the time in Bolivar, Mississippi, made it impossible to do the kind of shopping she knew the occasion required. As she put it, "there is no time or way down here to get ready and all my plans for clothes relate to another occasion."[47]

Bruce's concerns suggest that the club leaders' frequent calls for black female unity were more a political strategy than practical reality. Unity was neither existent nor anticipated, and this was recognized by club leaders again and again. As Terrell said of black social classes in Washington, D.C., there were "subdivisions ad infinitum" but there was "one general rule of admission into all, to which there has never been an exception":

> It would be as difficult for a bore or a moral leper to obtain social recognition among the educated, refined, colored at Washington, as it would be for a camel with a hump to pass literally through a cambric needle's eye.[48]

Besides being blunt about the distance between black social classes, Terrell and others were succinct about the tactical and strategic nature of the union of middle-class and poor black women. Middle-class educated black women were not free to reach their potential as long as the masses of black women were judged immoral and socially inferior, Terrell explained:

> . . . they know that they cannot escape altogether the consequences of the acts of their most depraved sisters. They see that even if they were wicked enough to turn a deaf ear to the call of duty, both policy and self-preservation demand that they go down among the lowly, the illiterate and even the vicious, to whom they

are bound by ties of race and sex, and put forth every possible effort to reclaim them.[49]

In separate *National Association Notes* articles both Ursula Wade and Addie Dickerson shared Terrell's perspective. Wade, from Mississippi, wrote that there were thousands of blacks who had "advanced to high planes" but that millions needed lifting from "degradation and ignorance." Wade warned club members that unless they could lift the masses up "they will be as a loadstone around our necks drawing us down to them. . . . " Citing the attention whites gave to the black women on Philadelphia's sleazy South Street, Dickerson told NACW women that "until we shall have helped this class, until we have raised them to our standard, there is danger of our being dragged to their level in the public eye by our enemies." Appealing to their sense of self-preservation, Dickerson reasoned, "If we can save and help this class we are saved and helped ourselves to all eternity."[50]

These sentiments compel an analysis of NACW women that goes beyond their altruism. Certainly the Association did accomplish much, but we need to understand that the different classes of black women were allied, not united; that their alliance was based on race and sex sameness and the sentiments that flowed from this kinship— not on social or cultural unity. Most black women were poor. They lived lives weighed down by agricultural and domestic labor. Pervasive discrimination left them with few choices. They did not have time to read, much less to cultivate an appreciation for Beethoven. For most, the church served an emotional need. It provided social activities, and the moral code they lived by. The clubwoman's intolerance for difference blinded them to these realities. Like white female reformers who heaped criticism on immigrants for holding on to their old world culture, black women reformers lacked compassion and a concept of cultural relativism. Given their program, the NACW motto "Lifting As We Climb" presumed race and sex sameness, but social and cultural distance.

In turn-of-the-century black America color mattered, too. While a light-skinned complexion was not a prerequisite for upper- or middle-class status, in the period before World War I, the black middle and upper classes were lighter than the black working and lower classes. These groups seldom mingled socially.[51] Owing mostly to their economic and blood ties to white America, the mulatto upper and middle classes were more familiar and more at ease with white cultural norms, and consequently were at once envied and distrusted by the black masses. No records speak of the complexion of the NACW's rank and file, but it seems clear that before 1920 most of the club leaders were light-skinned, and a few, like Mary Church Terrell, could and did occasionally pass for white.[52] That so many NACW leaders were light-skinned was problematic for some. After the 1906 election of Michigan clubwoman Lucy Thurman to the Association's presidency, one convention delegate suggested that Thurman was elected because of her dark complexion: "We prefer a woman who is altogether Negro, because while the lighter women have been the greatest leaders and are among the most brilliant of the association, their cleverness and ability is attributed to their white blood. We want to demonstrate that the African is as talented."[53] The comment, which referred to the defeat of Josephine Bruce and Mary Church Terrell, suggests that if color consciousness was pervasive within the Association's leadership, it did not disappear from the relationship that the upper classes formed with the black female masses. Indeed, with all the advice and criticism that the light-skinned women meted out to their darker skinned sisters, it is likely that at least some of the social service programs of the National Association of Colored Women exacerbated preexisting tensions. The term "colored" for instance, as opposed to "Negro" or "African-American" was much preferred by some mulattos because it allowed for recognition of white or Indian ancestry. Thus, the choice and persistence of the term "colored" in the NACW name suggest that the organization's leadership was out of step with the masses who displayed pride in their heritage by identifying themselves first as African Americans and then as Negroes.[54]

Such were the difficulties of nation-making. On paper, the National Association of Colored Women had race, class, and gender all worked out. While serving the lower classes they would demonstrate the equality, even the superiority of women, and solve the race problem, too. But in practice prejudice—their own prejudice—got in the way.

Before long its members' shortcomings caught up with the NACW. Many blacks believed that clubwomen, especially the leaders, came down to the level of ordinary black people only when they sought offices, honors, or political plums.[55] Alice Dunbar-Nelson understood this when the Fairmount Temple of the Daughter Elks refused to accept her overture for membership in 1926. Fairmount was a largely working-class lodge and Dunbar-Nelson reasoned that they did not want "dicties [a derogatory slang word for the black elite] coming out from town to tell them how to run their Temple!"[56] That rural blacks did not always appreciate the "high falutin" style of clubwomen is illustrated by one of Mamie Garvin Fields's experiences. Fields's club work went hand in hand with teaching. Having learned Madame C. J. Walker's hair straightening techniques in Charleston, she thought it progressive to bring the beauty process to the island. The mother of one of the girls whose hair she straightened thought differently, though. Standing in the middle of the road, arms flailing, the mother, as Fields put it, "la[id] me out." The mother, whose own hair was wrapped in a traditional multicolor head wrap, did not appreciate the standard of beauty that Fields brought with her from the city. Fields's job, the mother said, was to teach her daughter, not to do her hair. To Fields's credit she never again did a girl's hair without parental consent.[57]

Rebuke came also from black men. Speaking of the NACW's "big three," a male relative of a prominent Ohio clubwoman wrote to a friend in 1901, "Mary Church Terrell, Mrs. Washington and Mrs. Bruce all piss in the same pot through the National Women's Federation."[58] John Hope's less blunt commentary was equally derogatory. He thought that women's clubs were too self-indulgent. He was critical of "lazy women" who had built a clubhouse instead of a clean, safe home for working women, a home where women could get care and attention from "open-hearted, closed-mouthed women." Too many clubwomen and not enough club workers, he complained, and insisted that clubwomen made speeches when they "were not doing a great deal to talk about." He ridiculed Association women by citing one club meeting where the "clubwoman swagger" was particularly evident, and resolutions and bogus elections had accomplished nothing.[59]

To their credit, Association women listened to their detractors and sought to correct the shortcomings so detrimental to the NACW's reputation. In the process, however, they inadvertently admitted fault. For instance, the evenhandedly critical Fannie Williams said that the NACW "is of little value unless it can and does actually do the thing for which it was called into being." She cautioned against a tendency of some clubs to adopt the constitutions, bylaws, and programs of white clubs, and as early as 1904 called on the clubs of the NACW to abandon programs that its members had neither the talent nor money to carry forth.[60] Williams's voice was one among many. When the Association was only nine years old, Elizabeth Lindsay Davis, the organization's historian, wrote Margaret Murray Washington complaining of the "narrowness and selfishness so plainly manifest" in club members. In 1922, Mrs. Fayerweather—who had complained about the ineffectiveness of black men—advised New York State clubwomen to "let go of pretense, worry, discontent and self-seeking." Two years later a Washington, D.C., clubwoman, Mrs. Charles E. Hall, scolded clubwomen for practicing "rampant discrimination," which she said would "stigmatize the progressive element."[61]

Hall's complaint had to do with classism, pure and simple. By the 1920s, classism had become so pronounced that clubwomen like Hall and Fayerweather were willing to lodge public complaints. They probably took a cue from club member Katherine Macarthy's 1920 convention speech. Charging that clubwomen were more concerned with their members' ancestry than with the problems of the needy, she observed before the general assembly, that:

> It seems to be getting more and more the tendency of the club women to hold themselves aloof from others, to move around in a prescribed circle and to ostracize everybody else who does not happen to be in that circle.

Such exclusionary practices spawned "many places in which there are federated clubs, and in those very places there are hundreds of women, good women, intelligent women, who have never heard of our federation, either state or national." Issuing a most prophetic warning, Macarthy reminded her audience that "a pool that has no outlet and no inlet must become stagnant."[62]

Macarthy's charges—and advice and criticism from within and without the clubs—show how hard it was for clubwomen to satisfy everyone. The NACW's feminist strategy of race uplift enabled it to work effectively against racism. However, such a strategy encouraged an exclusiveness and eventually a damaging aloofness. While sorority and friendship—even sisterhood—flourished, so did social cliques.

Also regrettable—if predictable—were disputes over ideology. Club leaders disliked conflict of any kind, but as the woman's movement tackled suffrage, and the race question came down to whether blacks would vigorously protest disfranchisement and discrimination, ideological disputes were inevitable. The question came to dominate the 1904 National Association of Colored Women convention in St. Louis, Missouri. One session was to be held at the World's Fair ground, in the Hall of Congress. However, the day before the meeting a clubwoman and her escort were refused admittance to a local restaurant. This prompted Margaret Murray Washington to move that the NACW cancel its fairgrounds meeting. The motion passed but when the papers reported it, Washington denied sponsorship of this relatively militant action. Many Association women were livid. Washington's backpedaling denied their antisegregation position; further, Washington had made the NACW look disorganized and equivocal before the public. Lucy Thurman, a Michigan club leader and Washington's severest critic on this issue, thought that the real culprit was Booker T. Washington—she reasoned that Margaret Murray had issued her denial under pressure from her husband.[63]

North and South mostly thought alike within the NACW, but there were regional differences among these women. Northerners, Southerners, and Midwesterners were loyal to their section of the country when it came to elective office, and NACW leadership always tried to balance the executive board.[64] This was a good thing, but it ignored another tension—the different ideological leanings of the women in the different areas. By and large Southerners were more conservative in race and gender ideology than Northerners. Not that on any issue a Northern clubwoman was more activist or militant than a Southern clubwoman; rather, on average Southerners tended to be more tentative and less bold. This, no doubt, was a function of the severe hostility of Southern whites toward blacks. But it also grew out of the conservatism of Margaret Murray Washington. Until his death in 1915, her husband was *the* conservative force to be reckoned with in black America, and she herself opposed activism on behalf of female and black suffrage long after he died.[65] As founder of the Southern Federation of Club Women, Margaret was enormously popular. No doubt she spoke for a significant number of Southern clubwomen; clearly Josephine Yates thought she did. In one of her many letters to Washington, Missouri club leader Yates revealed her own regional and ideological biases when she opined that the South and the West were paired against the East as far as the way the race problem looked in the two regions. Stating her belief that clubwomen in the East were far too smug in their presumption of their civil rights she concluded that "the East . . . has something to learn."[66]

In particular, Yates wanted her Northern, and some of her fellow Midwestern, clubwomen to be less vocal about their rights. When Tom Dixon's antiblack play "The Clansmen" toured Northern and Midwestern cities early in the century, many clubwomen demonstrated against it.[67] Yates saw no point in this "ranting and tearing around," as she called it. Similarly, she agreed with Margaret Murray that the day of prayer Easterners had called for in support of black rights was too public and confrontational. Easterner Anna Cooper believed that blacks won nothing with silence; Yates, conversely, wrote that she did not believe in "going before the public with a wail, and a tale of woe."[68]

Even when regionalism was not a factor in ideological disputes, the different perspectives clubwomen had on race and gender issues was a source of unanticipated conflict. The debate over the *National Association Notes* is a case in point. After 1896, the NACW published its own newspaper, replacing *Woman's Era*, the newspaper that had been the organ of the New Era Club of Boston, under the chief oversight of Josephine St. Pierre Ruffin. Ruffin actually welcomed the new NACW publication because *Woman's Era* had become a financial burden for her.[69] The new paper, *National Association Notes*, would be published out of Tuskegee Institute, and would be able to rely on the resources of the college. It was, however, controlled by conservative Margaret Murray Washington.[70] As time passed, complaints about the *Notes* mounted. Subscribers did not always receive it; *Notes* was not always published according to schedule, and for many, it was too conservative.[71] Josephine Yates, of course, thought the paper's conservative bent was its salvation. In 1904, while she was president of the NACW, she wrote Washington congratulating her on the success of *Notes*: "it is just the conservative, dignified, tone in which they have been published, that has kept the Association out of wrangling without end and all sorts of undignified muddles." Two years later, in a letter that again demonstrated her conservative credentials, Yates reiterated, "our paper must be kept in a conservative tone that will show that we are not ranters, not seeking notoriety, that the matter of race elevation through intelligent and continuous work in the right direction is all we are seeking."[72]

Obviously, other club leaders disagreed. In 1910, at the NACW biennial meeting, Washington's editorship was challenged when antilynching and suffrage activist Ida Wells-Barnett moved that the *National Association Notes* editor be an elected rather than appointed post. Wells-Barnett's motion was voted down but not before many clubwomen voiced their opposition to Margaret Murray's failure to publish more radical, anti-Washington editorials. Ironically, it was at the NACW 1912 biennial meeting—the same meeting at which Washington was elected president—that activists carried the day, passing resolutions against Jim Crow cars, segregation, lynching, and in favor of full woman's suffrage.[73]

These actions say a lot about the Association. First, more united clubwomen than divided them; their shared race and gender identity formed the foundation of a sororal community that transcended ideology. Second, after sixteen years of defending black womanhood and fighting for the right to lead the race, these NACW goals still bound clubwomen together enough to withstand divisive ideological debates.

Yet, if the 1912 convention indicated a level of unity it also signaled current and future difficulties. Taken together, the resolutions and the election reflected divided loyalties and ambivalence. The civil rights and woman's suffrage resolutions signaled a new direction for the Association. The Northern and Midwestern leadership of the NACW were now convinced of a need for more vigorous opposition, in order to stem the tide of lynching, disfranchisement, and segregation. In 1910, as the *Notes* controversy flared, such top NACW leaders as Wells-Barnett, Terrell, Talbert, and Maria Baldwin were serving on the Committee of Forty on Permanent Organization, the group that organized the NAACP. By 1912, NAACP chapters multiplied with the help of black women's clubs, and by 1913 the Northeastern Federation of Women's Clubs was co-sponsoring NAACP antilynching rallies. Clubwomen were also involved in consolidating the organizations that in 1911 formed the National League on Urban Conditions Among Negroes (the Urban League), an organization dedicated to problems of housing, unemployment, health, crime, and the training of blacks in urban areas. The involvement of some clubwomen in interracial work also led them to seek a working relationship with the American Woman Suffrage Association and with white women of the YWCA.[74] By 1912, Addie Hunton was a national organizer for the Association, the leader of the Brooklyn Suffrage League, an organizer and spokesperson for the NAACP, and a strong advocate of black participation in YWCA work. In short, the Association, and its leadership, was growing in a new direction. Yet the election of Margaret Murray Washington reflected an unwillingness on the part of the NACW to move from the less confrontational community and individual oriented self-help social uplift programs. Pulled in both directions, would the NACW move at all? Its "uplift" ideology had proved increasingly out of step with a mainstream black America that was bolder in its demand for civil and political rights. Despite the broadened work of many Association members, as an institution the Association withered.

This was not the course of events envisioned during the Association's turn-of-the-century glory days. Then, NACW leaders had been so sure they had the answer to the race's woes. Beginning with women they would solve problems of race, poverty, and gender. Little could they know that the programs developed by black women, for the benefit of black women and the race, would generate enough gender and class conflict to destroy the goals themselves. No fault could be assigned in this. Issues simply pulled in different directions. Private needs added an additional layer of complications. Personal concerns, the needs of the NACW, the needs of other classes, the needs of black men, could not be met all at once. The NACW's epitaph might well read: Ideology is one thing, reality very much another.

Chapter 3

THEIR OWN BEST ARGUMENT

A life story should not be almost entirely propaganda.
—MARY ROBERTS RAUCHART

Clubwomen, no less than others, had the usual run of life's troubles and joys. But few NACW leaders saw any need to air them. When Mary Roberts Rauchart, a freelance editor, reviewed the first drafts of Mary Church Terrell's autobiography, eventually published as *A Colored Woman in a White World*, she counseled Terrell to open up, to write about her life as a woman, and not merely about her public persona. Terrell should, for instance, put more of her own problems into the manuscript, and address "the very problem of friends." No life was completely "a cause." The manuscript, thought Rauchart, needed more about family life; it needed more "heart"; as written, said Rauchart, "the book is a little cold."[1]

Rauchart's criticism was on the mark. Terrell's book reads like a list of accomplishments.[2] So do the memoirs of other African-American women. Most of them were cautious about putting their private lives and histories in the hands of a media that had for centuries stereotyped and slandered black women. Rather than take such a risk, black women learned to practice what historian Darlene Clark Hine called the art of dissemblance.[3] They let their public see only what they wanted them to see. As far as their audience was concerned, the public was the private.

Wanting the race to be judged by its best women, they had to become their own persuasive argument for the cause of race and black female advancement. When William Pickens, an admirer, was asked to say why Charlotte Hawkins Brown ought to be president of the National Association of Colored Women, he came up with a host of adjectives to describe the North Carolina club leader and school founder. It was not just that she was an unusually competent woman, and a clear-headed and effective speaker, who, according to Pickens, had made the world respect black women, but that she exemplified the ideal. Brown, he concluded, was "herself . . . the biggest argument she can make" for the cause of black womanhood.[4]

In order to be one's own best argument, however, clubwomen had to make "the cause" and their lives indistinguishable to themselves, their peers, and to future generations. Few left records that revealed their private selves; most of the collections left are filled with public memorabilia rather than personal materials. Even though it makes the historian's job of piecing together their private lives almost impossible, for women who wanted their public identity to stand in for the private, this was a good strategy.[5] Nevertheless, some private records have survived, and they point to a heavy and complex burden of being black, female, and a committed leader.

To OUTSIDERS MOST black club leaders must have looked remarkably alike. Most had been born in the South, then moved to the North and West. Most were married, but their low fertility suggests that they did not take seriously Du Bois's instructions to bear children for the race. According to historian Linda Gordon, forty-three percent of the NACW's leaders, and thirty-four percent of those who were married, had no children.[6] Being childless meant more time to manage marriage, club work, and a job outside of the home. Statistics on this last point show that even though most had husbands who could support them, seventy-three percent worked. More often than not, they taught in elementary and secondary schools. Their professional choices were indicative of the black woman's overall limited employment opportunities, as well as their own remarkably high level of education. Unlike the typical black American, who in the first part of the twentieth century had only a minimal education (in 1940, only one percent had a college degree), a third of all club leaders had completed college.[7]

As much as this profile highlights the differences between club leaders and the women they spoke for, it also underscores the similarities. Although club leaders had fewer children than the average black woman, black female fertility in general declined by one-third between 1880 and 1910, thus all black women were having fewer children, not just clubwomen. Furthermore, like countless black women, many Association leaders nurtured and raised the children of other relatives, even while working. Also, like countless black women, these women worked outside of the home. Well qualified by education to teach, they had few other opportunities. Few of any background could land employment in sales or clerical work, and even factory jobs were hard to come by. Unless they founded their own schools and/or libraries, hospitals, settlement houses, or employment agencies, club leaders were women who had class status but little else of special advantage. As with all black people, Jim Crow dogged their lives, and racism so limited their opportunities that they were depressed by it. Club leaders, thus, though different in particular ways from the women they served, had much in common with them.[8]

One commonality was domesticity and motherhood. Margaret Murray Washington, though childless herself, helped raise her husband's children. She also helped organize the Tuskegee mothers' club and the E. A. Russell Settlement. She did all this despite a confession that she was a "dull pupil" when it came to housekeeping, knew little about the care of children, and in fact disliked them.[9]

For Alice Dunbar-Nelson, domesticity meant double duty. Not only was she a high school teacher, and active in the Northeastern Federation of Colored Women's Clubs, but she helped raise both her husband's and her sister's children. She complained often of having little time for herself.[10] Once, after a very full day, which included early morning errands, laboring feverishly at work to make sure the day's commencement exercises went off without a hitch, and stopping to vote in a school board election on the way home, Dunbar-Nelson bristled at the thought of fixing dinner: "Tired as I am, have that to do."[11]

Double-duty was part of a larger problem—a feeling of being unappreciated and devalued. For all of their public statements about the race being saved by its women, Association leaders knew they were taken less seriously than whites or black men. Why else, they thought, would they be paid less for their lectures than everyone else. Sometimes, it was a matter of outright sexism. After speaking at a political rally in Chester, Pennsylvania, instead of being paid the money promised her, Dunbar-Nelson was given pats on the back along with what she called "well-done Girlie stuff."[12] Sometimes women were just cheated. This happened to Mary Church Terrell when the Chicago-based Woman's Civic League, a black woman's organization, refused to pay her the half of the proceeds they promised and handed her a flat twenty-five dollars.[13] Whatever the reason, club leaders knew they were being exploited, and they resented it.

Experiences like these sometimes made the influential Terrell doubt herself and the wisdom of her chosen course. The contradiction between her public pronouncements on the important role women played in the home, and the lecturing and organizational work that took her away from her home did not escape her. It was too "wearing on the nerves," she complained, to take five and six A.M. trains, travel all day to reach a destination by eleven P.M. or midnight, and then not be paid the previously agreed upon lecture fee.[14] Then there was always the unexpected. Long train delays sometimes wreaked havoc on her schedule. She once began menstruating on a train while hectically trying to meet an engagement in the Midwest. An exasperated Terrell considered giving up lecturing. To her husband Robert she wrote that she was "more and more convinced that a woman's place is at her own fireside. . . ."[15]

She felt especially guilty over her separation from her daughter Phyllis. Unlike Wells, who took her young son on lecture tours with her, Terrell left her daughter, the only one of her three children to survive infancy, behind in Washington, D.C.[16] Torn between the financial contribution she felt she should make to her household, the service she thought was her duty to perform for black women, and the desire to be at home with her daughter who "depends upon me to protect her," Terrell reasoned that the best compromise was to find ways of making money at home.[17]

But that was easier said than done. At home, her time was consumed with housekeeping and childcare. Terrell complained less about the latter than the former. She truly felt that if she did not spend time with her daughter, Phyllis, and Mary, her adopted niece, they would fall prey to the omnipresent forces of immorality.[18] Housework, though, was something else. Even though Terrell usually had household help, she generally managed her household and sewed, varnished woodwork, and upholstered chairs. This work she described as "a regular sepulcher in which a woman who wants to accomplish something burns her talent and time." Terrell had frequently lectured on the value of "homes, more homes, better homes, purer homes." She had praised the NACW for its mothers' clubs that taught black women "the best way to sweep, to dust, to cook and to wash." None of this softened her private view that, at home, she was a "prisoner bound with heavy iron chains which no amount of effort or determination or yearning of the intense kind can break."[19]

Ida B. Wells, though not as explicit about it as Terrell, also

expressed the conflict between her public and maternal duties. By
her own admission she did not long for children when she married.
Having raised her seven brothers and sisters when her parents died,
she preferred a public life over motherhood. Still, she opted not to
use available methods of birth control. When her two sons were
born she did what she felt was the proper thing, she nursed them.
This meant that a baby was always at hand on lecture tours, competing for Wells's time. Although Wells managed an extraordinary feat
for her time, Susan B. Anthony told Wells that marriage was a dis-
traction because it forced Wells to take attention away from her antilynching work and devote it to her eleven-month-old baby.
Anthony's comment probably hit a raw nerve, for Wells had already
concluded that if mothers wanted to influence their children's later
years they had to give them full attention during early childhood.
"Motherhood," she wrote, is "a profession by itself, just like school
teaching and lecturing. . . . , once one was launched on such a career,
she owed it to herself to become as expert as possible in the practice
of her profession." Accordingly, Wells several times tried to give up
public work altogether, but to no avail. Club work and antilynching
race work tugged at her as hard as the needs of her sons. Like Terrell,
she simply learned to live with her ambivalence.[20]

Wells also learned to live with Jim Crow. Forced segregation was
inescapable. No matter where Wells lived, as long as club business
forced her to ride trains, as long as she sought food and lodging,
rode an elevator, or entered a building, she would encounter Jim
Crow. Not all club leaders handled prejudice the same way, however.
Their personal responses reflected their different backgrounds and
the way color and class came together in their private lives.

Like Rosa Parks, the mid-century catalyst of the modern Civil
Rights movement, some black women resisted outright. In 1884,
Wells refused to move from her seat in a "whites only" railway car,
and was dragged away by three white men. She sued the railroad and
won her case only to have the Tennessee State Supreme Court over-
turn her victory.[21] Similarly, Charlotte Hawkins Brown sued the rail-

road after twelve white men forced her from her Pullman berth near Anniston, Alabama. She won a small settlement but found it a Pyrrhic victory. Especially painful was her feeling that, despite the compensation, "inconveniencing a Negro woman or humiliating her, in the eyes of the court, was never considered as any great outrage on personality."[22]

Jim Crow was such an outrage, however, that club leaders who could avoid the insult did so. Rather than use public accommodations and convention halls, they stayed with friends and held local and national meetings in black churches. On trips, they packed their own food or went hungry on trains that served food only to whites. For the few who could get away with it, there was always the option of passing.

Victoria Earle Matthews, founder of the White Rose Mission in New York, Josephine St. Pierre Ruffin, founder of the New Era Club in Boston and editor of the *Woman's Era* newspaper, Terrell of Washington, Fannie Williams of Chicago, Adella Hunt Logan of Alabama, Sylvanie Williams of New Orleans, Alice Dunbar-Nelson of Maryland—all were prominent Association women, who at one time or another were taken for, or deliberately passed for white. In many ways these women had the best of both worlds: They enjoyed elite status in black circles, while at least some of the time avoiding the insults meted out to most blacks. Someone like Terrell, for example, could sit in a train car reserved for whites and not expect to be dragged from her place by white men. Because she passed only some of the time, she did not have to cut off relationships and move away from her black family and friends. In short, even while being public advocates for black women, Association leaders like Terrell, unlike their darker counterparts like Wells and Brown, had some control over the degree to which color was an issue in their daily lives.

However, some control was not total control, as Terrell's records reveal. Terrell did sometimes travel in dirty and unventilated Jim Crow cars; while on the lecture circuit she was sometimes forced to enter back doors, take service elevators, and once, while lecturing in Athens, Georgia, she was forced to eat her dinner in the kitchen with a dog.[23] Additionally, Terrell was discriminated against during World War I when she landed a job in a government office. Her boss hired her thinking she was white, and when he later discovered his mistake, he dismissed her on false charges of incompetency and misconduct.[24] Late in life, in 1952, Terrell did initiate a widely publicized discrimination suit against a Washington, D.C., restaurant that had refused her service. Even so, in her young and middle-aged years she clearly had it both ways. [25]

Alice Dunbar-Nelson provides a more revealing look at the tension created by passing. Seemingly not as confident as Terrell, Dunbar-Nelson agonized over possible discovery on the night she, her niece, and her stepdaughter arrived to take their seats at an Atlantic City show. She had bought three tickets from an agent who thought she was white. When she arrived with her darker skinned companions she feared they would be turned away:

> I was conscious of misgivings, and a pounding in my throat when we approached the ticket taker. Suppose he should not let us take our seats? Suppose the ticket seller had sold the seats to me thinking I was white, and seeing Elizabeth and Ethel should make a scene. I choked with apprehension, realized that I was invoking trouble and must not think destructive things, and went on in.

There was no scene, but Dunbar-Nelson still wondered what life would be like without racial barriers. "How splendid it would be," she mused, "never to have any apprehension about one's treatment anywhere?"[26]

While this sentiment was no doubt echoed by blacks of all complexions, the club leader who could pass faced a peculiar dilemma, one especially revealing of the potential conflict between her public and private life. Should the near-white club leader go through her day telling her race to whites who did not know her so that she could be degraded by second-class treatment, or should she just not tell people she was black and agonize or feel guilty over her passive passing? As a race woman the club leader was pledged to fight racism. Passing might be seen as complicity with an obnoxious practice that others, like Wells and Brown, risked life and limb resisting. It might be viewed as a selfish indulgence that was inaccessible to the masses of black people. On the other hand, resistance, even a simple verbal objection, required nerves and courage that only a few possessed. Furthermore, the lone clubwoman, without the refuge of her organization, in a world where the black woman went unprotected by men or law, was vulnerable. If she put her personal needs first, did she necessarily forsake her public duty?

While there is clearly something paradoxical in the private passing for white of women striving to be model examples of black womanhood, on other levels it was perfectly consistent with their publicly avowed purpose to represent black women and speak for the race. What better agent of equality than a black who could be taken as a white. What better proof of racial equality than blacks functioning in a "whites only" capacity with no one the worse off for it. Rather than betraying the race, perhaps the passers exposed race in America as socially constructed to give whites an undeserved advantage over blacks.

This was Terrell's view. It would be foolish to ignore the comfort and safety she gained by passing for white, but it would be equally foolish to ignore the fact that she did not feel guilty for passing. She was not above moving from the Jim Crow railway car to the "whites only" car if the former was too crowded or dirty. More than once she traveled as a white women to a destination where she was to give a lecture on the virtues of black womanhood and was not at all disturbed by the puzzled look on the faces of her black hosts when she exited the train from the "whites only" section. In fact she once made light of her passing when she described her "leaps from the black to the white woman's role" as nothing short of "acrobatic."[27] In another incident revealing of her feelings, she traveled in the "whites only" car from Miami to Key West, Florida, in 1909, and talked freely with white women who wanted to know who she was. Rather than give her first and middle name she cagily replied that she was "a Terrell." They in turn wanted to know if she was related to Governor Terrell of Georgia, for they saw such a "resemblance in the eyes." The tone of the diary entry suggests that as these women searched for visible evidence that they were traveling with Southern aristocracy, Terrell was laughing at them.[28] To her, the episode was proof of the arbitrary, superficial, and constructed nature of race. After all, as a mulatto she was supposed to be a sensuous seductress, but here she was sharing a train car with Southern ladies who took her for a member of Georgia's ruling elite. Here in her private world was naked proof of her public pronouncement on the equality of the races.

This passing incident also makes sense if seen within the idiom of mediation.[29] Because the very light skinned could literally step in and out of the white world, they had a potentially broader and more grounded perspective than the darker skinned.[30] Norma Boyd, a founding member of Alpha Kappa Alpha, a black sorority organized during the NACW's heyday, thought the light mulatto's role as mediator something special. Had it not been for the "people who could pass for white and come back and report just how the other half does," the "darker people in our race would have had an awful time."[31] Whether Boyd was right or not is less important than her perception of her special role. She saw herself as an occasional spy in the enemy's camp. Apparently so did Terrell.

Their own self-conscious responses to passing made these near-white club leaders anything but "tragic" mulattos, like those literary figures hopelessly caught between the black and the white worlds, raised as whites, only to discover, to their downfall, that they were by blood connection, black.[32] If Terrell is any example, near-white Association leaders identified with black Americans and were sincere in their advocacy of black women. They made political connections with whites, and their education and exposure and general experiences made them more confident than most blacks around whites. Nevertheless, with one foot tenuously in the white world, their anchor was still in black America.

They were, perhaps, more securely black than many of darker complexion who accepted white cultural forms at the expense of black traditions. Charlotte Hawkins Brown took a brazen stand against Jim Crow, but one spots her deep insecurities about being black. She lectured blacks incessantly on the need for refinement and culture.[33] Moreover, this dark brown-skinned woman expressed a strange pride in revealing that she had an enslaved fair-skinned blue-eyed grandmother who was a blood descendant of John D. Hawkins, the English navigator; that the blood of great Southern slaveholders and railroad builders flowed in her veins, was a source of pride for Brown.[34]

Jane Edna Hunter, the founder of Cleveland's Phillis Wheatley Association, also seemed insecure in her racial identity. Born of a dark-skinned mother and near-white father, Hunter was determined to "escape the curse" of her dark heritage. According to her biographer, throughout her childhood and young adult years Hunter associated blackness with poverty, contempt, and subjugation. She was humiliated when she had to push her cousin's baby carriage through the streets of Charleston. The baby was dark, and Hunter felt her own light-brown skin made her superior to darker skinned relatives. Hunter eventually decided to dedicate her life to race work, despite a nagging insecurity. "Plagued by feelings of inadequacy" she "constantly worked to position herself to seem more important than she felt she really was."[35]

Of course, neither Brown nor Hunter were enveloped and protected by the black upper classes, and this had to make some difference in the way they handled personal issues of race. Unlike many of the near-white clubwomen whose economic status combined with their color to make their lives relatively comfortable, both Brown and Hunter came from humble backgrounds, and both had very short marriages to men who provided no entree to elite circles. Terrell's education had been planned by her parents, and her husband was a municipal court judge. But Hunter and Brown came by their education and life's work rather haphazardly. Brown went to Cambridge, Massachusetts, schools, but without the generosity of a white philanthropist she probably would have lacked even the one year of normal training she received before starting her own school in Sedalia, North Carolina. Hunter, on the other hand, lived with a variety of relatives and benefactors after her father died, and could not attend school steadily. Lacking the buffer and the anchorage that economic security and upper-class affiliation provided, Brown and Hunter practiced their own kind of "passing." They embraced white culture, or "passed" culturally, as a means of boosting their own sense of worth, and, ironically, as a way of legitimating their "race woman" status.[36]

Regardless of complexion, however, dealing with whites, especially white women, was never easy. All NACW leaders had to rein in their emotions and put on an artificial face before whites. Being their own best example usually meant being to whites something other than what they really were. Only in their private correspondence and in their diaries do a few Association leaders let go of "the cause" and express their real feelings.

At the heart lay a profound distrust of white people, this in spite of white benefactors and an occasional white friend. Terrell, for instance, had many white acquaintances, some dating back to her Oberlin days. Yet, she likened speaking before white audiences to going into battle. "I shall buckle on the armor," she wrote her husband before a talk to an Ohio audience. "It is a very nerve wracking performance this thing of representing my race and trying to please narrow minded white people too."[37] Margaret Murray Washington also had extensive white connections.[38] Still she kept white women at arm's length. She found those who visited Tuskegee to be especially untrustworthy and devious, so much so that she never let a white woman roam the Tuskegee campus without a carefully selected escort. In a 1911 letter she labeled "somewhat confidential" she instructed Emmett Scott, Booker T. Washington's secretary, to make sure that building attendants at Tuskegee knew when white women were visiting so that the latter could be properly courted. Revealing in private correspondence what she would not dare say in public, she wrote: "I always try to give Southern women special attention because they can be so nasty. . . . "[39]

Washington could have passed along the advice that Charlotte Hawkins Brown's mother gave to her: "Try to make friends of those southern white people, for they can make you or break you."[40] Brown, whose normal school training was financed by Alice Freeman Palmer, the first woman president of Wellesley College, found that all whites, Southern or Northern, deserved a wary eye. In their eagerness to appease their Southern friends, it struck her that Northerners were just as racist, and just as disrespectful of black women.[41]

During the first years of the century Brown began a relationship with Northern women who eventually founded the Sedalia Club, a Massachusetts-based organization formed in support of Brown's Sedalia, North Carolina, school. Correspondence between Brown and the white club members is interesting for its clear insensitivities. One Mary Grinnell, for example, had given large sums of money to the school. During the course of their relationship Brown made Grinnell into somewhat of a confidante. She asked Grinnell's advice on just about everything, from the running of the school, to love and matrimony. In 1910, shortly before her short-lived marriage, Brown asked Grinnell whether she should marry, and when the marriage quickly broke up, she again asked for advice. Grinnell's responses seemed sincere enough. Before the marriage she counseled Brown to consider whether she could turn herself away from her school and give full-time attention to her husband, and wondered if Brown's fiancé loved her to the point of suffering when not with her. After the couple separated, Grinnell wrote sympathetically about the trials of life, reminding Brown that she still had her work, and advising her to ignore the malicious gossip about the separation.[42]

What had to be troubling to Brown was Grinnell's avoidance of face-to-face encounters. In letters, Grinnell was a friend. But each time Brown tried to arrange a meeting, Grinnell gave her the cold shoulder. She rudely rejected invitations to visit Palmer, and discouraged Brown from visiting her.[43] One such snub occurred during the time when Grinnell was advising Brown on her impending marriage. Brown had suggested that she visit Grinnell in New Bedford, and Grinnell hedged. First she wrote in vague approval of the visit but added that she would assure her friends that Brown's visit was strictly business. Revealing a finer duplicity, Grinnell asked Brown, "Where would you stay?" She explained that she could not offer her one of her guest rooms because, as she put it, "my colored cook won't know what to think of me." Grinnell also claimed that she did not want to insult Brown by putting her in with the maid. Since, in any case, she did not want "to create any back-door gossip," Grinnell thought it best for Brown to stay overnight with a "respectable colored family," which Grinnell wrote she would be happy to find.[44]

Brown's records are silent on whether she traveled to New Bedford but they do show her relationships with other women of the Sedalia Club to be equally frustrating. From 1902 to the mid-1920s, the white women donors demanded almost obsequious obedience to their every request. First averring that they trusted Brown to make the school's major decisions, they went on to dictate instructions of the minutest detail.[45] Typical were curriculum guidelines sent by Mrs. Frances A. Guthrie, along with her $150 donation and boxes of boys' clothes. Along with personal cleanliness, modesty, and basic reading, writing, and arithmetic, Brown was instructed to teach girls sewing, table setting, and millinery so that they would be useful to their employers and to their husbands. The parents of Brown's pupils, Guthrie insisted, were "nearly all very ignorant people" and thus she advised Brown to abandon her dreams of providing "Higher Education" because "neither their parents, their possible husbands, or they themselves are yet ready to receive" such an education.[46]

An angry rebuttal would have been self-defeating, so Brown did what many clubwomen did when in need of white support—she dissembled. She begged and she begged humbly. She "Uncle Tom-med," but she kept her eye on "the cause" and over the objections of her contributors she expanded the building plant, the acreage, and the curriculum of Palmer Memorial.

And occasionally her true feelings came out. A hint of dissatisfac-tion with Helen Kimball, the initial donor of the school's land, was sparked by a discussion over the future of Kimball's maid, Mary. It seems that Kimball had sent fifteen-year-old Mary South to Palmer, keeping a promise made to the girl's mother to provide Mary's schooling. After a year, Kimball summoned Mary back to her domes-tic job, and Brown, knowing that Mary wanted to be a nurse, objected. Apparently, Brown, who was known for her feistiness, spoke plainly in a letter, which Kimball found objectionable. "I did not like the tone of your letter regarding Mary," wrote Kimball, who then proceeded to tell Brown that Mary would be a more "useful woman" earning money as a maid than she ever would be as a nurse; that the "longer she is kept upon books the harder work will be for her. . . ."[47] Brown's immediate response to Mary's leaving is not known. If, indeed, she did get up the nerve to write more than a bold letter there is no record of it.

In 1921, though, she exploded. Seeking more control over their contributions, the Sedalia Club decided to collect money from indi-vidual subscribers and send it in a lump sum. They withheld from Brown the contributors' names for fear that she might indepen-dently solicit their help; and when the club sent their money they dictated its use. Brown was livid. For a rare moment she did not sac-rifice self-respect for "the cause," instead she proclaimed that the two were inseparable. She wrote: "If the folks up there who give are not satisfied with the management of things they can withdraw. . . . I don't need anybody to help me."[48]

Brown also wrote revealingly of the personal stress behind recon-ciling the different "causes" in her life. Her Northern contributors were forever urging her to increase her Southern support. But Southern help came slowly, and only when she prostrated herself before Southerners with money. Aware that her self-effacing behavior often betrayed the efforts of other clubwomen to counter black stereotypes, she wondered in writing how far to go trading pride for cause:

> I have already gained the interest of some people who will give me money for the school, but absolutely have no regard for the rights of negro women in terms of courtesy. . . . The question in my heart and mind, and God only knows how it hurts, is just what are they going to ask me to submit to as a negro woman to get their interest, for there are some men who occupy high places who feel that no negro woman whether she be cook, criminal or principal of a school should ever be addressed as Mrs.[49]

Apparently, duty won out. Brown agonized privately, but in public she continued to "wear the mask"—and her school survived. Despite always unstable finances, Palmer Memorial remained a substantial black rural institution until the 1970s.

Brown was only one black woman whose credibility in her community was undermined by whites, or who made painful choices. Jane Edna Hunter's struggle on behalf of the Phillis Wheatley Association for Black Women is another case in point. Hunter tried through most of 1911 and 1912 to gain black support for her YWCA-like facility. Cleveland's blacks, including the local elite black clubwomen, were ambivalent about financing the all-black female home for fear that it would discourage integrated projects. Hunter therefore raised money initially from blacks like Booker T. Washington, who espoused economic nationalism. Still the project could not go forward without wealthy white supporters. From the start these whites compromised Hunter's integrity by insisting on control of the institution and make-up of the board of trustees. Faced with the choice of sacrificing the hard-won trust of the black community or the much-needed settlement facility, Hunter bitterly, but firmly endured the black community's rebuke.[50]

Over and over again, the pattern was repeated. In Chicago, in 1903, Wells and other black clubwomen enthusiastically joined with white women to finance a community center named for Frederick Douglass. To her chagrin Wells found that the white women involved in the project would not share leadership of the center with black women, nor the woman's club affiliated with it.

This was not Wells's first clash with a white woman. During her antilynching tour of England, Wells's efforts were undermined by Frances E. Willard, the American founder and president of the Women's Christian Temperance Union (WCTU). Willard scandalously assured the British public that Southern white women and children were menaced by black men. Wells shot back vitriolically, attacking Willard for her bigotry and duplicity and informing the British public of the racist practices of the American WCTU.[51]

Wells felt better about suffragist Susan B. Anthony, but the two did sometimes clash. One divisive issue was Anthony's support of the National American Woman Suffrage Association's (NAWSA) acceptance of Southern prejudices. Wells and many other club leaders were wary of supposedly progressive white women who around the turn of the century made the woman's vote their number-one priority. For many of these white women suffragists, it became expedient to drop any issue that would cost Southern congressional support. Chief among the causes they repudiated were the equal rights of blacks, the enfranchisement of black women, and the re-enfranchisement of black men. Individual white women might privately support black male and female suffrage, but once NAWSA went on record in 1903 in favor of suffrage as the "medium through which to retain supremacy of the white race over the African," NACW suffrage advocates, their credibility undermined, launched a desperate attack against NAWSA's official policy.[52]

Wells went on the attack early. Susan B. Anthony had asked Frederick Douglass not to attend an Atlanta, Georgia, NAWSA convention, even though Douglass had attended every previous meeting. Further, Anthony had also declined to help a group of black women form a suffrage association. Both actions angered Wells, who said in no uncertain terms that Anthony was wrong in confirming white women in their attitude of segregation.[53] In 1913, and in the face of continued discrimination by white suffrage organizations, Wells formed the Alpha Suffrage Club, the first such club formally organized by a black woman.[54]

More than a source of outrage and frustration, the racism of some of the nation's most progressive white women revealed a precarious situation that had trapped Association leaders. The NACW had come into being, in part, to combat the unofficial "whites only" policy of the General Federation of Women's Clubs. Black women could not be candid with most white women. In shared projects, club leaders usually found themselves adopting means that compromised their ends.[55] These problems only added to those club leaders had with their men. Black men involved in the race struggle and white suffragists should have been natural allies of the NACW, sources of private and public support. On occasion they were, black men more so than white women.[56] But club leaders were disappointed with both; neither provided the allegiance they needed. Cooper summarized the dilemma: The black woman of her day was "confronted with both a woman question and a race problem, and is as yet an unknown and unacknowledged factor in both."[57]

On such shifting sands, it would seem the bonds between the women of the National Association of Colored Women would be strong. Some enduring friendships did develop—Margaret Murray Washington and Josephine Yates for one—and some clubwomen served as role models for each other. Ursula Wade and Charlotte Hawkins Brown looked to fellow Southerner Washington; Mary McLeod Bethune inspired Alice Dunbar-Nelson.[58] And locally, close friendships often went hand in hand with community service. Overall, however, although the Association's national leaders shared common goals, although they struggled to reconcile their private needs with public demands, they were seldom friends.

Relationships established on the local level had the greatest potential to be exceptions to this general rule. Unlike national work, which demanded cooperation from women of diverse regions, local self-help projects brought women of the same community together for neighborhood or individual self-improvement. For Christia Adair, a Texas clubwoman, friends proved to be the source of strength she needed to help her survive the death of her husband. She thought that had it not been for their loving guidance she would not have known how to find and keep a job, or how to live on her own.[59] In Seattle, Tacoma, Spokane, and Yakima, Washington, club work cemented friendships. Both Eliza McCabe and Arline Yarbrough, moving club spirits in these lonely outposts of black America, spoke of their aim to nourish female friendships in these isolated Northwestern towns.[60]

Consider also Rosabelle S. Jones of the Kansas City Federation of Colored Women's Clubs and her emotional presidential farewell address. She listed the club's accomplishments and reminded fellow clubwomen that they supposedly lived by the motto, "Lifting As We Climb." Beyond this, Jones thought that if clubwomen were to:

> *Add to kindness amiability*
> *Subtract good from evil*
> *Multiply duty by love*
> *Divide cheerfulness with charitable deeds*
> *Reduce jealousy to its lowest denomination*
> *The result will be TRUE FRIENDSHIP.*[61]

Her poem was as much plea as it was statement of truth. Outsiders could not know how rife jealousy and bad feelings were in local club affairs. So insidious were the forces against amity and sorority that club leaders prayed for deliverance. "Keep us, O God, from pettiness. . . . ," was the first line of the Association's prayer. It went on to ask for freedom from fault-finding and self-seeking; for strength to make them calm, serene, and gentle. Knowing that they were more or less united on the large issues of race, class, and gender, they feared the repercussions of "mistrissism," and the damage of personality conflicts. Their prayer reflected their fears:

> Grant that we may realize that it is the little things that create differences; in the big things of life we are one. May we strive to touch and know the great common woman heart of us all, and, O Lord God, let us not forget to be kind.[62]

To be kind, gentle, calm, and serene were traits that were critical for women who strove to be examples of perfect black womanhood; they were also traits that easily escaped them. Why? Wells offered a thoughtful explanation. Discord ruled because every decision, she felt, was taken as a referendum on personality. Much later, in the 1960s, women learned to take private feelings and domestic experiences as points of departure for political awareness and action. The personal became political. In Wells's time just the opposite prevailed—women of the Association made the political personal, and made of every philosophical and tactical difference a personal slight. "Always the personal element," lamented Wells. "It seems disheartening to think that every move for progress and race advancement has to be blocked in this way."[63]

Wells's comment followed a clash—one of many—with NACW leaders. In 1900 she had a "falling out" with Agnes Moody, president of the Ida B. Wells Club (named in her honor) because Moody felt Wells usurped her power. Ten years later, after Wells had earned a reputation as a no-nonsense, uncompromising race leader, Wells was hissed off the Association's convention floor because delegates thought she was making a power play for editorship of National Association Notes. That episode led to her sound defeat in the Association's 1924 presidential election by Mary McLeod Bethune.[64]

Like Wells, Terrell had a stormy NACW career. She shot out stinging five- and six-page letters to fellow clubwomen over minor disagreements or incidents. Daisy Lampkins, Nannie Burroughs, Mary

McLeod Bethune, Addie Hunton, and Margaret Murray Washington—all of them received vitriolic letters from Terrell.[65]

Terrell could also be arrogant. In 1932, Bethune visited New York from Florida intending to visit Terrell. At the time Terrell was working for the Republican party and was staying at the Waldorf Astoria Hotel. When Bethune appeared, Terrell refused to see her, sending word to the reception desk that she was too tired. A shocked Bethune left New York the next day.[66] Terrell's silence in the Anna Cooper case was also reprehensible. Cooper and Terrell had graduated together from Oberlin in 1884. Although they had not been close friends in college, together they had pioneered the 1890s club movement, organizing the Washington Colored Woman's League. Cooper went on to become a teacher and then principal of Washington's M Street School, and Terrell served on the school board between 1895 and 1901 and again from 1906 to 1911. Suddenly, in 1900, the school fired Cooper—she had become a victim of infighting among Washington, D.C.'s black elite, who disliked her classical curriculum. Throughout Cooper's ordeal Terrell maintained an inexplicable silence, neither lifting a hand to help nor even offering a kind word in Cooper's behalf.[67]

The Cooper and Terrell estrangement dated back at least to the 1899 dispute over the NACW presidency, a time when many other Association leaders parted company with Terrell. Yates, Washington, Wells, and Cooper all kept Terrell at arm's-length after her re-election, a snub Terrell resented.[68] Wells accused Terrell of "selfish ambition," while Washington called her a warmonger. Yates described her as untrustworthy and manipulative. For her part, Cooper wrote an article in National Association Notes expressing opposition to Terrell's actions.[69] So stormy were Terrell's relationships that, by her own admission, she had not a friend in Washington, and her diaries speak often of later years spent in desperate loneliness.[70]

The 1899 and 1910 conventions that sealed the respective fates of Terrell and Wells within the NACW were typically combative. Almost all conventions or large meetings, national or otherwise, substantiated John Hope's view that the women were no better than men when it came to political bickering. However, NACW biennial election meetings were especially contentious. They were more akin to political conventions than conferences organized around self-help issues. How else can we describe the 1920 meeting where then-president Mary Talbert began campaigning against her aspiring successor, Hallie Q. Brown, fully a year before the election was held.[71] In 1933, Illinois club leader Mary Waring won out over Brown in a bitter struggle that saw Waring distributing handbill propaganda as far south as Alabama, and Brown campaigning all over the country.[72]

Enormous personal ego was invested in these partisan battles. The eleventh annual Washington State convention in 1928 was a case in point. The tension level was so high during a debate on who to send to the National Biennial that a delegate rose from her seat, walked to the podium, and knocked the chairwoman's bell (apparently used to maintain order) right out of her hands.[73] This episode was just a prelude to the bitterness that prevailed during the actual national meeting. Alice Dunbar-Nelson remembered the convention as one "too exhausting to think of." She called Brown a "dirty little rat" for using unscrupulous methods to gain office and described the contest for Executive Secretary (between Sallie Stewart and Rebecca Stiles Taylor) as a "bitter war." On top of everything else, during the three-and-a-half-hour Executive Board meeting so much "dirty linen washed" that some of the members were reduced to tears.[74] This was not unlike a meeting described by Terrell where some very "unkind and unpleasant" opinions were aired when a member submitted a personal finance voucher for reimbursement by the Association.[75]

Why was there so much discord? Why so much dissension among women who were natural allies? Wells was right about club leaders taking political and philosophical differences personally. But Wells only analyzed a symptom of the problem, not the problem itself. Central to the problem was the fact that the Association was too limiting, its goals too narrow to use all of the abilities of its leaders effectively. There were few other opportunities for talented black women. The clubs, therefore, became political arenas where leaders were very often mean and callous toward each other, venting anger and frustration that seemed to have no other outlet.

If this made Association leaders less than perfect, it certainly did not make them less worthy representatives of black women. In fact, their struggles demonstrated that they shared some everyday concerns and experiences of the women they spoke for. Like the average black women, Association leaders worked outside the home, chafed under double-duty, were torn between their work, their public duty, and their maternal responsibilities. Jim Crow was as much of an insult to them as it was to all black women, and though they did not work as domestics in the homes of white women, relationships with them were often trying. To the extent that they managed the exigencies of life under restraints imposed by sexism and racism, and managed as well to coordinate nationwide self-help projects, knowing all along that they were held to a higher standard than white women, they were indeed "their own best arguments."

But this was not the basis on which *they* sought to make themselves models of black womanhood. Club leaders wanted only the public person examined—the virtuous, self-sacrificing woman, articulate in defense of her sisters. No doubt, on some level they understood that if their private lives were examined along with the public, they would not pass their own very rigid test of perfect black womanhood. Contrary to their public statements and personae, their private lives revealed ambivalence regarding Victorian notions of homemaking and motherhood, a willingness to forsake resistance to racism for personal comfort, a tendency toward self-righteousness, and a penchant for the kind of politics which the Association officially denounced.

In setting themselves up as best arguments for the race and black female advancement, they were less than realistic. Just as balancing race, class, and gender was a difficult feat for the NACW, it was equally difficult for individuals to cope with all three variables. It was safer to conceal this reality than to reveal it.

Chapter 4

A NEW ERA

❖

Get ready, it is better to be ready and not have the chance, then [sic] to
have the chance and not be ready.

— Nannie Burroughs

On the afternoon of August 2, 1920, business in Harlem stopped
as thousands of cheering onlookers lined the sidewalks of
Lenox Avenue to view the spectacular parade of Marcus Garvey's
Universal Negro Improvement Association (UNIA). Such splendor
and pageantry was designed to mesmerize and astonish, not only
America's most renowned black community, but all of black and
white America. It stretched for miles. First came the mounted
African Legionnaires, followed by UNIA officials who rode in open
cars decorated with streamers. The African Legion followed, dressed
in spanking dark-blue uniforms with narrow red trouser stripes, its
members proudly conscious of the effect their colorful garb and
marching precision had on the marveling crowds. Although the
African Legion was unarmed except for its officers' dress swords, its
very existence hinted that the redemption of black people might
come through force, and the two hundred Black Cross Nurses that
followed them spoke of the readiness of UNIA women to come to

their aid should they fall in battle. The Nurses were followed by squads of children singing songs in praise of the African homeland. As Harlemites waved and cheered from windows and sidewalks, twelve marching bands and well-drilled drum majors passed. The banners carried by representatives of the many participating churches, lodges, and UNIA branches proclaimed a new era and announced the New Negro: "Down with Lynching," "Uncle Tom's Dead and Buried," "Join the Fight For Freedom," and "Africa Must Be Free." Two marchers at the head of the Woman's Auxiliary raised a large banner that read "God Give Us Real Men."[1]

Marcus Garvey himself had come from Jamaica, West Indies, to New York to bear witness to real manhood at the UNIA's International Convention of the Negro Peoples of the World. When the convention's first business session opened that evening at Madison Square Garden, there were, according to the *New York Times*, twenty-five thousand people in attendance, and thousands more stood outside. Garvey was greeted with a five-minute round of applause when he took the podium. Quieting the crowd, Garvey launched into a mesmerizing speech that heralded the new era:

> We New Negroes, we men who have returned from World War I, we will dispute every inch of the way until we win. We will begin by framing a Bill of Rights for the Negro race . . . The Constitution of the United States means that every white American should shed his blood to defend that Constitution. The Constitution of the Negro race will mean that every Negro will shed his blood to defend that Constitution. If Europe is for the Europeans, then Africa shall be for the black people of the world. We say it; we mean it.[2]

Garvey went on to preach his message of liberation, pressing it home throughout the convention: Africa was for Africans and people of African descent. Europeans had to leave the continent and recognize black people as sovereign. Black Americans must take pride in their race, their color, their contributions to America, and defend themselves, with arms if necessary, against racism. Garvey demanded political and civil rights, social and political separatism, and called for the solidarity of black people around the world.[3] These tenets were spelled out in a document called "The Declaration of Rights of the Negro People." After thirty days of deliberation on the future of the black populations around the world, the convention closed, leaving those who attended in a mood of self-confident defiance.

Garvey certainly reflected the period's potential and optimism, but he was not the only source of a new black pride; nor were African Americans the only group ripe for change. American women also oozed with the enthusiasm of post-World War I America. In 1920s advertising, glamorous women smiled behind America's newest toy—the automobile. They happily operated electric appliances, smoked cigarettes in romantic settings, and vacationed in exotic resorts. As their hemlines gradually rose, so did the proportion of female high-school graduates bound for college, and the number of college-educated women who combined marriage and career. The ratification of the Nineteenth Amendment, in 1920, was as symbolically important as Garvey's march through Harlem. It signaled a change in perspective, and marked the advent of the New Woman.[4]

These heady times presented new challenges for black women, and for the National Association of Colored Women. One might have thought that with the victory of woman's suffrage that the Association could have capitalized on the new political order. Surely the vote would abet its antilynching efforts, and strengthen the Association's claims for women's superior leadership. Organized as they were around local self-help issues, the clubs seemed situated to take advantage of the new black pride. The energy that catapulted Marcus Garvey onto center stage in black America might also have undergirded an organization pledged to save the race and defend black women. Not so. Instead this decade of transition in women's rights and black circumstances marked the permanent decline of the

National Association of Colored Women. With it went the idea that the progress of African Americans was marked by the progress of black women.

This fact was not immediately obvious, but it was not subtle either. It took no genie to predict that infighting and ever-growing classism would eventually undermine the NACW's effectiveness. Katherine Macarthy's 1920 biennial speech served notice of this danger. Nor did it take much foresight to realize that with the Depression creeping through black neighborhoods years before it hit white America, local clubs would struggle to meet local and national financial commitments. These were serious problems, but the most insurmountable was the Association's ideology. Put one way, the organization found itself with a philosophical foundation that could not withstand the assault it took during this period. Put colloquially, it was just not "ready" for the new age ushered in by the "New Negro" and the "New Woman."[5]

THOUGH IT MIGHT seem that the passage of the woman's suffrage amendment and the triumphant return from France of Negro regiments had little in common, both symbolized what women and blacks hoped would be a new era. White women of the middle and upper classes embraced the vote and partisan politics. The Women's Joint Congressional Committee successfully pushed legislation through Congress establishing joint federal-state programs of prenatal care and medical attention for babies, the so-called Sheppard-Towner Act. In states such as Virginia, women voters were able to lobby legislatures to push public health measures, prison reform, uniform guardianship and property laws, and limitations on the hours women worked. A new freedom of sexual expression arose. Sigmund Freud and Havelock Ellis wrote on the harmful effects of sexual repression; Margaret Sanger gave out birth control information and devices; woman had greater access to high school and college education—all helped to shape what was being described as the "New Woman." The term had come into use in the 1890s to signify women's new opportunities and roles. Women of the 1920s now need not choose between a career and marriage. With the help of new household labor saving devices they could have both. No longer forced to express her political ideas through the men of her family, the new woman held a job in the expanding job market, made decisions based on her own wants and needs, and generally embodied the spirit of individualism.[6]

Blacks, too, had reason for optimism. Black men had been ambivalent about fighting in World War I. Their country, after all, denied them basic human rights and forced them to fight under the French flag. Even so, men of the black regiments fought valiantly, earning the respect that should have been their birthright. The 1919 triumphant march of the 369th United States Infantry regiment down New York's Fifth Avenue and uptown in Harlem did what Garvey's parade did a year later, it heralded the arrival of the New Negro. The New Negro threw off the accommodationist views of Booker T. Washington. He was demanding and militant in search of civil rights and economic opportunities, and eagerly embraced a culture that celebrated its African origins and African-American traditions. The New Negro joined organizations that protested segregation, discrimination, and lynching—the NAACP, the National Race Congress, and the National Baptist Convention. Marcus Garvey's Universal Negro Improvement Association drew in the black working class. More than any leader of the period he inspired new hope for a brighter future. In his uniform of purple, green, and black, a white feather sticking from his cap, this Jamaican-born black man struck a noble pose, embodying possibilities of the age, as fully as the artists whose novels, poetry, music, painting, and sculpture made up the Harlem Renaissance.[7]

Taken together, the New Woman and the New Negro should have turned the status quo on its head. But for its promise, the 1920s was like the France of Dickens's *Tale of Two Cities*: It was the best, but also the worst of times. Blacks might fashion a new personality, but much of white America returned to old-fashioned racism, lynching, and terror. Called the Red Summer by novelist and poet James Weldon Johnson, the summer of 1919 saw some of the worst race riots this country had ever witnessed. Blacks and whites fought and died over parks, housing, and jobs. As if to say that no Negro, much less the New Negro, was welcome, black soldiers were singled out for special brutality. Southern rural blacks were also hit hard by the boll weevil, capping a despair already wrought by soil erosion and competition from foreign tobacco, cotton, and sugar cane. When rural migrants fled to urban enclaves, they fueled white hostility as well as resentment from blacks already there. A new approach to black rights was sorely needed but among other things that marked this period, the New Negro faced some age-old problems.

So too did the New Woman. At the beginning of the 1920s women reformers lobbied for and Congress passed the Packers and Stockyards Bill designed to increase consumer protection; the Cable Act in 1922 that reformed citizenship requirements for married women; the Lehlbach Act of 1923 that upgraded the merit system in the civil service; and the Child Labor Amendment to the Constitution in 1924. On the state level, twenty state legislatures granted women the right to serve on juries. Michigan and Montana enacted equal-pay laws, Wisconsin approved a far-reaching equal-rights bill and even in the South there was flexibility toward social legislation. By mid-decade, though, women's influence waned as Congress was tired of being asked to pass women's legislation. Subsequently, the Child Labor Amendment failed ratification in Massachusetts and New York, appropriations for the Women's Bureau and the Children's Bureau were cut, and reformers were able to get an extension on the Sheppard-Towner Act only by agreeing to let it expire in 1929.[8]

Female reform failed for a number of reasons, but chief among them was the failure of the suffrage campaign to unite women into a single voting bloc. In the years immediately following the passage of the Nineteenth Amendment politicians gave women's issues respect and recognition because they feared their numbers. When a woman's voting bloc did not materialize, and it became clear that women voted like men, indeed in lesser numbers, politicians returned to business as usual.

Black and other minority women could have predicted this turn of events. While supportive of suffrage they knew that they would not be voting in tandem with white women because few white women shared their preoccupation with civil rights, antilynching, job discrimination, and disfranchisement. By the time white women of the middle and upper classes realized that women of different races and classes were not united, they were deep into a divisive debate over the meaning of equality in America. What did being man's equal really mean? Did it mean equal civil and political rights, or equal opportunity for achievement in all realms? What, if any, difference did biology make? Those who supported the Equal Rights Amendment—framed by the National Woman's Party in 1923—downplayed the difference between men and women. They thought women could make their own way without special help. Others though, felt that women's lesser strength, their childbearing and nurturing roles, controlled their life chances. They wanted legislatures to act on woman's equality by protecting them against baneful industrial conditions. Like the problems that besieged the New Negro, these were age-old issues. What was new was the context, the generation, and the concern.

Also new was the mandate for change that the era presented the National Association of Colored Women. Although there was a lot that was symbolic, and much that was old, about the New Negro and the New Woman, the era did highlight the profound issues that would dominate black and women's rights movements of the future. As such, the era presented the Association with new challenges, the response to which would determine its future direction and place in black and black woman's history.

To begin with, the NACW needed somehow to address the underlying machismo of those who spoke for the New Negro.

Notwithstanding the advent of woman suffrage, the era of the New Negro contrasted markedly with the turn-of-the-century "woman's era" when black men had been admonished for their seeming cowardice in the face of white America. America now had many black men who had fought white men in battle, in Europe and in the riot-torn streets of America. Now, artists and race leaders celebrated a self-consciously militant black male. Claude McKay's poem "If We Must Die" was a call to arms. "O kinsmen!" he wrote, "we must meet the common foe!" The poem continued:

> Though far outnumbered let us show us brave,
> And for their thousand blows deal one deathblow!
> What though before us lies the open grave?
> Like men we'll face the murderous, cowardly pack,
> Pressed to the wall, dying, but fighting back![9]

While McKay revealed the black male's new militancy, J. E. McCall's poem "The New Negro" sculpted a truly majestic black man:

> He scans the world with calm and fearless eyes,
>   Conscious within of powers long since forgot;
> At every step, now man-made barriers rise
>   To bar his progress—but he heeds them not.
> He stands erect though tempests round him crash,
>   Though thunder burst and billows surge and roll;
> He laughs and forges on, while lightenings flash
>   Along the rocky pathway to his goal.
> Impassive as a Sphinx, he stares ahead—
>   Foresees new empires rise and old ones fall;
> While caste-mad nations lust for blood to shed,
>   He sees God's finger writing on the wall.
> With soul awakened, wise and strong he stands,
>   Holding his destiny within his hands.[10]

THIS COVER OF *THE MESSENGER*, THE JOURNAL OF THE BROTHERHOOD OF SLEEP-
ING CAR PORTERS, ILLUSTRATES THE MASCULINE ETHOS OF THE PERIOD. *Photo
courtesy of Photographs and Prints Division, Schomburg Center for Research in Black
Culture, the New York Public Library, Astor, Lenox and Tilden Foundations.*

Revisionist history also trumpeted the New Negro. Particular
attention was paid to Reconstruction. During the twenties no other
subject received as much print in the *Journal of Negro History*, or as
much session time at the Association for the Study of Negro Life and
History. Fully ten years before Du Bois's 1935 publication of the
monumental *Black Reconstruction in America, 1860–1880*, A. A. Taylor,
Rayford Logan, James Hugo Johnston, and John R. Lynch rewrote
the history of Southern reconstruction governments. Their story
was not of men who had sold their votes or lost it for the race, nor of

buffoons drunk with power. Rather these scholars unearthed the limited role black men played in government and politics during this period, a role that told a story of fiscal responsibility in pursuit of educational reforms and the extension of democracy.[11]

This new history was on George W. Woodson's mind when he addressed the Colored Women's League of St. Paul, Minnesota. Woodson, President Emeritus of the National Bar Association, thought it imperative that club women reject the idea that black men acted irresponsibly during Reconstruction, that they had, as Anna Cooper put it, sold their vote "for a mess of pottage." Woodson confessed an early belief that black politicians had proved themselves unworthy of respect, but now he understood that "there never was a word of truth in it. . . . " Woodson also told the clubwomen that though he had once believed that women would "stand up longer without pay for principals that are right, then [sic] a colored man will," he now believed that black men had been libeled and deserved the respect they had been denied.[12] Whether or not the members of St. Paul's Colored Women's League realized it, Woodson's comments signaled the waning of the "woman's era."

Though much more subtle, John E. Bruce's 1922 address before women at the White Rose Mission in New York sent a similar signal. Bruce reminisced about a speech delivered to members of the Mission twenty years earlier entitled "The Influence of Good Women." At that time the race's future looked "a trifle brighter" to him than it did in 1922; he had been very proud of the work that Victoria Earle Matthews and other club women were doing in establishing the mission. Now, in 1922, things had happened "to change the viewpoints of many . . . who see with tolerably clear vision." The gradual elimination of blacks from the political arena and the extension of segregation had made imperative a new tack. While Bruce never said that black women could no longer be of influence, he did imply that the twenties had brought adversity, which the influence of women alone could not overcome.[13]

Had more black women defined the period through literature

and poetry, Association leaders might have held their own; female Renaissance voices could have reiterated or redefined the NACW. But the Renaissance itself fell under masculine influence. Although not all of the literature and poetry of the era was written by men, most of it was. Black men also received most of the grants and patronage from philanthropists, and they were freer to frequent the bars where the intelligentsia gathered. More mobile than women, who were often tied to the home with familial responsibilities, men could travel, expand their experiences, and generally develop as artists. Literary critic Gloria Hull notes that the Renaissance was a time when men were " 'in vogue.' . . . They enjoyed the lion's share of all the available goods and, in the field of literature, were more apt to be seriously encouraged as professional writers."[14]

Women were discouraged from taking up their pens at the same time that they lost much of the rationale for female leadership that had been generated during the previous era. Club leaders had argued for race leadership on the grounds that black men had "lost" the vote. Not only was that history now being revised, but Southern whites now used the same terror, literacy tests, grandfather clauses, and poll taxes against black women and black men alike. Thus it was increasingly difficult to argue that African Americans would be better off under female stewardship. As black people looked to the future, more and more they focused on the ideas of John Hope, not those of Anna Cooper or Josephine Yates.

Perhaps the most crushing blow to the "woman's era" philosophy came from the black nationalism of the Garvey movement. Garvey captured more hearts and minds than any other New Negro leader, and to Garvey the age belonged to men: "this is the age of men, not pygmies, not of serfs and peons and dogs, but men, and we who make up the membership of the Universal Negro Improvement Association reflect the new manhood of the Negro."[15] The African Legion of the UNIA embodied the age. As noted by historian Barbara Bair, it personified the prestige and purpose associated with independent black manhood. It represented the ideas of power and dominance and the military might necessary to achieve and maintain Negro nationhood. Modeled on U.S. infantry protocol and regimentation, the paramilitary wing of the movement was made up primarily of World War I veterans.[16] When the African Legion marched in UNIA parades, supplied bodyguard and crowd control services at mass meetings, and added pomp and ceremony to the public appearances of UNIA officials, they, as Bair notes, served "as bodily symbols of the movement as a nation within a nation."[17] She might also have added that the African Legion picked up the gauntlet thrown down by Fannie Williams when she challenged black men to "stand out and say to all the world, 'Thus far and no farther in your attempt to insult and degrade our women!'"[18] Here, at last, was the promise of protection clubwomen had demanded. A promise the extended gloved hand of Mary Church Terrell could not fulfill.

The Garvey movement also promised to rescue black women from the labor force by giving them men who were providers. "The black man is tired of eating food and never selling it," said Garvey in 1923. He is "tired of laboring in the bowels of ships and not keeping watch on the bridge."[19] Like the captains of industry, Garvey promised that this new generation of men would be not just workers, but self-made black men who would take black women out of white people's kitchens.

Garveyite rhetoric, in fact, embraced the idea of Victorian womanhood, not the New Woman. The movement promised to exalt black women as white women had always been. The ideal was celebrated in an article in the Garveyite newspaper, The Negro World: "Let us go back to the days of true manhood when women truly reverenced us . . . let us again place our women upon the pedestal from whence they have been forced into the vortex of the seething world of business." According to the article, if the black man played his part as he should, "we would have many more mothers, many more virtuous wives, many more amiable and lovable daughters."[20]

Garvey's construction of womanhood impacted on black women and the philosophy of the "woman's era"; so did his ideas about racial purity, the foundation of his black nationalism. "We do not seek intermarriage," he insisted. "It is only the so-called 'colored' man who talks of social equality." "To be a Negro is no disgrace, but an honor," Garvey affirmed, "and we of the U.N.I.A. do not want to become white." For Garveyites, racial purity was the bedrock of the black nation. Black people, he claimed, had the right to "have a country of our own, and there foster and re-establish a culture and civilization exclusively ours."[21]

There was no room in Garvey's black country for mixed race leaders or integrated leadership, and Garvey seldom lost an opportunity to press the point. His vendetta against integrated civil rights organizations and light-skinned black leaders, especially W. E. B. Du Bois, had consequences for the NACW.[22] The NAACP, Garvey insisted, "wants us all to become white by amalgamation, but they are not honest enough to come out with the truth." "It is the duty of the virtuous and morally pure of both the white and black races," he continued, "to thoughtfully and actively protect the future of the two peoples, by vigorously opposing the destructive propaganda and vile efforts of the miscegenationists of the white race, and their associates, the hybrids of the Negro race."[23] Garvey's pronouncement placed him at odds with both the NAACP (and like organizations) and the NACW. If the integrated and mixed race leadership of the NAACP could not represent the aspirations of black Americans, certainly a *woman's* organization led largely by light-skinned members would be regarded by him as ludicrous. Even more than the NAACP, the National Association of Colored Women represented the antithesis of Garveyite ideas about black leadership.

Garvey's ideas of racial purity had other implications as well. Like the promise of protection, providership, and the pedestal, the ideology of racial purity gave black women a long-denied positive image of themselves. Garvey's poem, "The Black Woman," gave the dark-skinned woman the throne she had never had:

Black Queen of beauty, thou hast given colour to the world!
Among other women thou art royal and the fairest!
Like the brightest of jewels in the regal diadem,
Shin'st thou, Goddess of Africa, Nature's purest emblem!
Black men worship the virginal shrine in truest Love,
Because in thine eyes are virtue's steady and holy mark,
As we see in no other, clothed in silk or fine linen,
From ancient Venus, the Goddess to mythical Helen,
Superior Angels look like you in heaven above,
For thou art fairest, queen of the seasons, queen of our love:
No condition shall make us ever in life desert thee,
Sweet Goddess of the ever green land and placid blue sea.[24]

This poem painted more than a picture of regal black woman-hood; the black nationalism embedded within it offered black women something a woman's organization could not—male admiration. The poem not only negates the black woman's promiscuous image, but by celebrating them as the "fairest," the "brightest," and the "purest" object of male desire, it told them they were more beautiful than white women. Moreover, the poem comforts by ensuring black women that they are preferred over their white counterparts; that they will not be deserted and will preside as goddesses over the black nation. Garvey's black nationalism thus promised black women a life most could only imagine. It held forth the idealized existence many believed was the domain of white women. What black woman could turn her back on a life so ennobled, so free from hard labor, so protected from sexual violence? Garvey made black nationalism appealing to the masses of black women. He made them, as their banners attested, ask God for "real men."

In so doing, he, and the entire New Negro movement, offered a compelling counter-vision of black America to that offered by the Association. The turn of the century had seen racial violence, disfranchisement, and segregation collapse the public and political world of African Americans into a private world of community institutions—the traditional and expanding world of women. Although female leaders tackled national issues like lynching, and confronted white officials, they did so from their seat of strength—clubs and associations that had a community base and a community objective. Civil rights and black nationalism had not yet molded a public world for black men because accommodation rather than confrontation was the order of the day. In the post-World War I era, as real and figurative confrontation replaced accommodation, a new public and political role was created by and for black men. These roles rebutted women's allegations of male weakness by highlighting man's superior strength and fighting abilities. They promised to liberate black women from backbreaking work and sexual violence. Contrary to the Association's woman-centered race-progress ideology, the proponents of New Negro ideology made race progress dependent on virile masculinity. This irresistible vision threatened the very existence of the NACW.

But it was not the only threat. The twenties also attacked notions of strict sexual morality and female self-sacrifice. The cover to the 1926 July issue of *Opportunity Magazine*, the National Urban League's journal, is a case in point. Drawn by Gwendolyn Bennett, one of the few black women artists of the Harlem Renaissance, it featured a young black women in a pose that had sexual seduction etched all over it. Bennett's portrait hardly resembled a boyish looking flapper. While neither the flapper nor Bennett's seductress looked like most female Americans, black or white, both signaled the advent of new attitudes about female sexuality and individualism.

Evidence of these new attitudes was everywhere in black and white America. Supporters of the Equal Rights Amendment, as well as those who supported protective legislation, wanted women to be as independent and self-expressive as men. For decades women had lobbied for less physically restrictive dress. Although the fashionable short skirts, silk stockings, knickerbocker pants, and high heels were arguably not very functional or physically liberating, the decade saw America's emerging consumer culture begin to come around.

THIS COVER OF THE URBAN LEAGUE'S JOURNAL, *Opportunity*, SYMBOLIZED A NEW ERA. *Photo courtesy of Photographs and Prints Division, Schomburg Center for Research in Black Culture, the New York Public Library, Astor, Lenox and Tilden Foundations.*

The new consumer culture affected all women. Make-up, hair styling, dancing—everything changed. Madame C. J. Walker's hair straightening and beauty processes revolutionized standards of beauty among black women, and both black and white females turned to all sorts of skin creams and hair pomades, rouges, and lipsticks, to find their own special look.[25] If new dances like the fox-trot and the jitterbug amazed people, the lyrics to blues singer Ida Cox's 1920s hit, "Wild Women," shocked the daylights out of them:

> You never get nothing by being an angel child
> You'd better change your way an' get real wild.
> I wanta' tell you something. I wouldn't tell you
>   no lie,
> Wild women are the only kind that ever get by.
> Wild women don't worry.
> Wild women don't have the blues.[26]

Along with other blues singers, Ida Cox validated an image of black women very different from that cultivated by clubwomen, especially those who worked hard at being the best arguments for the race. Cox, Bessie Smith, and Ethel Waters sang songs about black women who were fallible, about women who were disgusted with the migrating, abandoning men who left them when times got hard. Their women were depressed living a life of never ending work and worry; they were sensual women, who enjoyed sex and used it for financial and emotional gain.[27] Although many songs, like Bessie Smith's "In House Blues," lamented the plight of women trapped at home, betrayed by the men they loved, other songs, like "Freight Train Blues," sung by Clara Smith, suggested that women could be as footloose as any male:

> I'm goin away just to wear you off my mind.
> I'm goin away just to wear you off my mind.
> And I may be gone for a doggone long long time.[28]

Another song called "Young Woman's Blues" assured women they had options. Written by Bessie Smith, it tells of a woman who, just like the man she used to date, decides not to marry or settle down. Smith's heroine must endure the ridicule of those who disapprove of her choices, but she continues to value her moonshine and running around more than matrimony and stability.[29]

In blues songs, women did not, like clubwomen, pray to be delivered from their jealousies and rages. In the face of men who were mean and untrustworthy, these women were arrogant and cynical. For instance, in another song sung by Clara Smith, a woman wants the world to know that she can be as insufferable as any man:

> . . .When I'm with a fella, it's simply for making a show.
> I keep a fella spending till his money's gone
> And tell him that he's nothing but a pure breed hog.[30]

One theme dominated blues songs in the 1920s—sex, mostly heterosexual, sometimes homosexual. While Ma Rainey's song "Prove It On Me Blues" had as its subject a woman who sings of friends who "must've been women, cause I don't like no men," most songs were about women who were passionate about men. Cox's "One Hour Mama" is as assertive about her sexual needs as she is confident about her sexual prowess:

> I want a slow and easy man;
> He needn't ever take the lead,
> Cause I work on that long time plan
> And I ain't alookin for no speed.
>
> I'm a one hour mama, so no one minute papa
> Ain't the kind of man for me.
> Set your alarm clock papa, one hour that's proper,
> Then love me like I like to be.[31]

Clearly, blues women offered black women self-images unlike any presented by clubwomen, in fact unlike any presented by blacks to America. In short, they did for black women what the flapper did for whites, they publicly affirmed black female sexuality with style and variety. As put by literary critic Hazel Carby, these singers had broken out of the boundaries of the home and taken their sensuality and sexuality into the public sphere. They were gorgeous and mesmerizing. Their physical presence was a crucial aspect of their power. Dressed in spangled dresses and furs, displaying their gold teeth and diamonds, they made black female sexuality desirable.[32]

Further, blues singers and their lyrics were not like anything in the flapper world. The flapper was white and boyishly feminine; the blues woman was black and sensual. Both shouted female independence and individualism, but the flapper was more of a coquette, virginal until won over by a man. Blues singers represented women who were more worldly—and more shapely. Like the flapper, they were men's partners, their equals, but unlike the flapper they were not naive, but knowing in ways of the flesh. They knew the pain of having no man and no money.[33]

Despite the differences, blues singers and their audiences were part of the sexual liberation movement, a movement as threatening to clubwomen as the New Negro movement. As John D'Emilio and Estelle Freedman note in their history of sexuality in America, the 1920s saw the country move toward a set of beliefs that affirmed heterosexual pleasure as a value in itself. Sexual satisfaction had become a critical component of personal happiness, something necessary for a successful marriage, and a healthy adolescence.[34] Such openness challenged club leaders' traditional ideas about the value of chastity and the black woman's duty to the race. In a very real way blues women removed the black woman's sexuality from the legacy of her slave past, and made it something of value and use for the present.

Therein lay a dilemma for the National Association of Colored Women. If clubwomen threw chastity to the wind, what happened to their time-honored belief that the race could rise no higher than its women? In the NACW creed black women had to be free of promiscuity. Now promiscuity was being proffered as something liberating, and black men were claiming race leadership as their domain. Confronted with new race and gender issues, the response of the NACW would determine its course for the rest of the century.

Unfortunately, club leaders could not adapt. They wanted no part of the new sexuality, whether flapper or blues woman. Throughout the twenties they railed against it. Moral purity and socially correct behavior became even more of a crusade than in the pre-war years. As the decade progressed, club leaders spoke more about women's power in the home and community, and less about their ability to write a "book of Acts for the race," or stamp "weal or woe" on its future. The change was often subtle. Femininity had always meant purity and morality, but before the twenties, club leaders stood against the legacy of the black woman's past. Now, they pitted themselves against both past and present, and struggled against the tide.

And an impassioned struggle it was. "The type of character held up to our girls as a model should be strong in prideful morality, strong in point of conduct prompted by a sense of self-respect and honor," wrote Iowa club leader Gertrude E. Rush. Revealing a very present-minded orientation, Rush wrote, "Mothers cannot be flappers and retain the respect of girls." She also implied that they could not be like the blues women. According to Rush, when "immoral women" were allowed to "float to the top" they spread "evil influence and disseminate their immorality. . . . " Rush warned that this made for delinquency in girls because they were impressionable and likely to imitate the "exalted immorality." Because she thought that immoral women were literally omnipresent, she encouraged clubwomen everywhere to purge their membership to ensure that there were none whose "tendency to moral perversion" has "completely swallowed their self-respect."[35]

Sallie Stewart, the NACW's president from 1928 to 1930, was also looking both ways. In her 1928 national biennial address she reminded clubwomen of the time when "the black woman was denied even the reputation of being chaste and virtuous." She recalled how with the help of the clubs they had "climbed," how the

NACW had made this climb "an object lesson before the world." Unlike the first generation of club leaders who put purity and morality in the context of female race leadership, Stewart begged only for clubwomen to "hold on to the quality of femininity." In so doing Stewart made the "climb" an end unto itself, a means to race recognition but not a prerequisite to female leadership.[36]

Throughout the 1920s, in fact for the remainder of the twentieth century, the National Association of Colored Women denounced female individuality and any expression of sexuality, while it held fast to femininity as an end to itself. Hallie Q. Brown testified that she "set her face like a flint against every thing that would dishonor the Negro woman." Black women, she insisted, could not become "obsessed with fashion and things of pleasure only." Rather, their concern had to be with uplift, child welfare legislation, health and sanitation, and higher standards in art and literature.[37]

Iowa club leader Mrs. S. Joe Brown agreed. Black women could not afford to "imitate" those white women who embraced the new individualism and sexuality. Brown claimed "they have not character. . . . the greatest need of the Negro Woman is to set up a standard of her own; that she may regain the confidence and respect of those of the opposite sex, many of whom are beginning to feel that women are losing their finer charms." Black women ought to "teach by example those higher ideals usually looked for in womanhood."[38]

Brown's response was typical of the club leaders concession to the masculine impulse of the New Negro movement. Here was a dramatic retrenchment in an ideology that had once accommodated Anna Cooper's sentiment that "no man can represent the race," and Fannie Williams's feeling that black men's conventions and councils began and ended with talk. John Hope had once asked black women for more Florence Nightingales and fewer Queen Elizabeths. Stewart and Brown were now willing to comply with his demand for black women to "hold on to femininity" and to not lose their "finer charms."[39] In short, where NACW leaders had once combined their race and gender ideology so that race work and feminism did not conflict, now they defined race work within the context of femininity.

To support this rhetoric the NACW, in 1928, launched a better homes drive, a program with significant class implications. Clubwomen were urged to form local committees that would go into schools and observe the dress, deportment, and hygiene of black children. The committees would report back to the local clubs, which in turn were to hold conferences emphasizing "Better Environment for Colored Children." According to Stewart, these conferences would gradually reach the homes "bringing first of all better personal appearances of the children." Stewart also urged blacks to avoid back alleys and kitchenette apartments. Spacious and sanitary homes, clean backyards, and mothers who read instructive materials were far more conducive, she argued, to "wholesome citizenship."[40]

Stewart's national project spawned a host of like-minded projects on the local level, among them a campaign for a delinquent home for girls and women sponsored by the New York City Federation of Colored Women's Clubs. For these clubwomen the new sexuality made this and other places of refuge even more essential than they had been before the twenties. In New York City especially, the flapper and the blues woman had painted such an enticing picture that it was easier than ever for the young black women "coming every day from the rural districts" to be waylaid by the silk and electric lights of the city. Afraid that they would be distracted by the "fine clothes, jewelry and finery" they saw for the first time, middle- and upper-class clubwomen worked to make sure that the unsophisticated newcomer would not get in with the wrong company, perhaps even wind up in jail with hardened criminals.[41]

Although the "Better Homes Projects" were well intentioned, the NACW's program and rhetoric fell on a black society now attuned to the militant language of the New Negro, and on a class of black women that had as much reason to ignore as to welcome it. Clubwomen could not, for example, make the same promises to black women that the New Negroes were making. They promised to provide for and protect black women. They fought for a world of racial equality free of sexual violence. Where Garvey offered black women reverence, clubwomen put the burden of protection on black women themselves: their code of morality would lead to self-esteem. The NACW may have been more realistic about the black woman's future, but ordinary black women now had a choice.

They were unlikely to choose the NACW because its leaders often seemed out of touch with ordinary black women. Most were poor, often migrants. Stewart's references to kitchenette apartments and back alleys, while not meant to be malicious, demeaned them. If a black female migrant had a house with a backyard, it was likely not her own, but that of the family who employed her as a domestic. If she was married with children, the children probably helped support the family and missed a lot of school. In fact, working long hours, and protected mostly by her own wits, many black women nonetheless now found a harsh but exhilarating independence, far from grinding rural life. Migrant Velma Davis said it was "like being untied and tickled at the same time!"[42] Davis and others like her were not closed to the message of race uplift, nor were they intent on losing what Brown called their "finer charms." Their reality simply did not allow them to focus on the NACW's issues. The mood and culture of the blues women and the New Negro more closely matched their situation.[43]

Take domestic work. Some club leaders had worked in white homes; all knew or were related to someone who had, but NACW women approached this subject very differently from those whose survival depended on it. Like their white counterparts, club leaders insisted that domestic work could be professionalized. Nannie Burroughs and others had founded the National Training School for Women and Girls in 1909. One mission of the school was the expert training of domestic workers. The idea was that with the proper instruction in the use of new household devices, and with proper professional behavior, black women could make an asset of their relegation to menial service.[44] Clubwoman Ezell Carter even insisted that black female service workers made their own way hard. From the floor of the 1933 biennial convention she warned cleaning women to be more reasonable in their demands. They "would have their afternoon off even if the President of the United States were to be entertained." Cooks, she added, "announce that they are 'taste' cooks and renounce the book with distressing results." Describing service workers in industry as sassy and lazy, she added, "they are Sunday dressers with little thought given to tidiness and neatness upon the everyday job."[45]

Portions of this speech appeared in major African-American newspapers and must have distressed domestic workers whose reality was quite different from that imagined by Carter. As one domestic said, it was "a job that you did and did, more and more—from one thing to another, early to late."[46] They knew, of course, that employers generally wanted to pay as little as possible for as much work as could be extracted. To them, uniforms were a badge of servility; if they did not wear their best clothes on the few Sundays they got off, they would not get to wear them. No amount of professional knowledge could change this. No matter what club leaders thought, domestic workers needed to gain some control—and most wished to leave live-in work altogether. Their isolation in their white employer's home, together with the plentiful supply of migrants looking for work, spelled exploitation that they could do little to prevent.[47]

Domestic workers could, however, avoid the NACW. After World War I, poor black women had more choices than ever before. Whether it was they who avoided the clubwomen or vice-versa, the fact was that Association women continued to have trouble dealing with them on their own terms. As young women moved out of the oppressive South by the thousands they changed the nature of domestic work from live-in to day work. They also adopted the new style of entertainment, behavior, and dress; in short, they responded to forces that created the New Negro and New Woman movements. Left behind were middle- and upper-class organizations like the NACW.

Middle-class women drifted away, too. Partly, increasing exclusivity was to blame. Some thought that clubs were populated by many a "wolf in sheep's clothing," the immoral clubwoman posing as a model of decency. Katherine Macarthy, though, was concerned that clubs were becoming overly choosy about their membership, intensively screening potential members. Taken together, these concerns suggest that the declining membership so obvious by the late 1920s could be traced to NACW clubs' inability to enroll just the "right" kind of women.

But the loss of members could also be traced to the NACW's increasingly narrow program and ideology. Like their poorer counterparts, middle-class black women, especially those in Northern urban areas, were branching out. Suffrage gave them a new way to participate in politics and a new tool for race work. The New Negro Movement made pan-Africanism attractive and stimulated an interest in women of other nations. To meet the needs of a new era many women shifted their race work to the NAACP, while they also created new organizations. Both the National League of Colored Republican Women and the International Council of Women of the Darker Races of the World were founded in the twenties by well-known Association leaders, including Mary Church Terrell and Mary McLeod Bethune. Both organizations represented efforts by middle-class women to carve out a place for themselves in the new era.

These new organizations underscored the limits of uplift. Take politics. Earlier disagreement over the relevance of woman's suffrage to black rights became moot after the passage of the Nineteenth Amendment. The vote was a reality for most Northern women, and club leaders were determined to use it in the struggle for black rights. Yet they could not organize politically within the NACW because it stood by its official non-partisanship in an effort to minimize political conflict. This was particularly exasperating in 1924. A year earlier, the United Daughters of the Confederacy had lobbied Congress on behalf of a bill proposing that a statue of Mammy be erected in Washington in tribute to "their" loyal black domestic help. Many Association leaders felt that if the Democrats won the White House in 1924 the solidly Democratic South would ram the dreaded bill through Congress. Despite their fears, widespread objection arose among clubwomen when the Association's newspaper, *National Association Notes*, was used by Republican clubwomen to support Republican candidates.[48] Since the NACW could not provide an outlet for their political energy, leading members met that same year and organized the National League of Republican Colored Women. This new group aimed to make black women a force in the Republican party through education and mobilization of the black female vote.[49] It also served notice that black women—including many Association leaders—would not yield leadership to black men so easily. Politics was not going to be an exclusively male domain.[50]

When the International Council of Women of the Darker Races of the World came along it sent a similar message. As a kind of think tank, the International Council focused on the conditions of women and children of color in countries as diverse as Nigeria, Brazil, the Philippines, Puerto Rico, and Haiti. Thus it became a vehicle for black American women to work with other women of color, improving the education and self-esteem of women worldwide. Like the League of Colored Republican Women, the International Council was founded by leading members of the NACW uncomfortable with the Association's narrowing focus.[51] It demonstrated not only the growth of pan-Africanism in black America, but also the growing respect that African Americans had for all non-Western people. By focusing on and respecting the racial consciousness of people of different cultures, the International Council took a step away from the elitism of the NACW clubs and their deference to Western mores. Taken together, the Republican League and the International Council demonstrated both the limits of uplift ideology in the new age, and women's resistance to the new masculine impulse.

The most determined resistance, however, came not from clubwomen, but from women in the Garvey movement. Female Garveyites prayed for "real men." They wanted to be revered by men, to build positive images of black women, and an end to sexual violence. But they also wanted gender equality and were unwilling to trade the pedestal for it. This was made clear at the 1922 UNIA convention. At one point, when Garvey had left the convention floor, Victoria Turner, a delegate from St. Louis, approached the podium bearing a set of five resolutions. Ratified by a majority of women delegates, the resolutions called for women to be granted greater recognition and authority as delegates, committee members, local officers, and field representatives. Finally they urged the need for women to be involved in setting internal policy "so that the Negro women all over the world can function without restriction from the men." Following Turner, women rose one by one to express their dissatisfaction with the limitations placed upon them in the movement. Clara Morgan, a Black Cross Nurse, declared that "she was not in favor of the women standing behind and pushing the men; they wanted to be placed in some of the executive positions because they felt they were entitled to them." Mrs. M. M. Scott of Detroit stated that "she found that whenever women began to function in the organization the men presumed to dictate to them." Another female delegate stated that "she believed the women were as competent as the men to be field representatives," and another made it clear that while women had no intention of taking the men's positions they "wanted to be by their side."[52]

When Garvey returned to the room he confidently dismissed the women's complaints. They need not have passed such resolutions, he claimed, for their interests were already protected under the UNIA constitution. During the same convention, when a woman delegate rose to nominate a woman as a member of the UNIA delegation to the League of Nations, Garvey again rejected the women's wishes as "entirely improper to send a lady as a delegate, since it would be contrary to diplomatic custom, ladies never being chosen as members of diplomatic missions."[53]

Garveyite women were not easily put off. Even Garvey realized that women were the stalwarts of the UNIA and the backbone of local divisions. Consequently, despite his chauvinism, a few women occupied important positions in the organization. Henrietta Vinton Davis became the international organizer and presided regularly at major mass meetings. In 1922 she became the fourth assistant president, and in 1924 she was the only woman member of the UNIA delegation to Liberia. Maymie De Mena served as a Spanish translator and organizer. In 1929 she became a female symbol of the crusading spirit of the organization. Throwing traditional femininity to the wind, she led a UNIA parade through the streets of Kingston, Jamaica, on horseback, brandishing a sword like a black Joan of Arc. That same year she succeeded Davis as fourth assistant president and international organizer.[54] In addition to Davis and De Mena, each local division of the UNIA had a "lady" president and a male president. The female ran woman's auxiliaries, including the Black Cross Nurses, who served as health care providers and launched community social welfare projects.

Just as they had at the 1922 convention, women persistently fought against the masculine impulse of the New Negro era. Eunice Lewis, of Chicago, said that Garvey women represented the "New Negro woman . . . revolutionizing the old type of male leadership."[55] De Mena called for support of women's rights when she noted that "very little, if anything, is said of the women who form such a large percentage of the membership of this great movement." "For seven years we have been lauding our men through the press, on the platform, and, in fact from every angle while in reality the backbone and sinew of the Universal Negro Improvement Association has been and is the real women of the organization." De Mena thought UNIA women had earned the right to be more than a Black Cross Nurse or secretary of a division, and she urged women to assert themselves. She also reminded the men that they could not meet the goals of the UNIA alone. Men, she urged, "seek and secure the co-operation of your women so that doors now closed against us may be open."[56] Gladys E. Holder of New York added to De Mena's advice, suggesting that there should be "the election and appointment of more women to the executive offices than heretofore." De Mena reminded the men that "there are scores of women workers, full of zeal, courage and initiative scattered throughout . . . who are capable of rendering greater service to the race if placed in higher positions."[57]

More than any other woman in the movement, Amy Jacques Garvey, Garvey's second wife, pushed on UNIA's doors on behalf of women workers. Amy Jacques Garvey could do this with impunity. Aside from being Garvey's wife, she served the UNIA as secretary, legal advisor, extemporaneous minister, journalist, and leading Garvey propagandist. In 1920 she became the business manager of the UNIA headquarters in Harlem. Amy achieved true influence in the UNIA, however, when she became Garvey's personal representative after he was convicted of mail fraud in 1923, and imprisoned in 1925–27.[58] Gradually Jacques Garvey became UNIA's feminist conscience, in tenor and tone often sounding like some of the early leaders of the National Association of Colored Women. For example, in her 1926 *The Black Women's Resolve*, Jacques Garvey wrote: "We serve notice on our men that Negro women will demand equal opportunity to fill any position in the Universal Negro Improvement Association or anywhere else without discrimination because of sex." "We are very sorry if it hurts your old-fashioned tyrannical feelings," she continued. "We not only make the demand but we intend to enforce it."[59] Jacques Garvey used the woman's page of the organization's newspaper, *Negro World*, to urge women to fight for their rights, not just as blacks, but as women. "Our Women and What They Think" ran from 1924 to 1928. Its very existence demonstrated that its editor, Jacques Garvey, and other UNIA women understood the inextricable connections between their sexual and racial identities, and wanted all who read the page to understand it as well.[60]

Indeed, Jacques Garvey's woman's page articles "represented the ideas of progressive black women seeking to understand the conditions of their sex and race."[61] It would not be a page "devoted solely to dress, home hints and love topics." "Our page is unique," Jacques

Garvey boasted, "it seeks to give out the thoughts of our women on all subjects affecting them in particular and others in general."[62] True to her word, the page ran feature articles on topics from home life to war, and clippings from other newspapers relevant to domestic and international women's struggles and achievements. Like members of the International Council of Women of the Darker Races of the World, Jacques Garvey was interested in the "world-wide movement for the enlargement of women's sphere."[63] Sensitive to the fact that "in all countries and in all ages men have arrogated to themselves the prerogative of regulating not only the domestic but civic and economic life of women," Jacques Garvey kept black women abreast of news about women in other countries. She wrote about Indian women entering politics, Egyptian women discarding the veil, about Madame Kemal, a Turkish woman who denounced harem relations, and Madame Sun Yat Sen's Chinese political schools that taught women about revolutionary thought, feminism, and political economy.[64]

Jacques Garvey and other UNIA women wanted to play a part in the New Negro era, not take a back seat. It was rare for black women to be celebrated as queens, to be promised protection and a life free of toil. Nevertheless, Jacques Garvey and others refused to trade their autonomy for a pedestal. UNIA women took to heart the lesson taught earlier by Anna Cooper—as long as sexual oppression hindered half the race, there could be no liberation for the race as a whole. Women had done too much for their families and communities to be designated second-class citizens by black men. UNIA women also understood that however much they needed protection from sexual violence, and freedom from never ending labor, such protection and freedom could not be bought by another oppression.[65] They wanted to carve for themselves an equal role in the race struggle, not because it was the "woman's era" and their superior sensibilities made them the best leaders, but because they could struggle as hard and fight as fiercely as men.

It was, thus, the middle- and working-class women of the Garvey movement who picked up the feminism of the early National Association of Colored Women and took it through the 1920s. Like Association leaders, the UNIA feminists insisted on equality with men and on woman's ability to lead when men did not. Their spokeswoman, Amy Jacques Garvey exhorted them to "take their places beside their men." If, for any reason, men did not lead the fight against colonialism and racism, then she urged women to go it alone. Sounding very much like Brooklyn clubwoman Mrs. Fayerweather, who wrote that "we are tired of hearing Negro men say, 'There is a better day coming' while they do nothing to usher in the day," Jacques Garvey kept her sights on women's abilities and served notice that they would "brush aside the halting cowardly men, and with prayer on our lips and arms, prepared for any fray, we will press on and on until victory is ours."[66]

Unfortunately, the times were against the UNIA. After 1929, the Depression pushed it into decline and prevented Garvey men and women from crafting a relationship and carrying forth a program that recognized all their strengths. By 1930, the triumphant Harlem parade of 1920 was but a distant memory. Organizational infighting, government harassment, and business fraud had taken its toll. After Garvey's imprisonment in 1925 and his deportation in 1927, the American chapters gradually declined. Black men were hit hard by the Depression, losing even low-wage, dead-end service jobs to white men desperate for work. Black women became providers in ever greater numbers.[67] Survival took priority over reform and improvement.

But much had changed forever. World War I and migration to the North had stimulated a new militancy, closing the age of accommodation. Racial equality and separatism were now well anchored in black consciousness. Men now challenged the idea that women stood at the center of the fight for equality. The twenties drove home the concept that the progress of the race rested on two things: black men's willingness to fight for racial justice, and their ability to provide for and protect—Garvey would say control—black women.

Less dramatic, but more central images of black women moved away from the legacies of slavery. In the twenties, black women became queens, even goddesses, on the one hand, and sexual sophisticates on the other.

The 1920s crippled the National Association of Colored Women. Rising from its ashes, however, were questions that would haunt the whole century. Does racial progress depend more on men to play patriarchal roles or on women to overcome sexual and racial oppression? How enticing was the black nationalist offer of the pedestal, and what, if anything, were black women willing to pay for it? Were black feminists and black nationalists really at odds or did they have common ground? As black women found ways to survive the century's worst economic crisis, they also began to resolve some of these questions. Predictably, black women did not all travel the same road to resolution.

Chapter 5

❀

RETHINKING PLACE

We must get away from the local idea. We must see the entire territory of the United States. We must see each State as a Union. We must see the city and State united. We must then send out the light that we have gotten.

—REBECCA STILES TAYLOR

Let us face our problems squarely and without fear. You shine as brightly as possible in your little corner and I in mine, and the meeting of our lights will soon emblazon the world and darkness will be dispelled.

—MARY McLEOD BETHUNE

The black people of Greenwood, Mississippi, had always had a "hard row to hoe," but the hoeing got harder during the Depression when the government paid landowners not to plant their crops, and landowners subsequently pushed tenant farmers off the land. Government programs like the Works Project Administration were supposed to provide work for unemployed black and white farm laborers. True to form, however, whites got most of the jobs, and blacks were left to fend for themselves. By the time Pinkie Pilcher wrote President Roosevelt in 1936, she had observed all manner of white deceit and meanness. In Greenwood, most of the WPA work seemed to go to white women. Pilcher saw blacks treated so badly that black men declared that "they would eat grass like a cow and drink water before they would go back to any of the relief offices, let them white people dog them again." Women applying at WPA offices were told that there were no government jobs and they should "go hunt washings," even though, as Pilcher noted, "white people dont

[sic] pay anything for their washing" and a woman "can't do enough washing to feed her family." Pilcher had a personal complaint. The white female WPA workers paid to look in and report on the sick cared little about what happened to sick black people. Pilcher told Roosevelt that "the money you all pay out for poor white women visiting the colored people you could throw it in the river or in the fire for what it do us." She wrote that she had always visited and helped ailing blacks, yet "I cant [sic] get work." She thought that the least the government could do was to "let the colored people look after the colored people old sick [sic] and the white look after white." "If we can't have colored home visitors," she wrote, "we dont [sic] want any."[1]

Lutensia Dillard had a similar complaint. She wrote to Roosevelt in 1941 because most of the men in Woodland Park and Bitely, Michigan, had been laid off and their families threatened with the loss of their homes. Apparently, they were unable to get WPA jobs, and they could only get government welfare by signing over their homes to the state. "Our men would work if they could only get work to do," she wrote. Explaining that when layoffs hit, "our group are always the first ones to get the first blow," she begged Roosevelt for help. Dillard felt Roosevelt owed them because she and the Colored Women's Democrat Club, on whose behalf she wrote, had campaigned vigorously for Roosevelt and supported him "one hundred percent." She also wanted Roosevelt to understand the despair the women felt over their men's situation. On the one hand, their husbands were out of work, and on the other, their sons were being drafted. It was not right, she wrote, that in a free land black men "are not aloud [sic] to work and make a living for their wives and childrens." Black people, she concluded, "aren't getting a fair deal."[2]

The raw deal black people *were* getting hit women hard. On any given morning in any large city one could find groups of black women with brown paper bags and cheap suitcases standing on street corners waiting for a chance to get work. They would get there as early as seven in the morning and wait into the late after-noon for someone to drive by and give them a day's, or half a day's, domestic labor. The lucky ones got about twenty to thirty cents an hour for scrubbing, cleaning, laundering, washing windows, and waxing floors and woodwork all day long. Once hired on the "slave market," the women often found that, after a day's backbreaking toil, they had worked longer than was arranged, were paid less than was promised, and were forced to accept clothing instead of cash.[3] As late as 1935, black women did housework and laundry for three dol-lars a week, and washerwomen did a week's wash for seventy-five cents.[4]

The story was much the same all over the country. When Arline Yarbrough, a high-school graduate and trained typist, looked for work in Seattle, Washington, she had doors slammed in her face "as soon as they'd seen we were black." In the early 1930s even domestic work was at a premium and employers gave preference to white domestics. Yarbrough had answered an ad over the phone and was told by the lady of the house that she was just the person she needed. When she arrived, however, the woman told her, "I don't think we'll need anybody after all." Together with a friend she went to all the hospitals, not to get jobs as nurse's aides but as orderlies. They also went to big restaurants looking for dishwasher jobs. As she recalled, "they practically laughed in our face. We couldn't get a thing, not a thing." The only jobs available were "little house jobs and baby sitting jobs, which would usually be for a day or two, a week at the most." She recalled that "it was a pretty cruel situation."[5]

Yarbrough did not get to use her typing skills until 1941 when World War II brought an end to the Depression, and jobs opened up. By that time, some things had become perfectly clear to black peo-ple, and black women in particular: They would have to put more energy into surviving than obtaining civil and political rights, or a separate black nation, or a trip back to Africa.

As hard as it was for black women to get work, it proved even harder for black men. Black women could always fall back on domestic labor, but black men had no such safety net. The Depression made it clear that there would be no pedestal for them, and if they had doubts that their labor was crucial to black family and community survival, the bad times erased them. Even when the war lifted the nation out of economic stagnation, black women who could escape domestic work for the factory found themselves doing the dirtiest and hardest jobs, work often reserved for men. No matter how hard they worked during the Depression, and no matter how patriotic they were during the war, race and sex discrimination combined to deprive most African-American females of a living wage at a time when black families needed their income more than ever.[6]

Clearly, the Depression and the war forced new ways of thinking about black women, the black masses, and gender relationships. Could African-American families attain the patriarchal structure demanded during the previous decade, and if so, could they risk it? Did black women need separate organizations to speak for them, or could race associations do as good a job? If African-American women did have their own representation, who should speak for them, and what kind of programs did they need to pursue? A myriad of new organizations sprouted during this period offering different strategies to cope with the crises. Two in particular—the National Council of Negro Women and the Ladies Auxiliary of the Brotherhood of Sleeping Car Porters—demonstrate how things had changed, and how black female leaders juggled their race and sex needs to meet the problems of the age.

GIVEN THE DIFFERENCES in priorities and programs, it's ironic that the women who ushered in the "woman's era" also birthed this new period of black female organizing. Terrell, Bethune, Brown, Hunton, Dickerson, and others could not have known that when they met to form the National Republican Colored Woman's League and the International Council of Women of the Darker Races, they were creating two of the first new black middle-class women's organizations. This is not to say that no new black women's associations formed between 1896 and 1924. On the contrary, during that period several Greek letter sororities were formed, including Alpha Kappa Alpha (AKA) and Delta Sigma Theta. Black women also continued to be active in the NAACP, the YWCA, lodges like the Eastern Star, and a host of other organizations.[7]

But the Republican League and the International Council represented a different kind of participation. Until the 1920s black women's organizations were basically devoted to self-help uplift and community development. This meant that although NACW women lobbied nationally for antilynching legislation, and used a national platform to defend black women, their fundamental approach was to create or support local institutions. The self-help work of sororities was quite similar; in fact, sororities modeled their service work after the NACW.[8]

The League and the International Council, however, broadened the scope of black women's work by concerning themselves with national issues and national identity. In addition, many black women's organizations would now do less theorizing about womanhood, and would defend the black woman's character without moralizing. Being one's own best argument increasingly meant belonging to an interest group that lobbied the government or big business in the interests of black women and the race. It meant staying abreast of current legislation and other national activities, and organizing along professional or labor lines in order to exert maximum pressure on the powerful. Founded in the 1920s, the Republican League and the International Council were a portent of things to come. As the League gave black women a voice in national politics, the International Council represented American black women in the world. No matter how one looked at it, black women's national organizations would never be the same.

In this they were like the white women's associations that emerged during the teens, twenties, and thirties. The General Federation of Women's Clubs, the organization after which the National Association of Colored Women was modeled, declined in membership during this period while numerous other special-interest women's organizations thrived. Through lobbying in Washington, organizations like the Women's Joint Congressional Committee (which represented a broad array of women's groups) were less community based and more connected with government bureaucracies, universities, research institutes, trade unions, and hospitals. Women in these new associations did less theorizing about womanhood. Says historian Nancy Cott, "the newer women's organizations were so more by habit and expedience than commitment." More important than their identity as women was their identity as voter, parent, coreligionist, ideologue, or citizen.[9]

Black women, however, were not mimicking their white counterparts. Like them, they were spurred to political lobbying by the Nineteenth Amendment. Yet black female activists were driven just as much by the migration of hundreds of thousands of blacks to urban areas, by the racism and discrimination that gave way to urban riots in the wake of that migration, and by the political tactics of the New Negro movement. While they too found new meaning in their identity as voter, citizen, and the like, American racism and the profound transformation the race was undergoing prevented these new identities from taking on a generic quality. The white woman could be a voter, citizen, or parent, but her darker sister would always be a black voter, black citizen, or black parent. New black women's organizations might depart from the philosophy and strategies of the NACW, but because African Americans were at a crossroads, they could never stray from the NAACP, the National Urban League, or the myriad other African-American groups. Whereas the Association had preceded the NAACP in organizing in the interest of black people, black women's organizations now followed its lead in emphasizing pressure-group politics.

And for good reason. Franklin Roosevelt had hired an unprecedented number of black advisors to deal with race issues, fueling

expectations that such tactics would yield results. Previous presidents had sought informal advice from one or two blacks whom
whites had deemed acceptable leaders. The most outstanding example, Booker T. Washington, was an occasional unofficial advisor to
Theodore Roosevelt and William Howard Taft. In breaking with previous practice, FDR used a few highly trained blacks in official positions. Not surprisingly, but definitely reinforcing the masculine
impulse of the New Negro movement, most of the intelligentsia
were male. Robert Weaver, William Hastie, Robert Vann, Eugene
Jones, Lawrence Oxley, Edgar Brown, and Frank Horne had already
established themselves as "race men." Now they were given more
attention and credibility by virtue of their relatively high-level government service. Alone among these highly visible African Americans was one woman, Mary McLeod Bethune, who from 1935 to
1942 served as the director of the Division of Negro Affairs of the
National Youth Administration (NYA).[10]

Bethune continued the tradition of female race leadership,
demonstrating professional versatility and seemingly limitless
energy. Like Cooper and Brown, she was divorced, and like them
she pursued several interests. Among these was the advancement of
black women. Besides the roles she played in government, and as
founder and president of the Daytona Educational and Industrial
Institute (later the Bethune Cookman College), Bethune was a former president of the Association (1924–1928) and a founding member of the Republican League and International Council. No doubt,
it was her participation in these new organizations, as well as the
insight she gained from her NYA position, that set the ideological
foundation on which the National Council of Negro Women was
based.

Of all the national black women's organizations to emerge during
this period, the Council was the most influential and, as it turned
out, the longest lived. Bethune conceived the Council to be a voice
for Negro womanhood in all the new agencies of the Roosevelt
administration. It was to represent women like Pilcher, and inter-

cede on behalf of black women's political groups like the Colored Women's Democrat Club of Woodland Park-Bitely, Michigan. Bethune felt black women needed an organization to look out for them as the National Council of Women looked out for white females. She was convinced that African-American women were overlooked by state and federal governments because the many black women's organizations did not present a unified front. "We need to corral the forces of our group," said New York City–based Clara Bruce at the 1935 December luncheon meeting that launched the National Council of Negro Women. "We must solidify," chimed in Addie Hunton, who was there representing the AKA sorority.[11] As founded, the NCNW proposed to do just that—to bring sororities, secret societies, and religious and professional organizations under one banner and speak on the national level for them all. It was, its brochures proclaimed, "an organization of organizations." It was to be "a clearinghouse for the dissemination of information concerning the activities of women." Demonstrating a move beyond the Association's localized self-help ideology, the Council promised to sponsor interracial development and support progressive labor movements.[12]

Judging from the minutes of its first fifteen years, the Council did what it proposed to do. Its most steadfast affiliates were the sororities, especially Alpha Kappa Alpha and Delta Sigma Theta. Church groups like the Woman's Home and Foreign Missionary Society of the A. M. E. Zion Church affiliated, and professional organizations and auxiliaries such as the National Jeanes Association (a teacher organization) also joined. In addition to these organizations the NCNW established local metropolitan Councils in major cities, councils whose members were from local branches of the national affiliates.

With the idea that the black urban masses now had political power that could be used to bring about change, Council leaders supplied affiliates and local Councils with information on legislation deemed important to black women. Women were taught how legislation and government policy affected them, and were advised to give or withhold their support. Some of the legislation the Council supported were Civil Rights measures, like repeal of the poll tax and passage of a federal antilynching law. Most of the Council's energy, however, aimed to increase black female employment and economic opportunity. Thus the National Council of Negro Women supported elimination of photographs from civil service job applications, nondiscriminatory public housing, fair and equal inclusion of blacks in all New Deal welfare and jobs programs, nondiscriminatory public housing, and price controls on consumer products. It also supported Social Security coverage and minimum wage and maximum hour legislation for domestic workers and farm laborers. During the war, the NCNW protested restrictions on the enlistment of black women in the armed forces, notably the WACS and WAVES. Because its leaders thought that without protective legislation black women would be exploited, it opposed the Equal Rights Amendment and instead favored giving women special status in the labor force.[13]

Unlike the locally oriented NACW, Council members made it their goal to study and speak out on world issues. The Depression and war were, after all, worldwide, and they thought African-American women needed to understand world issues, especially matters that affected black people. Accordingly, in 1944 they urged the United States to join the International Security Organization (later the United Nations) for the maintenance of lasting peace, supported the extension of United States economic and social benefits to Pan-American countries, and insisted that the United States fight against colonial subjugation of native peoples.[14]

Two strategies underpinned Council activities. One was what in the late 1970s would become known as "networking." In essence, the NCNW corresponded with other organizations and sent representatives to their policy-making meetings. In 1939, for instance, the Council corresponded with, or sent representatives to, the meetings of several organizations, including the League of Women Voters, the National Consumers League, the National Council of Family Relations, and the Council of National Defense. It urged the Social Secu-

rity Board of New York City to hire more black women, wrote the
Labor Department on behalf of the Chicago Domestic Workers
Union, and, generally, as one of its reports for that year stated, kept
the Council "before the public by public speeches, by area representatives and by newspaper publicity."[15] The strategy was the same for
the local councils. In 1943 the New York Metropolitan Council sent
a representative to virtually every political and social function held
by city officials.[16] The idea was that the more visible and persistent
Council women were, the less likely it was that government and private enterprise would ignore black women.

The second strategy was an extension of the first. Council women
hoped their networking would result in the hiring of black professionals, especially black female professionals, by the many national,
state, and local agencies that came into existence during the New
Deal and war years. Council women reasoned that black women
who had established kindergartens, libraries, reformatories, and settlements could now use their skills to direct national policy and
administer nationally funded community development New Deal
programs. During her many meetings with Eleanor Roosevelt,
Bethune pressed this point home, and all Council women were

MARY McLEOD BETHUNE AND ELEANOR ROOSEVELT. *Photo courtesy of National
Park Service—Mary McLeod Bethune Council House NHS, Washington D.C.*

relentless in their pursuit of policy-making jobs. In 1938, for example, the Council asked the Children's Bureau, the Women's Bureau,
the Bureau of Education, the Federal Housing Authority, and the
Social Security Board to hire black women to create and direct the
respective agency programs for blacks. It also lobbied the American
Red Cross and the Bureau of Public Health Service to get them to
hire black physicians, nurses, nutritionists, and other medical service workers.[17] Networking with an eye to influence and hiring was
the strategy of the National Council of Negro Women.

    This strategy was reflected in the Council's magazine, the *Aframer-
ican Woman's Journal*. Whereas *National Association Notes* carried an
endless number of editorials on the nature of African-American
womanhood and female leadership of the race, the Council's journal
offered more general reporting on the status of black women in arenas such as national defense, organized labor, and service industry
employment. Instead of stories on virtuous motherhood, the
Aframerican reported on prospects for world peace and the international status of women. Noticeably absent were the passionate testimonials defending black women. The Council did not entirely
abandon the Association's causes, but it now fought discrimination
and countered negative stereotypes by demonstrating black
women's connectedness to women and races across the nation and
world.[18]

    More than a product of the times, this strategy was the brainchild
of its founder, Bethune, who in many respects epitomized the era.
The fifteenth of seventeen children born to South Carolina ex-
slaves, she—like the majority of African-American migrants—was
born in the rural South and grew up working in cotton and rice
fields. Like Pilcher and Dillard and so many African Americans in the
1930s, Bethune identified the federal government as potentially
being black America's most powerful ally in the fight against racism.
Dark complexioned, practical minded, Bethune was as unlike Terrell, the first president of the Association, as the Association was different from the Council.[19]

THIS ISSUE OF THE NCNW JOURNAL IS TYPICAL OF THE BROAD PERSPECTIVE OF THE COUNCIL. *Photo courtesy of National Park Service—Mary McLeod Bethune Council House NHS, Washington D.C.*

In fact, even though Terrell and Bethune were only twelve years apart in age (Terrell was born in 1863, Bethune in 1875), their lives and careers reflect the differences between the two organizations, and the changes that took place in African-American female life and leadership during the first fifty years of the twentieth century. A major shift was party affiliation. When Terrell was president of the NACW, blacks were overwhelmingly Republican in sentiment. Terrell remained a Republican until her death, and worked assiduously for Republican candidates. By the mid-thirties, however, most black women, like Bethune, supported the Democrats.[20] By this time, too, most black leaders described themselves and all people of African descent as Negro, not "colored." Partly, this reflected the race pride and solidarity promoted by the New Negro movement. However, inasmuch as many light-skinned and more affluent blacks preferred the term "colored" to Negro, the popularity of "Negro" also reflected a rejection of the color/class hierarchy that existed at the beginning of the century, a hierarchy mirrored by Terrell and most of the early leadership of the Association. Unlike them, Bethune looked more like the black women daily crowding America's urban centers. Described by a biographer as a woman with "kinky-textured hair, flaring nose, full lips, and a coal black complexion," it is not surprising that Bethune rejected Terrell's advice to name the new organization "The National Council of *Colored* Women."[21][italics added]

There were other differences between Terrell and Bethune that reflected the end of one era and the beginning of another. Educated at a prep school and nationally renowned Oberlin College, Terrell wrote regularly about the characteristics, virtues, and perils of womanhood. Like so many of her contemporaries who produced treatises on gender, she was born into a class of people who were expected to represent the race by professional deeds and example. Bethune, however, more easily identified with the Pinkie Pilchers of the world. Her life was filled with toil and exploitation. Her mother combined farm labor and domestic work. No matter how hard their family worked getting the cotton crop in and out of the field, they were always cheated by the whites who weighed it. Bethune had the good luck to attend missionary schools but, unlike Terrell, whose education was classical, Bethune's schooling was based solidly on the three "R's," with a generous dose of cooking, sewing, and other "industrial" skills thrown in. Just as sensitive as earlier leaders about the nature of black womanhood and the injustices of racism, Bethune, nevertheless, was not compelled to expound upon the existential differences between men and women, blacks and whites. True to the education and experiences that had molded her, she emphasized the practical.[22] Bethune's leadership, therefore, signaled the end of the intellectual tradition of the "woman's era," and the entry of black women into the practical world of broker politics.

How effective Bethune and the Council were is difficult to judge. They did not conduct self-help service projects or found clubs to serve as tangible evidence of change and progress. Unlike the Association, the Council was dealing with the intangible. It aimed to insert black women into the nation's consciousness so that they would be factored into policy decisions and empowered to participate in decision-making processes. Theoretically the Council's program was sound. Lamentably, though, black women were not hired by private or government agencies in appreciable numbers, and the few who were would probably not have traced their employment solely, if at all, to the existence of the Council. Even Bethune did not owe her job as the head of the National Youth Administration's Division of Negro Affairs to the Council but to contacts she had made with black leaders and Eleanor Roosevelt years before the Council was formed.

It would be unfair, however, to judge the Council's success only by the number of black women hired in different social service and government agencies. To apply objective criteria to a task that was in many respects qualitatively subjective would be wrong. The Council charged itself with making the invisible visible. Wholesale hiring did not occur but the Council did begin the long and complex process of raising the consciousness level of the people and agencies with which it conferred.

The Council also helped ease the gender tension between black male and female leaders. This was partly due to Bethune's style. Best characterized as a chameleon, she was the consummate politician, always tailoring her remarks to please her audience. Unlike Terrell, Wells, Cooper, or Fannie Williams, Bethune did not challenge black men. Ever so infrequently she referred to black women as the "backbone" of the race. Never, though, was she as combative as many of the early female leaders of the NACW. No doubt Bethune's style was a by-product of the self-effacement that was necessary to raise funds for her school. (Brown and Washington also learned how to flatter men and whites to get what they wanted.) It was also related to the waning of Victorian theory about the superiority of woman and the decline of the NACW's passionate commitment to female leadership. Now that the strategy depended less on moralizing about women, and more on getting women jobs, the Council did not clash with men as had the Association.

The same could not be said about friction between black women. The Council was not well received by leaders of the Association. When president of the NACW, Bethune encumbered it with debt for its headquarters building.[23] During the Depression the building proved a drain on finances and local leaders resisted paying for it.[24] To Association members, Bethune seemed to be abandoning the Association after having financially ruined it. Moreover, the Council was perceived as competition. Recriminations abounded as Bethune was alternately praised by her supporters and cursed by her detractors. Among the latter was the NACW's then current president, Mary F. Waring. In an article dispatched to black newspapers by the American Negro Press (ANP), Waring questioned the wisdom of another black woman's organization. She thought the NACW and the International Council of Women of the Darker Races represented black women well enough. "Why in the name of good judgment should any woman seek to form a separate council?" she asked in the article, adding, "let us beware of what we do unless we walk backward." In the published article Waring politely admonished Bethune for what she called "separatist organizing," arguing that, contrary to Council member accusations, black women were in fact represented by the predominately white National Council of Women.[25] Waring's unpublished remarks were a lot angrier, revealing evidence of familiar infighting. Bethune, she wrote scornfully, founded the Council because Bethune's handpicked candidate for Association president, Charlotte Hawkins Brown, lost the bitterly contested election to Waring, leaving Bethune with no way to control the NACW. Waring demanded that Bethune abandon the National Council of Negro Women and drop the sour grapes. "Play the game squarely," she wrote, "you have been where you are going in the Association of Colored Women."[26]

Whatever the real reason for the Council's formation—genuine concern about the new needs of black women, another round of "mistrissism," or some combination of the two—many women in the Association viewed Bethune's founding of the Council as an act of betrayal. They took sides for and against her, and once again divided among themselves.[27] Bethune, for her part, kept her membership in the Association, but it never affiliated with the Council, and Bethune was not welcomed at NACW meetings. Eleven years after the Council's founding, a reporter covering the 1946 Association meeting wrote that Bethune was still a pariah. "Few tricks," he noted, "were left unturned by the old guard to keep Mrs. Mary McLeod Bethune from taking a prominent part."[28]

Like the NACW, the Council exacerbated class problems within black female America. Despite Bethune's more "common" background, classism was inherent in the networking strategy that made the middle-class black professional woman the conduit through which resources flowed into black communities. They were the immediate beneficiaries of the Council's work. Poor black women like Pinkie Pilcher and Lutensia Dillard benefited secondarily, only when and if problems were defined and resources allocated.

A related source of class tension was the organizational structure of the Council. It functioned as a clearinghouse for member organizations, the most prominent of which were professional associations and black Greek letter sororities. In 1945, for example, of eighteen affiliating organizations, six were sororities, two were teacher associations, and two were missionary associations of the traditionally middle-class African Methodist Episcopal and African Methodist

Episcopal Zion churches. In addition to the Woman's Auxiliary to the National Medical Association (the female relatives of black doctors) and the National Association of Colored Graduate Nurses, two beauticians' associations affiliated. The only organization that unequivocally defined itself as working class was the Ladies Auxiliary of the Brotherhood of Sleeping Car Porters, and that very year they withdrew from the Council.

The point is twofold. First, because the Council was a clearinghouse for middle-class women's organizations, to the extent that it spoke for and defined black women, it did so with the voice and frame of reference of the black middle class, not with the voices of the million or so domestic workers who barely made subsistence wages. Just as important was the fact that the Council took on the identity of its member organizations. Since the sororities composed the largest block of these, the Council, despite the impoverished rural background of its first leader, became identified with the sororities, which themselves had a reputation for exclusivity.

This reputation was in some respects undeserved. It is true that to be a sorority member, or soror, one had to have a college education. In the early years of the twentieth century, few outside the light-skinned black middle class went to colleges that had sorority chapters. However, during the 1930s and 1940s the two largest sororities, Alpha Kappa Alpha (AKA) and Delta Sigma Theta, turned their attention to race work. In 1930, the Deltas established a Vigilance Committee that protested lynching, segregation, and black unemployment. Like the Non-Partisan Council on Public Affairs established by AKA in 1938, it scrutinized and interpreted federal legislation, making sure that blacks understood how congressional bills affected them and their communities. Among AKA's many NACW-like service programs was its health project, conducted in Mississippi from 1935 to 1942. Under this program sorors went to Lexington, Mississippi, and established traveling clinics that immunized over two thousand adults and children and administered to the health needs of over twenty-six hundred other rural residents. Each summer saw the project expand until fifteen thousand people received medical attention, including prenatal care, blood testing, nutrition counseling, and dental care. Similarly, from 1945 through 1956, Delta Sigma Theta established libraries in towns in North and South Carolina and Georgia. In 1941, it inaugurated its jobs project. Local chapters researched, publicized, and developed strategies to get black women skilled and unskilled jobs in local industries.[29]

Numerous as they were, the service projects did not counter the sororities' elitist image. As Delta historian Paula Giddings has observed, the sororities were "one of the very few closed membership organizations in the Black community, and the only ones that required a college education." As such they were "particularly vulnerable to the stereotypes of a less than serious bourgeois class that was insensitive to the needs of the less fortunate."[30] Another part of their image problem was the perception that membership was open only to wealthy black women who were light-skinned enough to pass the infamous "brown bag test."[31]

Whether criticism centered around color, money, or complacency, many complaints leveled at the sororities came from members who were close enough to know the truth. Ida Jackson was one such person. She was head of the AKA's health project, and she complained bitterly about the air of noblesse oblige adopted by many participating sorors. In 1936, the project's second summer, she found fault with members she described as "narrow, small, petty people who want some group into which they can combine and become snobs." Despite the project's success, she wrote that she was "anything but inspired."[32] She was most bothered by what she called the "Better than Thou" attitude. Others located the problem in the sororities' seeming preoccupation with social activities often labeled "society" or "frivolity."[33] This image, which had plagued the Association, was one the Council could have done without. Unfortunately, because the sororities dominated the Council, and because the

Council's strategy depended heavily on black professional women, it could not escape their elitist image.

There was reason, therefore, for most black women to be skeptical of the Council. If women like Pilcher, Yarbrough, and Dillard asked themselves what this organization did for them, they might be hard pressed for an answer. Overall, black female labor force participation actually fell during the 1930s, from 42 percent to 37.8 percent. Inserting black women into the national consciousness and trying to get professional black women jobs so that they could in turn help the less fortunate was an admirable goal. It did not, however, feed, clothe, or provide shelter for the many who were stuck in towns like Greenwood, Mississippi. Likewise, the NCNW's program did not open secretarial "pink-collar" work to black women, nor did it decrease the numbers of black women who waited on the sidewalks of urban centers in the domestic worker "slave markets."[34]

Black women in other sectors of the economy did not fare much better. Only 5.5 percent worked in manufacturing. Compared to white women who made sixty-one cents for every dollar made by a white male, black women made only twenty-three cents, usually at work that was so tedious and dirty that it was earmarked only for them. In tobacco manufacturing, to take an example, the heat, humidity, and stench of the workplace was enough to make black women cry; cry because they had the job, and cry because they could not afford to quit it. The story was the same for commercial laundry employees, an occupation with a high percentage of black female workers. Low pay, long hours, speed-up operations, oppressive conditions—these conditions had to make average black women wonder what, if anything, the National Council of Negro Women was doing for them.[35]

Claiming that they spoke on behalf of black working women, the Ladies Auxiliary of the Brotherhood of Sleeping Car Porters asked just that. This group defined itself as a working-class organization, an organization of the Negro masses. After scrutinizing the Council's program and work, its top leadership found the Council's aims and objectives to be at odds with those of the Auxiliary. "I attended a session of the Council's Convention," wrote the Auxiliary's president, Helena Wilson, to the secretary-treasurer, Rosina Tucker, "and was not very satisfied with the discussions given to the lower income working groups."[36] This was in 1942, shortly after the Auxiliary's national convention had voted to affiliate with the Council. As Wilson's letter indicates, she was having second thoughts, thoughts that kept the Auxiliary from joining the Council for two years. Wilson's discontent surfaced during the 1942 NCNW convention when issues regarding workers were ignored by Bethune and NCNW delegates. In Wilson's opinion the Council paid too much attention to individuals with special training, especially government workers "and others in like positions." She needed assurances that the Council was definitely "interested in the unskilled and unorganized men and women of the race who are badly in need of the advantages and the protection which accrue from labor organizations."[37] At a time when the vast majority of laboring black women worked in some sort of domestic service, unprotected by national and state welfare policies, Wilson put the issue bluntly to Jeanetta Welsh Brown, the Council's executive secretary. The Auxiliary, she wrote, "wants to know if the Council intends to include the so called common man and woman in its plans."[38]

Both Bethune and Brown tried to reassure Wilson that it did indeed; that the Council's invitation to the Auxiliary evidenced its interest in ordinary working people. Brown pleaded her case by recounting her experience as an organizer for the United Automobile Workers in the Ford Motor Company in Detroit. Explaining that the Council understood that "most of the Congressmen that are Anti-labor are also Anti-Negro," she argued that no "serious thinking Negro in these days can afford to well deny the close tie-up of labor and the salvation of Negro people."[39] Countering Wilson's challenge, Brown put responsibility for the Negro masses right back on the Auxiliary: "you say that you represent the unskilled and unorganized women. Have you ever stopped to think that if your organization represents a certain group of people, that that group of people will be kept out of plans as long as you, yourself, keep them out?"[40]

Bethune was equally resolute. "The National Council of Negro Women has as its aim the bringing together of women of the Negro race for the united effort, in the things where we need to be united," she wrote Wilson in 1943. Addressing any fear of competition from the Council, Bethune added, "it does not aim to stand in the way of the program of any individual organization, but to pool our interests, in order to be able to show the activities of Negro women in this country whenever pressure is needed, on whatever needs to come together for the opening of doors for our group." Like Brown she pleaded her personal background, "I . . . am simply a common woman." Also like Brown she spoke of the need for cooperation: "we need one another."[41]

It took two years, from the autumn of 1942 to the autumn of 1944, before Wilson authorized the Auxiliary to join the Council. During that time, she wrote others about her concerns, and they shared their feelings with her. Tucker agreed with Wilson, not because she had done any research on the Council; in fact, she admitted, "I know nothing about this particular group. . . . " She simply had a negative image of Council women. To Wilson she wrote, "Such women are seldom interested in the economic side of our race, but interested rather in what the race can do for them."[42] Natalie Moorman, a life member of the Council, wrote Wilson imploring the Auxiliary to join to broaden the Council's base: "I have been inspired at the potentialities of that group and at the same time alarmed at the fact that the membership both of individuals and of affiliated organizations is largely made up of women of academic and professional pursuits."[43] Wilson concurred. Even though she let the Auxiliary join the Council, she expressed her concern that the Council was "composed of women who appear to be interested primarily in matters leading away from the Negro masses."[44]

Of course, to Wilson's mind, the Auxiliary's program best suited black America. The International Ladies Auxiliary of the Brotherhood of Sleeping Car Porters was established in 1938, when regional councils or auxiliaries combined to form a national organization. The first of these regionals was formed in 1925 in New York City, the same year the Brotherhood was formed with A. Philip Randolph as its leader. The auxiliaries organized so that female relatives of porters could formally support the Brotherhood. The philosophy was that if the wives, mothers, and daughters of Pullman porters helped raise money for strike funds, and helped withstand pressure from the Pullman Company and other antiunion forces, the Brotherhood could become black America's entry into the world of organized labor. Neither the Brotherhood nor its Auxiliary organized solely to gain better wages and working conditions for porters and maids on the railroads. The broader aims of Randolph, Wilson, and Tucker were to break down the barriers barring black workers from many unions. According to William H. Harris, a historian of the Brotherhood, "a union under black leadership strong enough to gain recognition from the Pullman Company and to wrest a charter from the AFL [American Federation of Labor] would serve as an example to other working-class blacks of the possibilities for improving their lives."[45]

During the 1920s and 1930s the Brotherhood and its Auxiliary set a stellar example for black people. Slavery had fixed the race in a servile role, and the kinds of jobs black people were forced into after slavery only reinforced that role in the minds of white Americans. No matter that racism had made porter work the only option available to some of the best-educated and most capable black men; servility was part of the porter's job definition. As Harris maintains, they "were seemingly obsequious men, always bowing and scraping in the presence of whites with their hands held out for a tip. . . ."[46] Although they seemed the most unlikely group to organize and win a charter from the all-white American Federation of Labor, and a contract from one of the quintessential symbols of white power, the Pullman Company, they persevered during the desperate times of the Depression, and won both. In winning these victories the Broth-

SEATED NEXT TO A. PHILLIP RANDOLPH (FIRST FROM THE LEFT), HELENA
WILSON POSES WITH OTHER BROTHERHOOD AND AUXILIARY LEADERS. *Photo
courtesy of the Chicago Historical Society.*

erhood and its Auxiliary demonstrated that perseverance and organization were the keys to the race's economic security.

Convinced of their critical role in the Brotherhood's victory, Auxiliary leaders felt their program was the best one for black women.
Although they supported some of the same causes as the Council—
nondiscriminatory public housing, a higher minimum wage, elimination of the poll tax, Social Security coverage for domestics and farm
workers, protective labor legislation for women in the labor force—
the heart and soul of their program was labor and consumer education.[47] Driven by their belief that trade unionism and consumer
cooperatives opened the door to economic opportunity, Auxiliary
women held classes in labor history. They taught black women the
relationship of blacks and women to the labor movement, and the

THE DENVER LADIES AUXILIARY, OFFICE OF PRICE ADMINISTRATION. *Photo courtesy of the Chicago Historical Society.*

benefits of paid-up union dues. In consumer cooperative study clubs, local Auxiliary members learned about credit unions, price controls, and the workings of the wartime Office of Price Administration. In fact, during the war, Auxiliary members tracked prices in neighborhood stores to enable community residents to bargain shop. In buying clubs like those established in Denver, Chicago, and the District of Columbia, members pooled their money and bought bulk goods for the best price. The Auxiliaries in Chicago and Portland established their own consumer cooperatives. In addition to operating its own store, the Chicago Auxiliary also joined the Union Cooperative Optical Center.[48]

This kind of economic nationalism did not originate with the Auxiliary. Trade unionism as a vehicle to African-American progress was relatively new, but the Auxiliary's consumer philosophy had its roots in nineteenth-century black thought. When Helena Wilson and Consumer Committee Chairman Alice Ward argued for coopera- tives on the basis that they kept "within the race the huge sums paid to the business concerns now operating in the Negro districts and from which he receives little if any return," they sounded much like Booker T. Washington.[49] They also echoed the thousands of other black women in urban centers who during the Depression and war years joined housewives leagues to support black businesses, buy black products, and patronize black professionals.[50] "The Negro must build race loyalty, race pride, race background and race secu- rity," Wilson wrote to the secretary-treasurer of the Atlanta Auxil- iary, "the day is rapidly passing when men or a race of men may hope to protect their interest without unity or solidarity of purpose."[51]

In practical terms this meant that men and women each had their own specific role to play in race advancement. All working men and women had to join a union, and where possible, as was the case with the Brotherhood, organize along racial lines. Beyond this, the Auxil- iary reinforced some very familiar relationships. Men, they believed, were the primary breadwinners and women their support. As Wil- son put it in 1941, "in the Auxiliary . . . women learn that the secu- rity and the happiness of their homes depend upon the security and the protection given the husband and father's job."[52] Like the wives of white trade unionists she argued "no working man can be a suc- cessful Union man . . . without the sympathetic understanding and loyal support of his family."[53] Women, however, were not thought of as men's subordinates. Their power lay in their role as chief pur- chasers of consumer products and as community organizers of neighborhood consumer activity. Furthermore, as wives and moth- ers, women could make a man join a union and keep his dues cur- rent. If a man's friends or hard economic times discouraged union membership, a man's wife could be the "greatest strike-breaker in the World" or a counterforce in support of the union. This made the home the place where the union began and ended. Women were piv- otal to its success. Since it was participation in unionism that would make blacks economically secure and collectively vital, and since the home was the center of the labor movement, wives and mothers were thought to be key to black survival and progress.[54]

This made for all the difference in the world between the Council and the Auxiliary. Besides the most obvious difference—labor unionism—the Auxiliary emphasized woman's power in the home and community, while the Council focused more on woman's role as worker and national and international citizen. Significantly, although Auxiliary women organized cooperatives, consumer leagues, and buying clubs, race, not gender, was their organizing issue. In contrast, as the "Voice for Negro Womanhood," the Council made black *women*, not black families or black communities, the hub of their program. Although neither organization challenged black patriarchy or black male leadership, the Auxiliary's emphasis on race unity through traditional symbiotic familial relationships left the least room for advancing the cause of black female autonomy.

In the 1930s, indeed through the 1960s, racial solidarity was a far more popular strategy than the Council's program of integrating black women into the nation's consciousness and professional labor force. Besides the fact that few black women could immediately benefit from the Council's program, the Auxiliary's impact was far more tangible. It helped lessen the gender tension between black men and women and, because it fell back on the time-proven self-help methods of the Association, it also gave African-American women a program they were familiar with—a hands-on uplift program that depended on the will of blacks rather than of whites. Instead of schools, hospitals, clinics, homes for the elderly, libraries, playgrounds, and settlement houses, the Auxiliary organized women to spend wisely and with race consciousness. Furthermore, even though the Auxiliary never organized more than fifteen hundred female relatives of porters, much of its program was fundamentally the same as that of the housewives leagues previously mentioned. In Cleveland, New York, Washington, Detroit, Baltimore, and Chicago, thousands of black working women and homemakers participated in league programs that steered black spending toward black businesses or businesses that hired blacks in significant numbers. The Detroit League alone had ten thousand members by 1935.[55] According to historian Jacqueline Jones, the combined efforts of the leagues "captured an estimated 75,000 new jobs for blacks during the depression decade, and together they had an economic impact comparable to that of the CIO in its organizing efforts. . . ."[56] In light of the number of black women who were organizing along the lines of the Auxiliary, Wilson and Tucker had good reason to believe that it, and not the Council, represented the heart and soul of African-American womanhood.

In keeping with that feeling Wilson withdrew the Auxiliary from the Council in 1945, after only one year of affiliation. Her stated reason was the Council's 1944 increase in membership dues from fifty to one hundred dollars, a fee she claimed the Auxiliary could not afford.[57] Yet, her correspondence with Auxiliary leaders throughout the country revealed that she never overcame her initial dissatisfaction with the Council.[58] For her part, Bethune continued to invite the Auxiliary to join but probably alienated Wilson even more with a 1948 letter that suggested that the Auxiliary's local approach was outdated and not gender-oriented enough. "These are the days now . . . when we must team together for the bigger national and international areas," Bethune wrote three years after the end of World War II. With the words "may your women broaden their vision and look beyond themselves to that great diamond of womanhood, meeting the world where we need to pull together and build together for the peace, freedom and economic security we all need so much," Bethune extended another invitation to the Auxiliary.[59] It was one of several that was not accepted.

In hindsight it probably should have been. Given the vacuum left by the weakened National Association of Colored Women, and the growing labor consciousness that accompanied the formation of the Congress of Industrial Organizations (CIO) in 1935, the Auxiliary's labor-oriented program was one from which the Council might have benefited. The Auxiliary might have helped the Council structure a program that had wider appeal among ordinary black women, and in time Wilson might have recognized that the two organizations had a lot in common.

That common ground was extensive. Like Council women, Auxiliary members valued female autonomy. Both the national and locals struggled to maintain an identity independent of, and equal to, the Brotherhood. Secure in their belief that without their help the Brotherhood would not have won its fight against the Pullman Company, Auxiliary members in cities as diverse as Baltimore, Spokane, Oakland, Pittsburgh, and Winnipeg, Canada, resisted Brotherhood attempts to control how Auxiliaries conducted their affairs and spent their hard-raised funds. When, for instance, the brothers of the Baltimore local tried to dictate policy to the president of the local Auxil-

THE AUXILIARY MAINTAINED ITS INDEPENDENCE FROM THE BROTHERHOOD. HERE DELEGATES TO ITS FIRST NATIONAL CONVENTION MEET. *Photo courtesy of the Chicago Historical Society.*

A GROUP PORTRAIT OF MEMBERS OF THE BROTHERHOOD OF SLEEPING CAR PORTERS. *Photo courtesy of the Chicago Historical Society.*

iary, the first vice president of the national body, Fannie Caviness, also a member of the Baltimore group, complained to Wilson: "I find that some of the men are doing more meddling into the Ladies and not enough of their own work. I am sure that you will have them to know that we are to take orders from you and it is their duty to work with their Zone Supervisors. Once they under stand [sic] I think ever thing will go all right."[60] In another instance, when the brothers of the Pittsburgh local called a joint meeting of the local and its Auxiliary on Mother's Day, the women balked. Many who attended walked out. Regarding that day, the local's president complained to Wilson that the men had been insensitive to the significance of the holiday. She recalled the "dark days" of union organizing when the women "played an important part, a vital role in the life of the Brotherhood." Auxiliary members, she said, knew "what a good

or bad influence from a woman means to the success of her husband," but it did seem that the men "failed miserably in helping in the
cause of the women."[61] The story was the same in every city where
the Porters tried to manage the affairs of its sister Auxiliary. In each
instance the Auxiliary proved that it would support the Brotherhood, but it would not be subordinate. Supporting their men's work
did not mean literally walking behind them.[62]

It also did not mean that the Auxiliary forsook the cause of black
women as a group. Like the Council, it too was a "voice for Negro
womanhood." Even though it put more emphasis on intraracial unity
than on gender identity, it rose to the black woman's defense. When
rock and roll came into vogue in the 1950s, Wilson, in the name of
the Auxiliary, railed against it "as an insult to and a degrading portrayal of Negro womanhood." Reminiscent of the Association's
response to blues lyrics, the Auxiliary's position was that the music
vilified black women by portraying them as "two-timing, loose-
living, . . . irresponsible persons."[63] Just as much as the Association or the
Council, the Auxiliary wanted black women to have a respectable
reputation. Its emphasis on woman's role in the family and community was one of its ways of making this very point.

The issue of respectability brings us back to Wilson's objection to
the Council's class orientation. She claimed that the Council did not
represent the masses of black women, that the Auxiliary's program
was more oriented toward blacks who did not have professional or
government jobs. This did not, however, mean that Auxiliary women
themselves were of a different "class" than Council women, especially during the Depression and war years when, in the absence of
jobs and money, respectability was all some people had. Considering
that after they won their contract, porters ranked among the highest
paid black workers in the country, that many of their wives did not
work outside the home, and that a significant number of both the
porters and their wives had college degrees, it is apparent that,
despite the disclaimers of Wilson and Tucker, the women of the Auxiliary and Council had much in common.[64]

In addition to these similarities, the two groups employed the same kinds of fund raisers and sororal relationships. Local Auxiliaries had just as many revenue-raising social affairs as did local Councils. Fashion shows, dances, teas, and brunches were staples of both organizations. There were probably more Council women who belonged to one of the national sororities, but Auxiliary women boasted memberships in lodges and national black women's secret societies like the Eastern Star and the Daughter Elks.[65] It also cannot be said that Auxiliary women got along with each other any better than did the women within the Council or Association. Rivalry for office and personality conflicts were as much a feature of the Auxiliary as of the others. Take the 1926 Constitution to the New York Economic Council (a local Auxiliary). One cannot read it without being reminded of the Association prayer cited earlier. Women were instructed to practice the biblical command that "ye love one another." From the 1940 convention floor, Rosina Tucker scolded, "There is going to be no cattiness or whispering campaign, but we are going to be sisters, loving each other and working together."[66] Members of the Washington, D.C., Auxiliary took Tucker's advice and applied it to working with the local metropolitan council. Over the reservations and objections of Wilson and Tucker, the president of the D.C. Auxiliary, Elizabeth Craig, established a working relationship with Bethune and participated in Council events in that city.[67]

That they could work together on the local level, and that differences seemed to be more perceived than real, suggest that gender and not class was the real divisive issue in their conflict. In other words, what these two organizations clashed over was the priority given to gender in the political strategy of race progress. By calling themselves working class, Auxiliary women strategically placed themselves within the new racial politics of black America, politics that paid less and less attention to black women as a group but that increasingly demanded civil and economic equality for the race. Already closer in spirit to the hundreds of thousands of women in the housewives leagues and "Don't Buy Where You Can't Work" action projects, the Auxiliary's working-class identity placed them in a better position than the Council to be the mouthpiece of American black women.

Unfortunately, the Auxiliary never achieved this goal. As the 1940s passed, Wilson and Tucker were making some of the same observations about Auxiliary women they had made about Council women. Both wanted working black people to develop a consciousness that embraced what Tucker called "the spiritual side of our Union."[68] Without defining its essence, by 1950 both she and Wilson lamented its absence. Auxiliary women seemed not to care any more about the underprivileged. The movement, they felt, suffered from a loss of energy and vitality. They complained that their members lacked enthusiasm for race work. There was too much socializing and general selfishness on the part of their membership, a membership that was fast declining. Tucker lamented that, across the nation, Auxiliary women and Brotherhood men "didn't know what 'it was all about.'" Most distressing was her observation that "among our women, . . . some consider themselves better than others to the extent that they refuse to join the auxiliary."[69] Wilson noted this, too, and faulted Auxiliary women for "supporting with all their might, various organizations of far less significance than the Ladies Auxiliary."[70]

The Council also fell on hard times. Bethune was the motor that drove the NCNW, and much of her energy was derived from her Washington connections, especially her connection with Eleanor Roosevelt. The Council's emphasis on professional employment, especially work tied to the government, did not bode well for it in the post-New Deal and postwar era. The end of the Roosevelt years, the decline of the Democrats, and the disappearance of many government agencies, left the Council adrift. By the time the Republicans took over the White House in 1952, the Council was in a state of confusion. Affiliate organizations questioned the need for its clearinghouse operations, and the local metropolitan councils found themselves in direct competition for membership with the sororities and church groups that affiliated with them.[71]

In short, by the end of the Depression and war decades there was no viable national black woman's organization that was truly the "Voice of Negro Womanhood." Indeed, there was reason to wonder if there ever had been. Of all the leaders discussed so far, Bethune seemed to understand how little unity there was among African-American women. Her organization tried to bring the disparate voices of black female America together under one banner. Her inability to pull in the Auxiliary was testimony to the real and imagined differences between black women, and to the difficulty of developing a philosophy that put together the issues of race, class, and gender in a way that made sense to all black women.

On the eve of the Civil Rights movement other facets of black women's organizational history were becoming painfully clear. Wilson and Tucker had objected to the Council because they believed it led away from the black masses, away from the tens of thousands of women in housewives' leagues. Migration had finally freed black women to work on the kinds of issues they felt helped them, and their overwhelming participation in Auxiliary-like programs bode well for the future of race movements. It spelled disaster, however, for organizations or movements that privileged female autonomy over racial solidarity. For women to put gender consciousness ahead of race consciousness was judged inherently selfish, divisive, and inimical to the race. Like Auxiliary members, most black women during the New Deal and war years seemed to think that their needs were served when they worked to raise the race, and they supported leaders who endorsed this principle. To get their support the Council would have to change. Just as the New Negro movement had crushed the feminist spirit of the NACW, the Civil Rights movement promised to turn the Council into something other than an organization that first and foremost represented black women.

The Council would also have to adjust to the inverse relationship developing between class and race. Before midcentury it had been expected that the "talented tenth" would speak for the race—not only that it was right for them to do so but that it was their duty. The massive movement of black people to urban centers changed this. More and more, women from humble backgrounds, from manual labor and service backgrounds, articulated the aspirations of the race, and those of more privileged background were judged elitist. As the perceived differences between Auxiliary leaders and the Council demonstrate, by midcentury it was no longer taken for granted that professional black women were the best arguments for the race. Increasingly, middle-class women had to show why others should follow their lead. The grassroots Civil Rights movement about to burst into full bloom would hasten this trend and create new hurdles for black women's organizations.

Chapter 6

❋

THE SACRIFICES OF UNITY

If we went out of business today, the nation wouldn't miss us.

—Dorothy Height

In her 1975 oral history, Dorothy Height told a story about a face-to-face encounter with Mississippi racists one summer evening in 1964 when she and two other black women went to a motel restaurant in Jackson. As she recalled, events took a mean turn the minute they took their seats. First, the waitress gave them the cold shoulder, and soon they were approached by the owner, who bombarded the middle-aged women with questions: "What are you girls doing here? Where are you from? You must be from out of town." It only infuriated him to discover that one of Height's companions was local. "You must know how dangerous it is for you to be in here. You know that your people are not supposed to be coming in here!" he yelled. One by one the white patrons left the restaurant and were replaced by uniformed white men who closed in on Height and her friends as they waited for dinner. As Height's mind raced to find a way out, one of her companions moved nervously toward a phone to call for help. Suddenly, Height noticed that the restaurant was slowly filling with black kitchen help who pretended to clean tables, while keeping watchful eyes on them. Somewhat relieved but still frightened, Height and her companions paid for their untouched meal and left. On their way out a uniformed white man scowled, "You know that you are not supposed to be in here." Relieved to escape this life-threatening situation, Height and her companions breathed even easier when they exited to find that all of the black men employed at the motel were lined up to form a protective corridor for them from the restaurant to the parking lot. One of these men told Height, "We want you to know that they know that we are watching them, and we heard what they were saying and what they plan to do, but we want you to know, it's not going to happen here."[1]

In 1964, Mississippi was the most dangerous site for Civil Rights activity, and, along with other organizations, the National Council of Negro Women braved white terror to help register black voters and set up freedom schools. Height remembered how important it was for the Council to be in Mississippi that fateful summer when white supremacists mounted the most violent resistance to black rights. Along with women from the YWCA, the National Council of Jewish Women, the National Council of Catholic Women, and Church Women United, the NCNW went to Mississippi as part of an interorganization effort to encourage Southern black and white women to work together on children's issues. They believed that if they could get Southern women to cross the interracial divide and quietly work together, Southern black children would benefit. This, thought Height, was the kind of work that Bethune, who had died in 1955, had endorsed. Bethune had wanted the Council to coordinate the activities of the many black women's associations, and also to be a sponsor of interracial work. Height took Bethune's vision as a mandate to gather representatives from the many different women's organizations, black and white, to sit down to discuss women's roles in Civil Rights work. Her thinking, she recalled, was that "if we could gather under the banner of the National Council of Negro

Women a really representative group of women . . . we could begin to work on some of the things that needed to be focused on."[2]

In her reminiscences, Height remembered how pivotal women were to the Civil Rights movement and how important it was that black women's issues be kept in focus. It struck her that "when you see an audience . . . you had predominantly women and children in the audience and predominantly male leadership on the platform."[3] She felt that if a woman's organization was not in the forefront of activity, women's issues would be lost in the push for voting rights and desegregation. As she put it, "I found that it was very difficult to get people, who are oriented toward laws and practices like that to accept the fact that the conditions affecting children, and affecting youth, and affecting women, whether they were services like child care, or whether they were things related to employment opportunities . . . was all a part of civil rights."[4] Height's fear, expressed years after the movement faded, was that "the things that the National Council of Negro Women was organized to deal with . . . somehow got subdued as you were thinking purely of getting a Voting Rights Act passed." Years later, Height also expressed the opinion that the Council lost touch with teenagers and young adults who were pushing so hard for change. She had wanted to "get some kind of linkage to these young people" as a "way of building some bridges of understanding."[5]

Height's 1975 recollections are crucial to understanding what was at stake for black women and the Council during the Civil Rights movement. It is not clear whether she realized it during the sixties, or after the movement had ended, but at some point Height saw that the task before the NCNW was to not let the drive for integration and voting rights preempt concerns like child care, women's employment, and sexual exploitation.[6] She had to get Civil Rights organizations to see that women's issues *were* race issues.

This was not easy. At the turn of the century, the National Association of Colored Women brought race and sex together by arguing that the race could rise no higher than its women, that racial issues had to be addressed in the context of black women's concerns. It was difficult to make the same argument in the 1960s. At the century's start there was little Civil Rights agitation. Black people had adopted the strategy of racial uplift, and the location of activity was the family and the community—women's traditional domains. In the sixty years that had passed, and especially since the 1920s, Civil Rights had gradually become a priority and its locus had become national. The thrust was on "fighting back," on courage in the face of violence, on voting—long a prerogative of men before it was of women.[7] The 1960s was a "masculine decade," and Height's concerns suggest she knew it.[8] Yet, if any organization could keep the sexual discrimination of black women in focus, it was the National Council of Negro Women, the most viable, open, secular black woman's organization. The problem was, how?

The masculine ethos of the era was certainly an impediment, but so was the Civil Rights movement's subsumption of gender and class issues. The movement was at once a black woman's movement, a black movement, and a class-based movement, and it was not easy to define what was, and was not, a woman's issue. As a race movement, the fight for integration and voting rights aimed to open all the privileges of citizenship to African Americans and to end the daily humiliation that generated black self-hatred. It also aimed to break down the negative stereotypes used to justify the oppression of black people. As a race and class movement, the fight against segregation sought to redistribute tax-funded resources so that blacks could access the same opportunities as whites. Because Jim Crow ignored black class structure and put all blacks on the same level, it made them all part of an underclass vis-à-vis whites, and made getting along with white people an important determinant of class status in black America. For better or worse, the movement strove to make individual accomplishment, not race, and not ties to whites, the primary basis for class differentiation.

Embedded in these race issues were gendered concerns. Segregation, with its prohibitions against trying on clothes in store fitting

rooms and using public restrooms, denied black women basic dignity. Finding ways of telling hungry children why they could not eat
or drink at restaurants and soda fountains was almost as trying as
riding the segregated buses that extended the oppression of the
black domestic's workday. In fact, because most black women had to
work, and usually worked at the dirtiest, hardest, lowest paying jobs,
any change the movement brought in black employment, whether
for men or women, improved the black woman's economic well-
being. Even male leadership and dominance could paradoxically be
viewed as liberating to women who had historically been overbur-
dened with wage work and maternal and domestic responsibilities.
Male protection, such as that extended to Height by the motel
workers in Jackson, could be welcomed by women who had had few
protectors. In short, the Civil Rights movement promised to meet
many black female needs and demands. To work for the race was to
work for black women.

And this is what the National Council of Negro Women did. By
the end of the 1960s it had a lot to be proud of. It had registered voters and ended segregation. It had protected young Civil Rights
workers against imprisonment, and had built understanding between
black and white women. It had also established community service
programs like day care.

But the Council had also sacrificed a lot. By the middle of the
1960s, it, like other Civil Rights organizations, suffered the rebuke
of young blacks who turned away from the movement's nonviolent
direct-action campaigns to militant black nationalism. It was also
repudiated on the grounds that it was a middle-class organization
seeking self-serving middle-class goals. Most of all, the NCNW lost
part of its mission. Bethune founded the Council with the idea that
the race was served when black women's needs were met. Under
Height a subtle shift occurred. Its Civil Rights work privileged race
over gender such that black women's needs were perceived to be
met when the race was served. By the middle of the 1960s, therefore, the Council, indeed black America in general, had supplanted

the principle that a race could rise no higher than its women with the idea that women could rise no higher than the race. As the race became more male defined, the ethos of the "woman's era" all but disappeared. By the end of the decade, black Americans were endorsing the concept that the race could rise no higher than its men.

THE GROUNDWORK FOR the Civil Rights movement was laid in the 1940s. At the very beginning of the war, in 1941, A. Philip Randolph's March on Washington Movement forced the Roosevelt administration to outlaw discrimination in war industries. Though imperfect in many ways, Executive Order 8802 loosened the white stronghold on employment and extended at least the promise of equal work opportunity.[9] Taking the initiative, blacks supported "Don't Buy Where You Can't Work" boycotts and organized the first restaurant sit-ins. Persistent protest against segregation in the armed forces, the 1943 founding of the Congress of Racial Equality as a nonviolent direct-action civil rights organization, and the NAACP's successful litigation against Jim Crow all paid dividends in the post–World War II era.

Indeed, compared to the past, real change seemed to snowball. In 1948, President Truman desegregated the armed forces, and by 1951, blacks and whites fought side by side in the Korean conflict. Also in 1948, the Supreme Court outlawed restrictive housing covenants. This ruling combined with newly available nonsegregated public housing to provide access to better living accommodations than had previously existed. By the middle of the 1950s, Washington, D.C., had desegregated most of its restaurants, parks, hotels, and theaters, and the Interstate Commerce Commission had outlawed all racial segregation on interstate trains and buses. When, in its landmark *Brown* decision, the Supreme Court declared that those things that were "separate but equal" were inherently unequal, the foundation for the modern Civil Rights movement was completed.[10]

The Council and the Auxiliary, however, did not directly benefit from these Civil Rights advances. If anything, the Civil Rights movement drew to itself resources and energy that might otherwise have been channeled into these organizations. Few things frustrated Helena Wilson more than the attention members gave to the church and to NAACP activities. That Auxiliary women supported "with all their might" organizations she considered to be of "less significance than the Auxiliary" was embittering. She thought Walter White, the NAACP's executive secretary, was insincere, and she derided other NAACP people as "the unintelligentsia."[11] Rosina Tucker was similarly resentful. In 1955, a time of crisis for the Auxiliary, it pained her to realize that while they neglected their own organization's meetings, "members of the Brotherhood and auxiliary were . . . spending much time actually meeting and working for the NAACP. . . ."[12]

Wilson and Tucker were hostile because the Auxiliary was in a live or die situation in the 1950s. Besides the loss of members to Civil Rights organizations, the transformation of the nation's travel industry away from rail travel wreaked havoc on the Auxiliary. Its labor and consumer education programs could go nowhere without dues-paying members. They were disappearing as fast as the automobile, bus, and airplane were making railroad travel obsolete.[13] The defection of bona fide members to Civil Rights organizations only made the situation worse.

The defection also evidenced a significant shift in members' ideological perspective. During the 1930s and 1940s, blacks, like other Americans, focused on economic problems. In the prosperous 1950s, blacks turned from price watching, cooperative purchasing, and labor organizing to civil and political rights. As integration and voter registration became the new focus, the Auxiliary's influence among African-American women waned.[14]

Its diminished following sparked new conflict between Auxiliary leaders and the men of the Brotherhood. In 1956, in response to the Auxiliary's declining membership and deteriorating financial status, the Brotherhood's international executive board proposed to reorganize the Auxiliary so that the Brotherhood could control it with an eye to increasing its membership. The men felt that the Auxiliary needed "new strength and vitality." To that end they sought to reorganize the Auxiliary into a smaller but more effective organization, one that could keep its old members and aggressively recruit new ones.[15]

Of course, Auxiliary leaders had no intention of giving up their autonomy. They saw the reorganization plan as the men's way of destroying the Auxiliary and they balked. The confrontation that followed foreshadowed the intense male/female conflict of the 1960s and 1970s. So effective was their rebuttal that the Board withdrew its reorganization plan. Randolph, in turn, defended the Brotherhood at the Auxiliary's convention that same year. Reminiscent of John Hope's chastening remarks before Georgia clubwomen, Randolph called the women's response to the plan "too drastic and too severe and too bitter." The executive board, he reported, thought the women's unwarranted suspicions evidence of their distrust and disrespect. On behalf of the women, Elizabeth Craig pleaded that they "did want to live," that they were fighting for what Rosina Tucker said "has been my heart." In the end, the Auxiliary passed a motion of apology that assured the executive board of its loyalty, respect, and support. However, it was clear that the Auxiliary intended to remain the autonomous black woman's organization it had always been.[16]

And, in fact, it did, but as a shadow of its former self, and as an early casualty of the Civil Rights era. The organization never regained the vitality it had had during the 1930s and 1940s. In 1968, the fifteen delegates who attended the annual convention lamented their diminished numbers and the dissolution of many city divisions.[17]

Like the Auxiliary, the Council had a near-death experience in the 1950s. The decade found it in such financial straits that it struggled to pay even its utility bills. It too lost members to Civil Rights organizations. Unlike the Auxiliary, however, whose loss was tied to changes in the transportation industry, the Council's loss was exacerbated by its inability to keep young members and its failure to open its organization to poor black women.[18]

In the South, in particular, the NCNW competed with other Civil Rights groups for members. For example, the Council established but was unable to maintain its Metropolitan Council in Montgomery, Alabama, because potential affiliates—sororities, church groups, and professional organizations—felt they were already represented by the Montgomery Improvement Association, the organization that led the successful antisegregation bus boycott. In New Orleans the Council could hardly compete with the NAACP and the Urban League. Council members devoted so much time and energy to these organizations that the local president, Mattie Grant, refused to allow her members to even discuss Civil Rights activities at Council meetings. By 1964 the New Orleans' Metropolitan Council was defunct.[19]

To boost its membership and ensure its future, the Council tried to attract young black women. This group, it was thought, would impart needed energy and innovation, and also guarantee the Council's long-term survival. The problem, as Council leaders quickly discovered, was that it needed young black women more than they needed the Council.

This became apparent in 1954 when Helen Meade, the director of junior Councils, issued a report on the status of young female members of the junior groups sponsored by local metropolitan Councils. The report told of adolescents and young adults who resented the interference of anyone older than thirty-nine. Young women, she said, thought older Council members lacked understanding of young people; they felt the older women condescended to them. Younger members, anywhere from sixteen to thirty-two, complained that when they took up local Council membership, they were relegated to "second-rate citizenship," and too often were given legwork assignments such as "running errands, and menial chores." In their minds, Council women spent too much time "wrangling," and "trying to get the best spots." Young women also resented older

THE MARY MCLEOD BETHUNE YOUTH SECTION OF ST. LOUIS, MISSOURI. *Photo courtesy of the National Park Service—Mary McLeod Bethune Council House NHS, Washington, D.C.*

members' attempts to control money they had raised. They felt that they were "'grown-up' enough to handle their own money since they had been 'grown-up' enough to raise it." How they raised their money, however, was also a sore spot in relations between the generations. Older Council members found the young women's dances, cocktail parties, and soirees inappropriate fund-raisers. In fact, one local Council publicly canceled a junior dance by calling in the tickets that the juniors had issued.[20]

The effect of the generational conflict on the Council was a devastating failure to attract young women or even keep the ones it had. On paper there were twenty-one junior Councils but in reality there were only eight nationwide. A junior Council that was expected to yield sixty-six new young members in fact got only three.[21] This was a problem. The Council was the largest open national secular organization that explicitly represented black women. At the very moment when young blacks were making the nation stand and face its overt racism, the Council appeared to many young women as an archaic "do-nothing" organization—a relic of a generation that had failed them. The Council needed their financial support as much as it needed their vitality. Unfortunately, it got neither.

To survive, and most of the Council's 1950s activities were dedicated to doing just that, the Council fell back on its tried and trusted constituency, middle-aged to older women of the black middle class. The same year it got the disheartening report on the juniors, the Council's leadership created the Life Members Guild for members who paid at least half of a hundred-dollar membership fee. The Guild's job was to encourage women who were already members to pay lifetime dues, and to attract influential new members. Guild members were given more status because of their ability to underwrite projects and to become public spokeswomen for the Council. To meet their recruitment obligations Guild leaders were encouraged to host social activities that would attract potential life members. As outlined by Vivian Mason, the third president of the National Council of Negro Women, these activities included garden parties, barbecues, and summer fashion promenades.[22] It went without saying that soirees and cocktail parties such as those held by junior Councils were to be avoided.

All but a few Council members thought the Life Members Guild a good way to stimulate membership and pay bills. Among those with reservations was Dollie Alexander, an active life member, who felt the Guild's impetus was misplaced. "Money should not be the main issue of the Life Members Guild," she wrote Mason, service should be the major consideration. According to Alexander, as one of the Council's main "strengthening cords" the Guild needed to be "made up of women who want to work and make contributions of service, and not name only."[23] Mason seconded Alexander's assertions about the strengthening value of the Guild, but, keeping an eye on the financial straits of the Council, Mason sidestepped Alexander's point about money versus work and went on to list some of the people she thought would be "able, competent, highly qualified . . . life members." Predictably, she opted for women of the entrenched black middle and upper classes: the "wives of college presidents, wives of executives of Negro businesses, wives of college deans, wives of notable professional men, Negro women in business and the like."[24]

Mason's strategy was understandable but unfortunate. It came at a time when black America was in the throes of a major shift in attitude about its middle class. As the Civil Rights movement depended more and more on young people's grassroots organizing and nonviolent direct-action sit-ins and freedom marches, the tactic of relying on relatively well-to-do individuals and spotlighting high-profile social events was being abandoned.

Evidence of the changing attitude toward the black middle class, and in particular its women, could be found in the correspondence of Claude A. Barnett, head of the Associated Negro Press. In 1951, he wrote the Grand Basileus (or president) of the Zeta Phi Beta (Zeta) Sorority that henceforth the sorority's press releases had to reflect activities that demonstrated significant service to black society. With the warning that the "old social clichés which made organizations slightly snobbish are passé," Barnett went on record as one who opposed articles that detailed only social events.[25] The head of a national news service, Barnett both shaped and reflected opinions. It is likely he was doing both when, later in the year, he wrote a similar letter to the National Sorority of Phi Delta Kappa. He told this organization of black teachers that their meetings were not newsworthy and that "the cycle when a sorority or fraternity was readily accepted as a basis for social prominence has passed."[26] Two years later he wrote another, more caustic, letter to Zeta: "Don't be dreaming of a lot of feature stories revolving around your organization . . . . " Revealing again his reading of the times, he noted that "there has been considerable tempering of the idea that social stature and prestige gained though that source was an end to itself." Barnett told Zeta that he would take news releases and pictures that demonstrated real service but sardonically added that he was rejecting pictures of "staid dames drawn up posing."[27]

Barnett's remarks were restrained when compared to E. Franklin Frazier's critique of black women's associations. Barnett's criticism at least mirrored those of Council life member Dollie Alexander, whose concern about the Life Members Guild reflected an understanding of the difference between service and social posturing. Frazier, on the other hand, summarily dismissed the work black women's groups had done. He saw them only as a significant component of a black middle class that was concerned more with conspicuous consumption than with the civil rights and economic progress of all black "folk." What he faulted them most for was what he called their singular preoccupation with social life, or what he called "society."[28]

In a vicious attack in his widely read book, *Black Bourgeoisie: The Rise of a New Middle Class in the United States*, Frazier criticized every facet of the black middle class. Some of his most malicious criticism targeted black association women. Describing them as frustrated people who led ineffectual lives, Frazier dismissed their service as minimal. He accused them of using service to justify their exclusivity, which in turn was perpetuated as compensation for their rejection by white America. Belittling their club work as nothing more than their way of finding an excuse to play poker, he heaped ridicule on them in a very personal way:

> The idle, overfed women among the black bourgeoisie are generally to use their language, 'dripping with diamonds.' They are forever dieting and reducing only to put on more weight. . . . Even the women . . . who work exhibit the same frustrations. Generally, they have no real interest in their work and only engage in it in order to be able to provide the conspicuous consumption demanded by society.[29]

As singularly vicious as was this assault on black middle-aged association women, it nevertheless echoed the criticism of Barnett and young women. All repudiated traditional styles of black leadership and middle-class consumption. All signified a rejection of the time-honored methods of people who thought of themselves as the talented tenth, and an embrace of new criteria for leadership. Race leaders now had to live among and seek the advice of people at the grass roots. They had to confront segregation with a direct action such as a sit-in, boycott, march, or freedom ride. These were the new requirements of a new leadership class that was increasingly younger and more vociferous than ever before.

By the late 1950s, therefore, it was clear that the National Council of Negro Women faced a crisis similar to that faced by the Association in the 1920s. Its very existence depended on how well it could adapt to the transformations taking place in black America. Dorothy Ferebee and Vivian Mason, the two women who succeeded Bethune, were competent leaders, but seemed unable to stem the flow of members out of the Council, or to attract new members into it. The Council needed someone with energy and vision, if not to transform the organization, at least to help it survive. In Dorothy Height they found such a leader.

Born in 1912 in Virginia and raised in the coal mining town of Rankin, Pennsylvania, Height was everything that the NCNW wanted from members of its junior Council. She was a former president of the Pennsylvania State Federation of Girls Clubs, and had been a very conscientious student. Even though her mother missed many school events, because her work as a private duty nurse usually kept her close to her employers, Dorothy never let her resentment keep her from excelling in her studies. Instead, she drew on other sources for inspiration, in particular, two Delta Sigma Theta women who worked at the Christian Center to which she belonged. They coaxed her out of her shyness and gave her her first pair of silk stockings. Later, in young adulthood, it was none other than Mary McLeod Bethune who, through extended conversations, helped her

DOROTHY HEIGHT IN 1965. *Photo courtesy of the National Park Service—Mary McLeod Bethune Council House NHS, Washington, D.C.*

to identify her talents. With the help of a scholarship from the Daughter Elks, she got bachelors and masters degrees from New York University in 1933. Like most other black women who found work hard to come by during the Depression, Height took temporary jobs to make ends meet. She waitressed, did laundry and factory work, and even wrote obituaries for a funeral parlor in Harlem, her adopted home.[30]

Height's unmarried status and her seeming casualness about it reflected changes in women's lives. Most past leaders and members of the Association and the Council were married, or had been, if only for a short time. Upon reflection, Height said she never wanted to be like so many other women who married just to lay claim to the status. She thought the Depression and war had made it difficult to find a man who had had opportunities similar to hers, and she was afraid that marriage would leave her always worrying about whether she was overshadowing her spouse. Since most of the men she had known could not accept the fact that she had a career and interests she wanted to pursue, that she was, as she put it, her own "person," she decided she wanted no part of a marriage where "the woman has to become part of the background for the man."[31]

It is not surprising that Bethune helped her make these decisions about marriage and career. Bethune's husband had been unsupportive in her drive to establish a girls' school, and it was for women like Height that Bethune founded the National Council of Negro Women. She wanted black women to be able to be independent, and to have the means to make it possible for others to be so as well. With the limited employment opportunities open to black women, Height would have been hard pressed to utilize her degree in educational psychology if she had not found work first as a welfare investigator and then as an administrator for the YWCA. In both jobs she served as a representative of black concerns, but at the "Y" she became an advocate for black women's issues, using her position to protest New York's domestic worker slave markets and the limited housing available to single black women in Washington, D.C.[32]

Height was, in Bethune's view, one of the best arguments for black womanhood and the Council. Neither Bethune nor Terrell had had the opportunity to work for black women from within the government or private service agency until late in their lives. Not only did they begin their careers as "race women" in institutions they founded or helped to create, but at the time they went to college, schools like New York University were not accessible to women of any status, much less to a black woman of small means from a coal mining town. Bethune knew the value of the schools, kindergartens, libraries, boarding houses, and settlements created by the clubs of the National Association of Colored Women, but she also knew the value of jobs and their connection to the power and independence black women could have if they commanded extensive government and private resources. As a member of the NCNW, and as vice-president and then president of the Deltas, Height worked for the same goals as Bethune. She called this shared goal the "equitable exposure of Negro women to job opportunities." This meant "not only trying to get women into jobs, but also giving people a sense of what kinds of opportunities there were."[33]

Height's tenure as the head of Delta Sigma Theta sorority prepared her for the presidency of the Council. As an affiliate of the NCNW, Delta had already been moving in the same direction as Bethune, and Height's presidency made sure there was no backsliding. In the same way that Bethune designed the Council to extend the black woman's influence beyond the local community, Height made sure that Delta's program was expansive. For example, Height initiated the Delta Jobs Project in 1944 to expand black women's opportunities beyond the fields of teaching, nursing, and social work. Height also transformed the sorority's National Library Project. Under her leadership the state of Georgia was persuaded to assume responsibility for the bookmobile and libraries that the Deltas had established in local areas.[34] To keep Delta members abreast of national and international issues, Height involved people who were not directly tied to race issues. By having people like Admiral Chester Nimitz, Madame Rajan Nehru, City College president Buell Gallagher, and Reader's Digest editor Stanley High participate in Delta conventions and forums, Height encouraged a broadened perspective. The establishment of its first international chapter in Haiti in 1951, its 1952 scholarship at the University of Delhi for two Hindu women, its 1954 Haitian Relief Fund, through which it aided the relief efforts in that country after Hurricane Hazel, helped maintain that perspective.[35]

Unfortunately, activities like these did not change the minds of people like Frazier, or of young black Americans. Height had her work cut out for her at the Council. In 1958, when she became NCNW president, she inherited not only an organization that was unable to attract women under the age of thirty, but one that was financially crippled and losing members to Civil Rights groups. To make matters worse, the Council was unable to shake its elitist image, especially now that the third president to succeed Bethune was a former high-ranking sorority officer.[36]

Another real problem was the doubts of sorority members themselves. As the most steadfast affiliates of the Council, their support, though problematic, was nevertheless crucial to its survival. Yet sorors questioned the need for the Council. They claimed it only duplicated the work of the sororities.[37] Having joined with black Greek letter fraternities in 1948 to create the American Council on Human Rights, a lobbying and clearinghouse organization through which black sororities and fraternities did Civil Rights work, the NCNW seemed a superfluous organization whose time had passed.[38]

These problems were exacerbated by the suspicions surrounding Height herself. When she was president of the Deltas she manipulated its executive board, conventions, and constitution to serve an unprecedented four terms, and generally imposed her will on the sorority.[39] Many, like soror and historian Helen Edmonds, found her ruthless and domineering. Edmonds claimed that under Height, there was "not one iota of fairness, democracy, justice nor integrity."[40] Height, therefore, brought experienced leadership to the Council, but it was leadership that was tainted. Added to Frazier's highly publicized criticism of black association women, and to the omnipresent idea that the NCNW served only the selfish interest of middle-class professional black women, it was not surprising to find, as did a chagrined Height, that black women would say, "I don't belong to the National Council of Negro Women," and say it "as if it's something to be proud of . . . ."[41]

Height did not let these problems discourage her. Undaunted she set to work to make the NCNW something black women could take pride in. She began by broadening the membership. Bethune had always encouraged an integrated membership but Height made it reality as never before. Height brought in figures like Lena Horne to head up membership drives, and women like Gladys Zales of Hadassah, Mary Rockefeller, Jackie Kennedy, and Eleanor Roosevelt to lend their names and support to the drives. The Council held gala benefits to honor people as diverse as A. Philip Randolph, Walter Reuther, and Mrs. Arthur Goldberg.[42] When membership drives yielded insufficient funds to run Council programs, Height sought and received hundreds of thousands of dollars from government and foundation grants. By the end of the sixties, among the organizations that held life memberships were Lockheed Aircraft Company, the Kilimanjaro Coffee Company, and the Emma Lazarus Federation of Jewish Women's Clubs of New York.[43]

As money came in from these sources the Council's focus gradually shifted. In 1960, it sponsored a benefit to memorialize Bethune, and in 1963, the Council set up a fund to send members to Selma to investigate and publicize the strip searches and rapes of young black women arrested during Civil Rights demonstrations.[44] Nineteen-sixty-four saw a very subtle shift in the Council's focus. To encourage women of different faiths and races to work together for change in the South, the Council helped initiate WICS, or Women in Community Service. This project brought together women from the NCNW, the National Council of Catholic Women, the National Council of Jewish Women, and Church Women United to work on community projects like Head Start and low-income housing. It also focused on Civil Rights initiatives like desegregation and voter registration. Although some of WICS's resources were used to educate and place poor young women in newly created government Job Corps programs, most of its energy was devoted to breaking down the barriers of communication between white and black women and to helping them coordinate integrated service projects.[45]

This shift to general community service and integration was helped along by the Council's 1964 Wednesdays in Mississippi (WIMS) project, a program that grew directly out of Women in Community Service. Once a week, WIMS sent integrated teams of women to different towns in Mississippi to work in the freedom schools that had sprouted in the wake of school closings brought on by desegregation. In Jackson, Mississippi, an integrated group of women initiated and ran what became the first of many Head Start programs that WIMS and Council women established. WIMS women also served as Civil Rights emissaries. They visited small groups of women of their own race, urged them to accept and work for desegregation and black voting, and invited them to see, by their own example, the benefits of interracial cooperation. In 1967, these community development programs were extended to Danville, Virginia, Paterson, New Jersey, and Boston, Massachusetts.[46]

Just what the NCNW could do in community development was demonstrated in Mississippi, one of the poorest states in the country, with perhaps the most deprived black population. The Council's efforts in developing Head Start programs, homes for unwed moth-

UNDER THE AUSPICES OF THE NATIONAL COUNCIL OF NEGRO WOMEN THIS INTEGRATED GROUP WORKED TOGETHER IN MISSISSIPPI. *Photo courtesy of the National Park Service, Mary McLeod Bethune Council House NHS, Washington, D.C.*

ers, pig farms, and victory gardens were much appreciated by black Mississippians. Its efforts in Sunflower County are a case in point. Although Sunflower residents were sometimes called on to testify before Senate Committees on hunger, the government did little about the problem. Fannie Lou Hamer, a renowned grass-roots Civil Rights organizer, was convinced that testimony was all the government really wanted. She appeared before Senators Joseph Clark and Robert Kennedy, and also testified before the Department of Agriculture, but to no avail.[47] The NCNW, however, initiated the first program in the county aimed at ending hunger. Using public and private money, it established the "Freedom Farm Co-op" program in 1968. Under Hamer's guidance the NCNW purchased forty acres of land on which cooperative members planted vegetables and raised pigs. Although the only part of the program to survive was the Head Start center, the initiative brought hope, and meat, to the families in Sunflower County.[48]

The Council also spearheaded voter registration campaigns. In the South it coordinated its efforts with associations like the Southern Regional Council.[49] However, in Northern cities it conducted independent programs. One such initiative was the "WMCA Call for Action" in New York City, a program that let people anonymously call in to a radio station for voting information. The response was so overwhelming that at the Council's prompting the city's board of elections opened neighborhood firehouses to disseminate information and facilitate registration.[50]

These NCNW programs underscore how difficult it was to stay focused on black women during the Civil Rights era, a time that highlighted racial injustice and community needs. Like women's groups before them, the Council stepped in to do what it could on both fronts. Scorned as exclusive and removed from real black people, the Council's new grass-roots focus was strategically smart, heartfelt, and sincere. Furthermore, programs like WICS and WIMS helped establish the Council's credentials as a bona fide Civil Rights organization. Indeed, Height often used the NAACP as the standard

HEIGHT WITH TOP CIVIL RIGHTS LEADERS. FROM THE LEFT: ROY WILKINS, FLOYD MCKISSICK, A. PHILLIP RANDOLPH, WHITNEY YOUNG, AND DR. MAR-TIN LUTHER KING, JR. *Photo courtesy of the National Park Service—Mary McLeod Bethune Council House NHS, Washington, D.C.*

of comparison in her efforts to make the Council a reputable organization.[51] Just like Bethune, Height was often the lone black woman in meetings that brought major Civil Rights leaders together. In 1963, for instance, she was the only woman to attend organizing sessions for the March on Washington, and throughout the 1960s Height represented the Council at meetings of major Civil Rights leaders.[52]

Although beneficial, the Council's shift to Civil Rights and community service left black women without an organization that spotlighted their particular struggles with sexual discrimination. Bethune had created the NCNW first and foremost as a vehicle to integrate black women into the nation's job structure and consciousness. But the Civil Rights movement necessitated an organization that focused primarily on race matters. Because the Civil Rights movement addressed concerns that all blacks, including black

women, had about the race, the subtle shift in focus occurred without debate or interrogation, almost unconsciously. But it occurred.
Under Bethune black women's distinct needs took precedence. The
underlying assumption was that the race was served when black
women were. Under Height, general concerns of the race became a
priority, the unspoken presumption was that black women were
served when the race was.

This subtle shift had monumental consequences. For at the very
moment that the Council was shifting its focus to Civil Rights and
community development, Daniel Patrick Moynihan's 1965 report
on the black family was legitimizing a stereotype of black women
that was as damaging to their image as that which cast them as
promiscuous. Assistant Secretary of Labor Daniel Patrick Moynihan
wrote *The Negro Family: The Case for National Action* to alert government policy makers to the problems in black America that went
beyond desegregation and voting. He aimed to demonstrate that neither the Civil Rights movement nor Civil Rights legislation had
made an impact on black everyday life.[53] Indeed, the report's survey
of unemployment, housing, school dropout rates, crime and delinquency, and intelligence tests revealed that over ten years of Civil
Rights protests and national upheaval had not changed the fundamental living conditions of most African Americans.[54] Moynihan
blamed past and present racism for the alarming conditions. No one
should suppose, he warned, that "the Negro American community
has not paid a fearful price for the incredible mistreatment to which
it has been subjected over the past three centuries."[55] The price, he
concluded, was a "tangle of pathology," the fundamental feature of
which was a "matriarchal structure" that "seriously retards the
progress of the group as a whole, and imposes a crushing burden on
the Negro male and, in consequence on a great many Negro women
as well."[56]

Even though Moynihan's goal was to highlight the instability of
the black family and thereby encourage the government to systemat-
ically design programs to strengthen black families and communi-

ties, he inadvertently placed black women at the center of black America's problems. In essence, Moynihan argued that black women had done better against racism than had black men, and that their advantaged position had crippled black men and black communities. According to the report, "a fundamental fact of Negro American family life is the often reversed roles of husband and wife."[57] Black females, the report claimed, surpassed black males in school and were generally better educated. They had a stronger position in white-collar and professional employment, and were less inclined toward criminal behavior than black men. On the negative side, black women had more illegitimate children than did white women. Taken together, these factors alienated black men and forced them out of the house, leaving the community without strong male figures and without a strong family base.[58]

The report was devastating to the black woman's image. It seemed to say that if only black women could be less dominant and domi-neering, the black man would have a chance. This is how many read Civil Rights leader Whitney Young's comments. Cited in the report as an expert on the black family, Young claimed that black mothers "made sure that if one of their children had a chance for higher educa-tion the daughter was the one to pursue it." The consequence was that "both as a husband and as a father the Negro male is made to feel inadequate. . . ." Moynihan also quoted psychologist Thomas Petti-grew, who claimed that the black wife became so disgusted with her financially dependent husband that "her rejection of him further alienates the male from family life."[59] Black men, argued Moynihan, needed to get away from black women. They needed a male-domi-nated world. He suggested they join the armed services. There they would find what they needed, a "world away from women, a world run by strong men of unquestioned authority. . . ."[60]

Whatever else the report did it erased over seventy years of image-building on the part of black women's organizations. On top of the media's healthy dose of the "strong black woman"—the many portrayals of Mammy, and the Sapphire image made popular by the radio and television sitcom *Amos and Andy*——the Moynihan report legitimized the perception of black women as unnaturally strong and emasculating. The reverberations were disastrous.[61]

The ripple effect hit black male/female relationships hard. As we have seen, gender tension had been persistent in African-American life. Now it was exacerbated because Moynihan told the nation that the black man's lack of authority in his household retarded the progress of the group and this was the black woman's fault. As he put it, "Ours is a society which presumes male leadership in private and public affairs. The arrangements of society facilitate and reward it. A subculture, such as that of the Negro American, in which this is not the pattern, is placed at a distinct disadvantage."[62] Like the entire report, this statement put black women on the defensive. Writer and critic Michelle Wallace explained the impact best when she noted that the report brought the black man's resentment of the black woman to the surface: "The result was a brainshattering explosion upon the heads of black women, the accumulation of over three hundred years of rage."[63] Indeed, Moynihan had underscored John Hope's indictment of the black woman's femininity, and given government backing to Hope's early insistence that "the only way for our men to be more manly is for our women to be more womanly." As the Black Power movement gained momentum this idea became one of its major supporting tenets.

In effect, the Moynihan report damaged the black woman's image as much as did James Jacks's 1895 characterization of her as sexually promiscuous. However, unlike the earlier period, when the National Association of Colored Women mounted a national campaign in support of black women, this new slander met no such organized resistance. Although individuals protested the report, there was no nationally coordinated effort to show how Moynihan had distorted the black woman's history of defending herself and her community in times of hardship. No national organization defended black women against vilification for the role that racism had forced upon them. Whereas the Association had provided the historical context by which to counter sexually promiscuous stereotypes, no national black women's organization explained that black women still predominated in domestic service and low-paying, nonsecure, service-sector jobs. Few Americans learned that black women were hardly represented in white-collar and professional occupations, that those in this sector were stuck in entry-level clerk and secretarial positions, or in the relatively low-paid, traditional female professions of teaching, nursing, and social work.[64] Why? Wallace maintains that "the black woman did not, could not, effectively fight back [because] no one had written a report for her."[65]

The reasons though went deeper. The one organization that could have been expected to write a report was the National Council of Negro Women, but it had never been given to NACW-like testimonials defending black womanhood. It was unlikely to start now because, like African Americans in general, it had shifted its attention to Civil Rights. Moreover, its leader, Dorothy Height, was as much on the defensive as most black women. Height never repudiated the report. Instead, like Moynihan, she emphasized the father's position in the family. Along with Whitney Young and Thomas Pettigrew, Height was quoted in the 1965 Moynihan report. Then, and again in 1969, Height went on record saying that the "Negro woman's major underlying concern" is "the status of the Negro man and his position in the community and his need for feeling himself an important person."[66] In the absence of comments that recognized the critical role black women played in the black family's survival, *their* need to feel appreciated, and the need for black men and women *together* to fight racism—the real enemy of the black family—Height's comments were injurious to black women. Rather than leading the opposition to the report, as Ida B. Wells, Mary Church Terrell, and others had done in opposition to James Jacks's deleterious remarks, Height and the Council lined up with those who blamed black women.

It also put the Council in the camp of those who, like Moynihan, believed that the race would rise only when its men did. Moynihan was strongly influenced by Catholic welfare philosophy, which made patriarchal family interests the central objective of social welfare and social policy in general. Thus he believed that President Johnson's War on Poverty had to focus on the black family (hence the report on the family), and that the best way for the government to serve the black family was to find black men jobs. He felt African Americans would have a chance to reach economic parity with whites if employment opportunities for black men were combined with decent housing and birth control. Central, though, were jobs for men. They would marry women and provide support for them and their children. Even if it meant that women's jobs had to be redesigned to enable men to fill them, Moynihan felt it was a necessary move against black matriarchy.[67]

Height was not among the women who objected to this policy direction. The writer and lawyer Pauli Murray, for example, was quite dismayed over the possibility that black women would be ignored in the effort to create career opportunities for black men in government and industry. Earnestly she asked: "At the very moment in history when there is an international movement to raise the status of women and a recognition that women generally are underemployed, are Negro women to be passed over in the social arrangements which are to create new job opportunities for Negroes? Moreover, when American women are seeking partnership in our society, are Negro women to take a backward step and sacrifice their equalitarian tradition?" Citing statistics demonstrating that black women had a harder time finding a mate, remained single more often than white women, raised more children, and stayed in the job market longer, she noted that black men deserved to develop their potential and feel secure in marital relationships, but that "as a matter of sheer survival," black women had to "insist upon equal opportunities without regard to sex in training, education and employment at every level."[68] Margaret Wright, an activist mother of four children, concurred. She knew that work was not necessarily liberating, that black women had worked "at mopping floors and stuff like that" because "they wouldn't give our men jobs." She was appalled, though, at the matriarchy theory: "Black men used to admire the black women for all they'd endured to keep the race going. Now the black man is saying he wants a family structure like the white man's. He's got to be head of the family and women have to be submissive and all that nonsense. . . . Hell," she scoffed, "the white woman is already oppressed in that setup."[69]

Wright wanted no part of this kind of family, but there were many who agreed with Height. Singer Majorie Barnes argued that black women could not afford to be competitive with their men because "competing with them for jobs would just add to the problems that already exist." Black women had not chosen to be the steadier provider, "it happened out of economic necessity."[70] Barnes welcomed men who could finally take the burden off women, and she was joined by many black women, including Height.[71]

Considering how much of the Council's original mission had been sacrificed during the 1960s, it was unfortunate that neither Height's position nor the Council's Civil Rights activities endeared the Council to the masses of black women. When black nationalism caught the hearts and minds of black Americans around 1965, black women were still suspicious of the Council's middle-class orientation, and young black women distrusted its middle-aged constituency. The integrated Council projects actually repelled the young. Height did not realize this until years after the Civil Rights movement ended. Only then did she see that her 1966 declaration on behalf of the Council that "we do not want black power for American Negroes," that "freedom knows no color," helped alienate black youth.[72] Only later was she able to surmise that young blacks resented the compromises that older generations of African Americans had made through the years and they distrusted anything whites were connected with. As she put it, "they began to . . . accuse the elders of the civil rights movement of maintaining for them a heritage . . . an inheritance of dependency."[73]

Ann Moody, who grew up and joined the movement in Mississippi, certainly felt this way. Bright eyed and sure that nonviolent direct-action protest would bring about a new era of economic and personal freedom in the South, Moody joined the movement in the 1950s. Like other young people who participated against their parents' wishes, Moody thought that "the future of the Negroes in Mississippi didn't depend upon the older people" because "they were too scared and suspicious." She felt the period belonged to the young, whose minds were "susceptible to change . . . open, inquisitive and eager to learn."[74] Throughout all of her harrowing experiences as a Civil Rights worker, she never retreated from this idea. She did, however, change her mind about Civil Rights leadership. After the murder of NAACP leader Medgar Evers, after a beating she received during a sit-down strike at a Woolworth's store, and after living in perpetual fear for many years, she became totally disillusioned with Civil Rights ideology. At the 1963 March on Washington, she thought the way some of the leaders were leading, "the people were better off leading themselves."[75] Her heart sank as she listened to Martin Luther King, Jr.'s "I Have a Dream" speech. "We had 'dreamers' instead of leaders," she thought. It sank even further when two weeks after the march four black girls were killed in a church bombing in Birmingham, Alabama. That was the last straw: "Nonviolence is out," she said in an angry prayer. "Tell [Martin Luther King, Jr.] that nonviolence has served its purpose." By the end of 1963, Moody's feeling was that "we've been praying too long. . . . all we got is a lot of religion and the white man's got everything else. . . ."[76] The 1964 summer project that brought Height and the Council to her area of Mississippi did not change her mind. Her uncle and three other blacks had been murdered by whites that May, and as they joined the long list of martyrs she had known, she lost faith. She felt that as long as whites could shoot and butcher blacks like hogs, Civil Rights organizations could never bring about change.[77] In turning toward black nationalism, Moody, like millions of other dissenting black youth, struck a deathblow to the Civil Rights movement and organizations like the National Council of

Negro Women. Despite Height's efforts young black women remained unimpressed, alienated, and outside the Council.

So did poor black women. Time bore out Civil Rights leader Andrew Young's conclusion that "up until 1968 [the Civil Rights movement] was really a middle-class movement. There were middle-class goals, middle-class aspirations, middle-class membership, and even though a lot of poor people went to jail . . . it was still essentially a middle-class operation."[78] Poor black women made similar assessments. "The poor black woman still occupies the position of domestic in this society, rising no higher than public welfare, when the frustrated male deserts her and the children," argued a group of poor women from Mount Vernon, New York, in 1968. The Civil Rights movement did not change that, because, they argued, "the capitalist system was not supposed to be overturned," but rather, "reformed so the Negro caricatures of a middle class could enjoy the crumbs of what the U.S. pillaged from Latin America, Africa, and Asia.[79] Although they did not specifically indict the NCNW, like other Civil Rights organizations, its record with poor people was not exemplary. It had worked with many poor women in its service projects, but few poor women became members. Height and other leaders were proud of their ability to attract poverty-stricken Mississippi activists Fannie Lou Hamer and Unita Blackwell to the Council. They knew, however, that these were the exceptions. Like young black women, the poor stayed away.

Only when the country's politics turned conservative in 1968 did the Council take steps to attract poor women. It took Richard Nixon's election, the subsequent relaxation of school desegregation guidelines, the call for law and order, the priority given the Vietnam War, and the cutback of federal funds earmarked for social programs, including those of the NCNW, to convince Council leaders that a new direction was in order. Once they realized how conservative, or, as Mildred Goodman, the national program coordinator, put it, "repressive," the new climate was, they acted immediately.[80] Six months after Nixon's inauguration Height called Council leaders together in Nassau, Bahamas, to "chart out a new course of action constituting a complete departure from their traditional approaches to problem solving."[81]

Surprisingly, the complete departure took a black nationalist direction. At first, this was indicated by press releases and speeches that abandoned the word "Negro" in favor of "black." Then, just three years after Height had declared that the NCNW wanted no part of Black Power, Height proclaimed that the "Civil Rights victories of the fifties and sixties were far too limited to provide black people the minimum level of protection which our people require."[82] Stating that "now we understand better what our black youth have been saying to us . . . that our commitment must be total and unrelenting," the Council made an astounding concession to young blacks and stepped away from policies that, despite their shortcomings, had revived and sustained the NCNW.[83]

Council members now asked black women to commit to a "Black Women's Movement" dedicated to the liberation of the black people in America.[84] It asked its local sections to promote black pride through use of the media, libraries, and black history projects, and instructed them to design programs to help solve problems in the areas of drugs, police-community relationships, and community control of schools.[85] The Council's call for the elimination of white racism through "personal" contacts, and "through . . . seminars for white women on the meaning of black pride," signaled a move away from integrated projects, toward a more separatist black female organization. This new NCNW promised to promote consumer education to "halt the exploitation of the black ghetto market," and to promote the creation of cooperatives and credit unions to break "the financial barriers in the local financial institutions."[86]

If these last policy statements sound an ironic chord, it is because they were so similar to the community-based program the Auxiliary had initiated thirty years before when the Council was concentrating on a national gender policy for black women. Now, more than a generation later, the Council was retreating back to a local orientation, calling for Auxiliary-like programs that privileged racial over gender identity.[87]

The new program demanded a different constituency, different financing, and different spokespersons. Since the Republicans were a lot more parsimonious with money for social programs than were the Democrats, the Council resolved to focus less on public funding and more on contributions from corporations and private foundations.[88] It also realized that a black woman's movement premised on black nationalist principles could go nowhere without young black

THIS COVER OF THE NATIONAL COUNCIL OF NEGRO WOMEN'S NEW JOURNAL WAS SYMBOLIC OF ITS NEW IDEOLOGICAL DIRECTION AND ITS ATTEMPT TO BRING TOGETHER WOMEN OF ALL GENERATIONAL AND SOCIOECONOMIC BACKGROUNDS. *Photo courtesy of the National Park Service—Mary McLeod Bethune Council House NHS, Washington, D.C.*

women and those who were poor. By the late 1960s these two groups were among the most outspoken about the failures of the Civil Rights movement. The Council, therefore, aggressively recruited them along with middle-class black women.[89] Accordingly, in 1968, its leaders conducted a confidential search for young articulate "militant" women to serve as Council spokeswomen. The average age of the women suggested was twenty-nine.[90] Based on the recognition that "the NCNW is dependent on its ability to attract and retain young women," leaders also initiated a pilot project to form NCNW college sections, and explored the possibility of creating a staff position for a young person to help develop and execute programs relevant to the needs of the young.[91]

The Council also moved to broaden its social-economic base. In fact, its leaders declared their intention to "create a membership program that will retain persons reached through our service programs for membership in the NCNW."[92] To this end, as well as to increase overall membership, the NCNW instituted a direct membership policy, which allowed members of affiliates to pay dues directly to the Council. Earlier, black women had to pay five dollars to a regional council, a portion of which would be sent to the national body to cover both regional and national dues. Now, for two dollars it was possible to become a member of the national body. This was a significant change, for not only did it promise to increase overall membership by bringing in women who did not care to belong to a regional council, but since the regionals were dominated by sorority members, it seemed likely to increase the numbers of women not of the black middle class.

Perhaps the most significant aspect of direct membership was the way it changed the essential nature of the Council. In 1935, it was founded as "an organization of organizations" to enable different kinds of black women's groups to speak in unison. Unlike the Association, the Council did not bind black women together in a tight alliance that made the fortunate responsible for the unfortunate. It aimed to bring together different kinds of associations and place them on an equal footing so that together they could lobby on behalf of black women's interests. Now, in 1969, direct membership would move the Council away from a "loosely knit Council of organizations" to what the Council hoped would be an organization of individuals ready to mount a "strong black Woman's Movement."[93] To facilitate the new initiative the Council changed the location of its 1968 convention. Instead of holding it at its usual site in Washington, D.C., it was held in Los Angeles, California, to bring the Council in closer touch with issues confronting large urban black areas, and particularly to "strengthen the hand of . . . the newly formed Watts Section of NCNW."[94]

Council leaders hoped that these measures would not just strengthen the NCNW but actually protect and save it from the late 1960s conservative backlash. After all, Council women did not want to be missed if they went out of business, they did not want to go out of business at all. In this they proved how different they were from the National Association of Colored Women. In the 1920s, when it was first confronted with a young migrant black female population that embraced different ideas about blackness and womanhood, and a middle class eager to use new methods to tackle old problems, the Association resisted change. It clung to a past that was increasingly unusable to a new generation of black women. The Council was taking a different tack. With their "Black Woman's movement" they looked forward and tried to change.

Indeed, most of black America was changing. The optimism that marked the early years of the 1960s waned as the sit-ins, freedom rides, marches, demonstrations, and voter registration drives failed to end racial inequality. As hope turned into bitterness, the Civil Rights movement gave way to the separatism of Black Power. By the decade's end most blacks could see that for all the South's newly registered voters, for all the lunch counters and front seats of buses now accessible, black unemployment rates were still higher than those of whites, housing was still substandard, and education was still inferior. En masse, African Americans sought other ways of tackling these entrenched problems. Some, like Martin Luther King, Jr., focused more directly on the problems of the poor, and sought answers in a poor people's movement. Some endorsed the "Black Power" that Stokely Carmichael proclaimed in 1966, others supported the black nationalist Black Panther party or the extreme separatism of the Black Muslims. The Council endorsed separatism and a black woman's movement, and did their best to change their constituency. In doing so it moved with, and in the same direction as, the rest of black America.

This is not surprising since during the 1960s the Council struggled with some of the same issues that gripped African Americans generally, and indeed all of American society. The generational conflict, for example, was not just a Council problem but one that in black America led to the creation of the Student Non-Violent Coordinating Committee (SNCC). Just as the junior Council members resented the control exerted by the older members, the SNCC was born out of black students' desire for autonomy and their opposition to any hierarchy of authority.[95] Similarly, the Council's struggle with class issues, even its image problem, mirrored black America's adjustment to new ideas about the nature of leadership, and the responsibility of the black middle class. In the SNCC the philosophy of leadership allowed the privileged to inspire, convince, and nudge, but required local people to lead.[96] Like the SNCC, the Council's work in Sunflower County, Mississippi, demonstrated its responsiveness to the criticism of the black middle class and its willingness to try a new way of leading. On the whole, therefore, the Council's program and problems reflected the concerns that consumed African Americans, and paralleled the direction that the race took.

It was, therefore, left to other organizations to focus on black women, particularly the problems confronting the young and the poor. It was not mere coincidence that the National Welfare Rights Organization was founded in 1966, and the National Black Feminist Organization materialized in 1973. The former was made up mostly of poor black women, and the latter's members were mostly young and college educated. Just as the National League of Republican Colored Women, the International Council of Women of the Darker Races of the World, and the Ladies Auxiliary of the Brotherhood of Sleeping Car Porters signaled the dawn of a new era in the 1920s, so these new organizations were created out of the new needs of different classes and generations of black women in the 1960s.

One of these needs was for organizations to defend the image of the black woman and to act as a mouthpiece for her causes. For all of the burden that the turn-of-the-century Association placed on black women to be chaste and moral, for all its elitism, it did not allow them to be slandered without rebuttal. Association leaders were outspoken about the burdens of being black *and* female, about black women's contributions to community development, the shortcomings of black male leaders, and the present and future progress of the race. Under Bethune, the Council moved away from moralizing about the black woman's character but still lobbied on her behalf. Under Height, the Council represented black women in the Civil Rights movement, but did not speak exclusively for nor defend them. Welfare rights advocates and black feminists took up the cause of defending black women. As we will see, they did so in an atmosphere that was decidedly misogynist, one in which black women had few defenders.

Chapter 7

❈

MAKING A WAY OUT OF NO WAY

Many people had the same feelings but never expressed them in a unified way. Suddenly they began to admit that they were on welfare and
they were relieved and willing to go out and express the community
feeling to the state and city.

—WELFARE RECIPIENT

I went through periods of being afraid that my feelings were latent lesbian feelings. I wanted to examine myself hard before I turned to a
group or organization for political as well as moral support. I realize
now that the feelings I have (that of the mere fact that I should be able to
do what I feel I am capable of doing and not doing what is expected of
me because of the "peculiarities of womanhood") are my own and have
always been within me for as long as I can recall.

—COLLEGE STUDENT

Jane Galvin-Lewis joined the staff of the Women's Action Alliance
sure that she had found a community of women who, like herself,
were committed to ending sex discrimination and stereotyping.
Founded as a resource center to help women handle job discrimination, child care, welfare rights, and health needs, the Alliance's
stated goals were to "encourage a united working relationship
among all women—educated women and uneducated women,
black, white, Chicana, Native American, Puerto Rican and other
ethnic minority women, young women and old women, rich women
and poor women." On the board of directors were some of the

country's most well-known black and white human rights advocates and feminists, including Johnnie Tillmon and George Wiley, leaders of the national welfare rights movement. For Galvin-Lewis, the Alliance was the vehicle to take the principles of the woman's liberation movement into local communities and apply them to the problems of average women.[1]

Despite her initial enthusiasm, Lewis's tenure with the Alliance was short-lived. As a volunteer for the Alliance she answered mail from women from across the country, and sent out referrals and information. She worked as an outreach person to local women's groups, and was the liaison between volunteers and the paid staff. She felt she had done a good job and expected to continue this line of work when she became a paid staff member. Once on staff, however, she felt invisible and superfluous. She was ignored to the point where she felt that all of the approaches she made to "become active . . . were intrusions." "I was consulted about nothing and planning never involved me," she explained. "My job became totally unclear. I had no job description and I never received an evaluation. I was treated as a total non-person." Galvin-Lewis did not understand why.[2]

Slowly, she began to suspect her marginalization was connected to her membership in the National Black Feminist Organization (NBFO). Since an Alliance goal was to expand the woman's liberation movement beyond white middle-class women, Galvin-Lewis thought that black feminists would be welcome at the Alliance. She was unprepared for what she considered the staff's negative response when the NBFO started using one of the Alliance's rooms for their meetings. From her perspective, "people tended to be very uncomfortable" around the black women, a reaction that "was not the same when large numbers of white women were present." It seemed to her that the office gossip surrounding her, and the communication problems she was having with Marlene Krauss, the director, could be traced to this involvement. When she was dismissed in the Spring of 1974, she blamed it on the racism of the entire white staff.[3]

Galvin-Lewis did not go quietly. In a stinging grievance statement she blasted the Alliance for losing sight of its founding principles. Bitterly she accused the white women of betraying Alliance goals. The staff, she said, had "not dealt with their racism and do not realize the subtleties of its functioning in their feelings and actions." Black people at the Alliance needed to be forewarned: "her or his role will be exclusive of decision making or policy making." In Galvin-Lewis's opinion a white male would have been treated better—"free of deception, deceit and total lack of respect." Given the hypocrisy at the Woman's Action Alliance she felt it did not "deserve to posture as a sisterhood."[4]

Galvin-Lewis was not alone in her mistrust of white women. Rather, like the vast majority of African-American women, she had come to believe that white women could not and would not represent her; that woman's liberation was a white woman's bid to share power with white men. Importantly, Galvin-Lewis did not turn to the National Council of Negro Women or other civil rights or Black Power groups for support, but put her faith in the organization she had helped found: the National Black Feminist Organization.

Johnnie Tillmon's actions were similar. In 1968, a year after she helped organize the national welfare rights movement, she and other welfare activists met with Dr. Martin Luther King, Jr., to discuss the Poor People's campaign being launched by the Southern Christian Leadership Conference. The welfare rights activists were angry that welfare issues had been deliberately ignored in the new drive for poor people's rights, and had called a meeting to grill the civil rights leaders as to why. Andrew Young, King's assistant at the time, remembered that the welfare mothers made King visibly uncomfortable. In fact, according to Young, they "jumped on Martin like no one ever had before."[5] After a barrage of questions on welfare legislation that he obviously could not answer, Tillmon, who sat next to King with her grandchild on her lap, said, "You know, Dr. King, if you don't know about these questions, you should say you don't know, and then we could go on with the meeting." King replied,

"You're right, Mrs. Tillmon, we don't know anything about welfare. We are here to learn."[6]

Indeed, the late 1960s and early 1970s were a period of learning for many groups, including black women who felt betrayed or somehow unrepresented by the black and woman's movements of the civil rights era. The creation of the National Welfare Rights Organization in 1967 and the National Black Feminist Organization in 1973 manifested a new kind of thinking about black womanhood. Both organizations were created out of a need to deal with aspects of contemporary black female life that had been neglected. They supported the African-American woman's right to work at a decent wage, her rights to education and job training, her right to medical care for herself and her children, her right to be safeguarded against sterilization. They made children's day care and the media's portrayal of black women a priority.

In doing this, these two new organizations put black women back at the center of race progress. Like founders and members of the National Association of Colored Women and the early National Council of Negro Women, members of the National Welfare Rights Organization and the National Black Feminist Organization did not feel their programs betrayed the race when they worked on these issues. In their eyes, gender and class issues *were* race issues. For the welfare mothers, the race was best served when poor people were; for the feminists, black people of all classes were served best when black women were.

A major difference between these two national organizations and those that preceded them was their unabashed attention to issues of sexuality. For good reason, black women's national organizations had portrayed black women as moral but essentially asexual. Now, new technologies of birth control, new powers and responsibilities of government, and, above all, new stereotypes of black women demanded a departure from this traditional approach to black female sexuality.

The late sixties and early seventies were, therefore, an era much like that of the 1920s. Just as women of that period presented new challenges to the National Association of Colored Women, so too did black women in this period manifest needs that fell beyond the scope of programs offered by the National Council of Negro Women. In defining themselves and in meeting their needs, organized black feminists and women on welfare defined black women to the nation. Their definition differed from that offered by the Council and contemporary white women's groups, for both organizations brought together issues of race, class, and gender differently. If ever the nation could see the variety of black womanhood, now was the time. Sadly, only the Council survived the seventies. Not only was the country unaccepting of new organizations that heralded the diverse identities of black women, but African Americans also had trouble dealing with the emerging autonomy of individual black women and the national groups they forged. This period proved how difficult it was to make a way out of no way.

THE EARLY 1970s witnessed the entrenchment of black nationalism. Despite the government's effective infiltration and destruction of the Black Panther Party and like organizations, black nationalism persisted.[7] What was infectious about it was the idea that black people, without white help and its implicit sense of obligation, could and would change the way they experienced America. The concept was broad enough to be embraced by anyone and any group that expressed black pride, self-sufficiency, independence, and self-worth. Thus, groups like the automobile workers who established Revolutionary Union Movements (Dodge Revolutionary Union Movement, Ford Revolutionary Union Movement, and General Motors Revolutionary Union Movement) to resist racist hiring practices and racial inequities in the automobile industry were black nationalists. So were black capitalists, who promoted black property ownership and black business development. And so was the Nation of Islam, whose religion supported a strong black family, black separatism, black-owned businesses, and a rhetoric that was antiwhite.

Sadly, many of the words and ideas of black nationalism were misogynist. This misogyny had been in the making at least since Frazier's critique of black middle-class women and Moynihan's matriarchy thesis. African-American men, from Black Panther Eldridge Cleaver and sociologist Calvin Hernton, to psychiatrists William Grier and Price Cobbs, to ideologue Frantz Fanon, accused black women of harming and holding back the race. Hernton, for example, explored black female history and concluded that it had produced in her a "sort of 'studism'," which expressed itself in a "strong matriarchal drive." The black woman could be expected to be "too dominating, too demanding, too strict, too inconsiderate, and too masculine," said Hernton, because her history of being "alone and unprotected" had produced in her a "rigidity," and a "quality of austerity."[8] Hernton was joined by Grier and Cobbs who traced these defects to the black woman's self-hatred. She is "the antithesis of American beauty," explained the two psychiatrists. "Depreciated by her own kind, judged grotesque by her society, and valued only as a sexually convenient laboring animal," the black girl, they reasoned, had the cards stacked against her as far as "the achievement of a healthy, mature womanhood." The failure of a black female to develop a healthy narcissism in girlhood caused her, later in life, to neglect her figure, allow herself to become obese, concern herself more with the utility of clothing and less with style, and resign herself to the "asexual maternal role in which work and a hovering concern for the family" occupied her entirely. According to the argument, the black woman's concern with family was emasculating because black women were all too good at preparing their black boys for a manhood that demanded they curb their aggressiveness, mute their assertiveness, and accept a subordinate place in the world.[9]

This put black women in league with white men in their attempt to destroy black men, or so the critique went. A character in

Cleaver's 1968 best-selling book, *Soul on Ice,* exclaimed that the black woman was "the silent ally, indirectly but effectively, of the white man." Whether she knew it or not, the white man had chosen her as his instrument to destroy black men. He had, said the black male character to his black male audience, "propped her up economically above you and me, to strengthen her hand against us."[10] No wonder, the argument held that black women secretly desired white men. Speaking in an international vein, Frantz Fanon, an Algerian psychologist, lent the viewpoint a universality that seemed to cement its validity. Women of color, he wrote, in *Black Skin, White Masks*, desired white men because they hated the inferiority attached to black men. To marry a white man was to marry whiteness and therefore free oneself from the self-hatred born of being female and black.[11] Hernton agreed. Black women, especially middle-class women, revealed a "suppressed sexual desire for white men" because the white man was the embodiment of sociomasculine prestige.[12] In psychoanalytic language Grier and Cobbs explained that the thwarted narcissism of black women motivated their drive to find fulfillment in lovers who had limitless opportunities. Identification with the white male, they wrote, allowed black women to view themselves as white and therefore beautiful.[13]

As we have seen, this was not the first time that black men had accused black women of desiring white men and of wanting to be white. This contemporary assault was, however, far stronger than the attacks at the turn of the century. It had a different quality. Earlier critiques were grounded in sociology, but the modern critiques relied heavily on Freudian psychology, lending a "scientific" dimension absent earlier in the century. For Grier and Cobbs, black women were born deficient because they had no penis. Race was just an additional burden.[14] The difference in the two periods also turned on the issue of motherhood. At the turn of the century—indeed, for most of the century—black people celebrated black motherhood. When lynching and castration occurred regularly, the idea that black women emasculated their sons when they taught them how to avoid the lynch mob was not an issue. Moreover, the early years of the century found black women engaged in spirited debate with black men over who should lead. Amy Jacques Garvey never missed an opportunity to counter her husband's views on the superiority of black men, but neither Garvey nor the men of the period lashed into black women so. Earlier in the century black women had many more male defenders. In more ways than one, and by more than a few, black women were told to "write a book of Acts" for the race. Black women themselves stood up for their sex. When black men claimed that men were natural leaders, women challenged them to put their action where their words were.

In the absence of defenders, black women became tentative. Women in organizations like the Southern Christian Leadership Conference, the Student Non-Violent Coordinating Committee, the Congress of Racial Equality, and the Black Panthers were bombarded with demands that they stop competing with black men for jobs, and that they stay at home and have babies "for the revolution."[15] Although compliance would have left them proverbially barefoot and pregnant, black women could not aggressively object without reinforcing the image of the emasculating matriarch they sought to challenge. As put by activist Angela Davis, the late sixties and early seventies were "a period in which one of the unfortunate hallmarks of some nationalist groups was their determination to push women into the background. The brothers opposing us leaned heavily on male supremacist trends which were winding their way through the movement."[16]

Black Panther Elaine Brown had a lot more to say. She thought macho attitudes destroyed the Black Panthers. Her initiation into misogynist black nationalist circles came one evening when she and a friend sat discussing the movement in a house in Los Angeles. Both women had contributed money to pay for the chicken dinner the group was serving, but when they got up to help themselves to food they were told that the "Sisters" had to wait until the "Brothers" were served because the "Brothers" were the "warriors" and they had to eat first. Brown's protest that "nobody said anything about 'our war-riors' when money was changing hands," fell on hostile ears, and she was summarily read the "rules" by a "Brother" who explained that "Sisters . . . did not challenge Brothers." Sisters, he said, "stood behind their black men, supported their men, and respected them." That evening Brown learned that not only was it "unsisterly" of her to want to eat with the "Brothers," but "it was sacrilege for which blood could be shed." In the several years that she spent with the Black Panthers, she and other black women were regularly beaten by black men in the name of "black manhood." According to Brown, women in the Black Panther party were expected to clean up after "their" men, to have sex with them on demand, and to never ques-tion their authority or the decisions they made. A woman in the Black Power movement, Brown concluded, "was considered, at best, irrelevant. A woman asserting herself was a pariah. A woman attempting the role of leadership was . . . making an alliance with the counter-revolutionary, man-hating, lesbian, feminist white bitches. If a black woman assumed a role of leadership, she was said to be eroding black manhood, to be hindering the progress of the black race. She was an enemy of black people."[17]

Sixty some odd years earlier, Addie Hunton had expressed a fear that black women would be blamed for all the problems of the race, and now in the late 1960s and early 1970s her prophecy had come true. Never had the conflict between black men and women been so venomous. Never had black women capitulated so easily.

Why? Black men were no more disabled than they had been at previous times during the century; in fact, they were probably doing better than ever before. There were also very capable black women who sacrificed much and worked very hard for African-American causes—Angela Davis and Elaine Brown were cases in point. One factor that was different about the late sixties and early seventies was the lack of an organized effort to support black women and defend their name.

The National Council of Negro Women was as unresponsive to

the misogyny as it was to the Moynihan report. There was no open discussion about the black woman's image in the NCNW, mostly because debate did not occur in the Council. In the National Association of Colored Women, although elections always gave rise to bitterness, the Association was fueled in part by the fierce exchange of ideas that women from different regions with different ideological perspectives brought to national meetings. The Council did not function this way because it did not hold elections. Height, in fact, never yielded the presidency.[18] The late sixties and early seventies gave rise to some independent supporters of African-American women, but the Council did not incubate or nourish them.[19]

For better or worse, Dorothy Height continued to adhere to a policy of expediency that left her following the tide rather than leading it. Height's biggest accomplishment was that she saved the moribund Council with a politic shift toward Civil Rights that brought in public and private money. The Council moved toward black nationalism only after the white conservative backlash made imperative a more nationalist stance, and only after most Civil Rights organizations had made militant demands for economic parity. Unlike her turn-of-the-century counterparts who praised the black woman's fortitude, and unlike Helena Wilson and Rosina Tucker who suffered no male to dictate the programs of the Auxiliary, Height was equivocal. Despite her regret that the "black woman has had to struggle against being a person of great strength," in 1969 she reiterated her belief that the black woman's primary concern had to be the status of the Negro man.[20]

Height's position was unfortunate not just because the Council did not provide an organized defense of black women in the wake of malicious attacks from white and black men, and not just because the Council did not offer a program for bolstering the black woman's self-esteem, but also because it did not offer much guidance on what to do about the burgeoning woman's movement. When the woman's liberation movement blossomed in the late sixties, black women looked at it askance. Many could not identify with the white middle-class professional woman's demand for work and equal pay, or the white suburban housewife's revolt against leisure living. Although a few black women—Pauli Murray, Aileen Hernandez, and Shirley Chisholm, for example—joined the movement, and a few like Jane Galvin-Lewis tried forging alliances between black and white women, most black women stayed away. The white woman's demand for a more "meaningful" existence was not taken seriously by African-American women who had more experience as the domestic employees of these women than as their political allies. African-American women were constantly found wanting when compared to white women, even by their own men; naturally they preferred membership in black organizations than in the likes of the National Organization of Women (NOW), which had emerged in 1966 in the vanguard of women's drive for equal rights and equal pay. The fact that NOW women did not at first identify issues of poverty as women's issues was as alienating as their tendency to compare themselves to minorities and call themselves oppressed.[21] Black women, wrote Toni Morrison, in 1971, "look at White women and see the enemy, for they know that racism is not confined to white men and that there are more white women than men in this country." Moreover, explained Morrison, black women had "no abiding admiration of white women as competent, complete people." Black women regarded them "as willful children, pretty children, mean children, ugly children, but never as real adults."[22] These feelings were validated when sexual discrimination was prohibited under Title VII of the 1964 Civil Rights bill. Most African Americans felt that white women had not fought and sacrificed as had blacks, had not shown their mettle, had not proven themselves. Rather, like spoiled children, they had gained something for nothing. As the 1970s progressed, and the woman's movement got stronger, while the black movement was attacked and weakened, these feelings only deepened.

They also left many black women in a quandary. At odds with both black men and white women, they could have used more guidance through the maze of ideas on race and gender. In times past, black women felt freer to work for their vision of black liberation, freer to assert an independent role, even the central role, for themselves in that liberation. Now race and gender issues seemed oppositional. It seemed that black women could not work on both fronts at the same time, could not embrace one part of their identity without denying the other. They needed new organizations to represent the parts of their identities that had gone unrepresented, the needs that had been ignored.

One new organization was the National Welfare Rights Organization (NWRO). Formed in 1967, the black women of the NWRO identified their poverty, not their race or sex, as the most determining feature of their lives. Their blackness and femaleness was understood within the context of their status as welfare recipients. When they spoke against substandard housing, of their need for clothing and food for their children and for respect from welfare caseworkers, they expressed concerns that had received little attention from either middle-class blacks or white women. When they talked about poverty as a function of male desertion, they addressed concerns that the middle-class women of the Council and the macho black nationalists purposely avoided. By approaching their gender concerns from their class perspective, they made visible many of the circumstances that were unique to black women and women who were poor.

By the time the first welfare rights organization (WRO) was founded in 1962, in Alameda County, California, the Civil Rights movement had given local people a sense of empowerment.[23] Thus, when a fire destroyed the roof of the home of a thirty-eight-year-old mother of seven and the Alameda welfare department canceled her support because her housing was deemed unfit, other recipients organized on her behalf. With the help and aid of a social work student at the University of California, the mother questioned the legal basis of the welfare department's action and had her aid restored. In the process, the first local welfare rights organization was born.[24]

A year after the Alameda County WRO was formed, Johnnie Till-

JOHNNIE TILLMON. *Photo courtesy of the Photographer, Collection, Moorland-Spingarn Research Center, Howard University.*

mon, the future chairperson of the National Welfare Rights Organization, organized Aid to Needy Children-Mothers Anonymous, in Watts, Los Angeles. She was motivated by not just the diabetes, arthritis, and tonsillitis that caused her to lose her job as a laundress and go on welfare, but conversations she had heard on her way to work when she was employed. "Domestics," she recalled, "would complain that all you had to do was have a baby and you could get on welfare." Those already on welfare complained about caseworkers who searched their apartments at midnight looking for evidence of extra support. They would check recipients' laundry baskets and clothes hampers, look in refrigerators, wake up kids with flashlights, and look for men under beds and in closets.[25] Since aid was denied to anyone suspected of getting outside help, this was a perennial complaint of recipients.[26] Tillmon wanted people to know that welfare did not pay an adequate income, that most women on welfare did not have children just to get a bigger check, that welfare recipients wanted job training so they could make a living wage. She, herself, at age forty-five, had worked all her life but was only making "90-some cents an hour." Had illness not forced her onto welfare, she would have continued to work her laundry job for pitiful wages just to stay *off* welfare.[27]

Tillmon did not know a lot about organizing but she knew that something needed to be done. She went to the manager of the housing project where she lived and he asked her to gather five other women of similar sentiment. Together they wrote and mailed an open letter to welfare recipients requesting "that they come to a certain place, a certain time, a certain day at a certain hour to discuss your check and your housing lease." The letter went out to over five hundred recipients and the turnout was amazing. According to Tillmon, the welfare mothers were suspicious when they first arrived, thinking "who the hell are you?" But Tillmon talked fast, calmed them down, and soon had them electing officers for an organization. They called themselves ANC-Mothers Anonymous because the dictionary definition of anonymous was "nameless." They thought that word fit them because, as Tillmon explained, "we understood that what people thought about welfare recipients and women on welfare was that they had no rights, they didn't exist, they was [sic] a statistic and not a human being."[28]

For the next year or so the group worked quietly, afraid of investigation and retaliation by the welfare department. Slowly but surely they got welfare mothers to believe that they could have some control over their lives. They told mothers who were accustomed to staying at home, cooking and taking care of their children, that "cooking is all right, you're supposed to cook for your children, and you can have a day for washing and ironing, but then you can do something else that's beneficial to you and your children. You can participate in voter's registration, voter's education, you can work in some political campaigns or civil rights demonstrations because that'd benefit us too." Besides encouraging women to become active in civil rights, ANC-Mothers Anonymous also helped people threatened with eviction, people with problems collecting all their aid, and people cut off from aid for any number of reasons. They taught people how to appeal decisions made by the welfare department and became liaisons between recipients and welfare supervisors.[29] As a local action group they used their resources to affect the behavior of local supervisors:

> We felt like we was [sic] isolated, that there was maybe a conspiracy, to maybe keep us where we were. We didn't want to be where we were and maybe we didn't really feel that it was the entire country . . . trying to keep us there, because we didn't have contact with . . . big folk. The people we had contact with were the social workers, and of course you strike out at whatever is close to you.[30]

All over the country women on Aid to Families with Dependent Children (AFDC) struck out at local welfare departments. From cities in California, local WRO's spread to Colorado, Cleveland, Boston, and New York. Jeanette Washington got involved in organizing poor people in New York when, after losing her factory job, the seventh she had held in a year, welfare officials forced her to live in a hotel room with her three children. Along with Beulah Sanders, another future chairperson of the National Welfare Rights Organization, she helped organize the West Side Welfare Recipients League. Washington recalled how meeting collectively helped individual recipients overcome the shame attached to welfare, and made them conscious of their rights as citizens. When they sat down to discuss their basic needs they found them wanting. "Families were being moved in and out and we found five or six people were living in one room. . . . We sat down and looked in the welfare manual and it said there were minimum standards."[31]

The minimum standards and special needs provisions written into most state welfare laws provided the foundation on which most local welfare groups built their protest movement.[32] According to most laws, AFDC clients were entitled to a certain standard of living, which included allocations of furniture, clothing, health care, and other necessities. Other laws provided that recipients could apply for additional benefits should a "special need" present itself. The first action that local welfare organizations took was to inform recipients of their entitlements under these provisions. That most recipients did not receive benefits that matched the minimum standard or their basic needs, that once applied for these benefits could be received fairly quickly, and that local protest at welfare offices often forced welfare agencies to comply with the law, were the basis on which most local organizers built their initial campaign for welfare reform. Organizers would canvass an area, get a core group to attend meetings, confront welfare officials with demands for additional aid, and then stage a demonstration if necessary. In Boston, for example, Mothers for Adequate Welfare, a Roxbury group, staged a three-day sit-in to protest the summary termination of recipients without hearings. After three days, police attempts to remove demonstrators from the Boston welfare office resulted in a weekend of rioting.[33]

The Boston demonstration occurred just two months before the National Welfare Rights Organization held its first convention in August of 1967. The groundwork was laid by George Wiley, who became the organization's first Executive Director. In May 1966, shortly after resigning from the post of Associate National Director of the Congress of Racial Equality, he and a staff of four opened an office called the Poverty/Rights Action Center. Its purpose was to coordinate the activities of different grass-roots community groups that worked on issues like health care, education, the control of antipoverty programs, and the public welfare system. For Wiley, welfare rights groups were ripe for organizing, and they also provided him with a means of working toward his ultimate goal of racial justice through economic opportunity. In June 1966, he organized a series of demonstrations around the country that culminated in a call for the formation of a national meeting of welfare recipients and organizers. In August, and then again in December, the recipients and organizers formed a National Coordinating Committee, and at the later meeting made the Poverty/Rights Action Center its headquarters and fund-raising center. By August, the founding convention of the National Welfare Rights Organization was held in Washington, D.C. The convention brought together 178 locally elected delegates and alternates representing approximately seventy-five WRO's in forty-five cities and twenty-one states.[34]

By and large the aims of the National Welfare Rights Organization were threefold: to provide a national voice for local concerns, to coordinate the activities of the local organizations, and to work on establishing for poor people their right to dignity, justice, and democracy. A good example of the way the NWRO functioned is illustrated in the "Winter Action Campaign" of 1968. In November, the NWRO called on local welfare rights groups to refuse to pay their December rents and instead to use the money to buy necessities not provided by welfare. It also directed WROs to demand special Christmas grants of fifty dollars to one hundred dollars per person for family gifts; to underpay utility companies by giving them only the meager amount of money welfare departments allocated for utilities; and to demand that large department stores extend credit to recipients to enable them to escape unscrupulous ghetto merchants. The rationale behind the National Welfare Rights Organization's call for action was its leaders' belief that the poor had a *right* to live decently and with dignity.[35]

This belief was also at the heart of two other initiatives undertaken by the NWRO. The first was their 1969 call for a nationwide boycott of Sears if it did not extend low-interest revolving credit to welfare recipients.[36] The second was their vocal and persistent opposition to work incentive programs and flat grant proposals, opposition that went hand in hand with their support of a guaranteed annual and adequate income. The National Welfare Rights Organization opposed forced work programs out of several fears. Its leaders had worked for years at dead-end jobs. They believed that mothers would be forced into similar jobs, jobs that paid the minimum wage or less. If they refused to work, they would be thrown off welfare. Welfare rights leaders also felt that there were not enough jobs to go around, and that, at most, work incentive programs prepared people for unskilled jobs that no one else wanted. Such jobs never covered the expense of child care, and by the time mothers paid those costs, actual take-home pay was lower than their welfare check. Leaders and members of the welfare rights organizations repeatedly articulated their desire to work. They insisted, however, on skilled jobs and the training that they needed to fill them. They felt that mothers with large families or with small children had a right to stay home and care for their children just like women with more means. And they felt poor women had a right to quality child care, and that any job a poor women was forced to take ought to enable her to pay for it.[37]

The right to work at a good job was central to their program, but since they doubted the existence of such jobs for everyone, they demanded the government institute a guaranteed annual income. The income would be based on need and would include cost-of-living increases. Families with men would be treated the same as those with only women. Additionally, single women with children would be treated the same as the blind, the aged, and the disabled.[38] This was important because, as the welfare law was written under the 1935 Social Security Act, these latter groups were considered more deserving of aid and thus were granted more money.[39] In 1968, the National Welfare Rights Organization lobbied for a $4,000 income for a family of four; by the early 1970s it was $6,500; by 1974 they supported a $7,500 guaranteed annual income.[40]

The similarities and differences between the National Welfare Rights Organization and the National Council of Negro Women spotlight the divergent ways black women of different social and economic classes brought their race, class, and gender to bear on their organizations and self-identification.[41]

As noted, the middle-class Council represented black women and endorsed a program of "woman power," but it did not undertake an explicit defense of black womanhood nor did it put black women at the center of its program. Through Height, it addressed black women's concerns from a race rather than gender perspective. Welfare rights organizers addressed black women's concerns from a class perspective. The National Welfare Rights Organization was not a "black" organization per se, but by virtue of the poverty issues it handled it was overwhelmingly composed of African-American women. This meant that although it worked on issues critical to blacks, it did so from its concern with the poor. Unlike the Council, the NWRO never made race an explicit priority. Although their numbers were smaller, poor people of other races belonged. The National Welfare Rights Organization was also not a "woman's," nor a "black woman's organization." Its members were almost entirely black and female, and the issues it addressed touched the lives of most black women. Still, it had been organized to serve poor people who were welfare recipients, and thus class was prioritized over race and sex. Its members were black and female because black women were disproportionately poor. Their status explained the prominence of male leaders. Before Johnnie Tillmon became chairperson of the NWRO it was directed by a middle-class black man named George Wiley, whose advisors were mostly white men. This leadership confirmed the poor black woman's powerlessness to effect change without the help of white or male guardians.

The different thrusts of these organizations reflected real differences between their leaders and members. Dorothy Height and Johnnie Tillmon were as different as Mary Church Terrell and Mary McLeod Bethune. Height had grown up in an upwardly mobile working-class family in Pennsylvania and she attended school regularly. Tillmon had been born into a sharecropping family in Arkansas and grew up picking cotton. Poverty chased her all her life, not because she did not work, but because she could not make a living wage from the sharecropping, maid, or laundry jobs she held. Height made a decision not to marry or have children because she did not want to compromise her freedom or stand in the shadow of a man. Tillmon, on the other hand, became autonomous when she and her husband separated, but her separation did not translate into freedom. Unlike Height, who was healthy and had no children to support, Tillmon had six children and suffered from chronic illness. Both became national leaders, and their organizations reflected the differences between them.[42]

The most obvious difference was social class. Here the differences were very real, far more dramatic than the political differences that existed between women of the Auxiliary and the Council. Council and Auxiliary women were *really* middle-class, welfare women were *really* poor. Most Council women who worked held white-collar or professional jobs. Unlike Height, most were married. Whatever emotional and intimate relationship they had with their husbands, they benefited economically from their marital connection. Welfare women did not work for a wage, did not have a legal income outside that provided by the government, and in general their welfare status had to do with personal relationships with men who did not help them economically. Some were widowed, but more were separated, divorced, abused, and abandoned by the men whose children the government supported.[43]

In other words, they had no men to fall back on. Johnnie Tillmon, for example, was left with the support of six children when she and her husband separated.[44] Like Tillmon, Espanola Jackson, the president of the San Francisco WRO, raised her six children alone. When left by her merchant marine husband to fend for herself, she tried unsuccessfully to have him prosecuted to make him help support his children. When her efforts proved futile, she turned to welfare.[45] So did Elizabeth Perry of Washington, D.C., who raised eleven children alone for several years before illness forced her to leave her government job and join the welfare rolls.[46] A woman in Aiken, South Carolina, found herself in a similar situation. She turned to welfare when her philandering husband left her and her children in debt for the purchase of his girlfriend's washing machine.[47]

The actions of thousands of women like these, who did not accept

their abandonment or aloneness as a personal or moral failing, but
were instead propelled to demand economic assistance as a right,
flew in the face of prevailing national attitudes. Historically, single
mothers were, as historian Linda Gordon notes, "pitied but not entitled." Their circumstances had never been dissociated from moral
values surrounding sex, reproduction, and family. Even though special consideration had always been accorded widows with young
children, single mothers were always considered guilty of something—of failing their husbands, of sexual immorality, of self-
destructive assertive behavior.[48] The 1960s were no different;
welfare mothers were considered lazy, irresponsible, and immoral.
Historically and contemporaneously, single motherhood contra-
dicted conventional mores that defined a "proper" family as male
headed, and the proper relationship of women to men as dependent.
Social policy conformed to conventional ideals. Even when it was
conceded that the single mother's poverty had nothing to do with
her character, policy makers feared that public welfare would
encourage immorality and women's independence from men. Welfare was thus always stigmatized, if not condemned.[49]

This attitude prevailed not only in the nation at large, but was
widespread among black people.[50] For the century between emancipation and the Civil Rights movement, African Americans struggled
to get jobs, wages, and civil rights equal to whites. During World
War II, A. Phillip Randolph threatened a march on Washington if the
Roosevelt administration did not end discrimination in the war
industries, and African Americans launched "Don't Buy Where You
Can't Work" campaigns throughout Northern communities. The
1940s and 1950s saw civil rights lawyers chip away at segregation,
and in the 1950s and 1960s African Americans mounted a battle for
full citizenship rights, the likes of which this country had never seen.
In the late 1960s, when civil rights groups turned their attention
from civil rights to economic issues, they avoided welfare like the
plague.

Welfare carried too much stigma. As Andrew Young explained

when he was Dr. Martin Luther King, Jr.'s aide, the Southern Christian Leadership Conference (SCLC) was afraid of tackling welfare: "Everything we did was considered Communist, and I think almost to survive we tended to phrase everything in religious terms and to avoid issues that smacked of economic change." When the SCLC did turn toward economics, it focused on hunger, and on improving government food-aid programs rather than on welfare. Andrew Young thought it was an issue of tactics. Whites, he argued, would accept hunger as an issue but not welfare. "I guess in the back of our minds we thought asking for welfare was tactically unsound. You asked for jobs, you asked for food. You might get something. If you asked for welfare, you might not get anything." George Wiley thought the problem was not so much tactics as the black middle class's lack of understanding of lower-class life. In the late 1960s he told a group of young blacks, "I find so frequently that black students aspire to greater things than dealing with the welfare issue. I'm often told: 'We don't want to deal with welfare; people should get off of welfare. We want to get away from that.'"[51]

As the contentious episode quoted at the beginning of this chapter attests, even Dr. King shied away from welfare. Not the least of his reasons was the focus it put on women. His Southern Christian Leadership Conference, for example, had no women in high-level positions. Ella Baker was the exception that proved the rule. She had helped organize the SCLC, and had served as its director from 1958 through 1960. She left in 1960, in part because she realized that the SCLC wanted a man and a minister to head the organization. Moreover, she was a woman who spoke bluntly and she felt that King would not tolerate her because he "wasn't the kind of person you could engage in dialogue with . . . if the dialogue questioned the almost exclusive rightness of his position."[52]

In this, King was like a lot of black men of the post–Moynihan report years who disdained any organization that gave agency to black women. The last thing they wanted was for welfare mothers to appear to confirm Moynihan's contention that the "strong black woman" was out of control. According to welfare organizer Edwin Day, the Black Power men were against the organization of women because they "were very intent on freeing themselves from the idea of a maternalistic, matriarchal Black society."[53]

With both the black middle class and black men aligned against her, Johnnie Tillmon knew that she was between the proverbial "rock and a hard place." As she put it, "I'm a woman, I'm a black woman. I'm a poor woman. I'm a fat woman. I'm a middle-aged woman. And I'm on welfare. In this country, if you're any one of those things—poor, black, fat, female, middle-aged, on welfare—you count less as a human being. If you're all those things, you don't count at all."[54] Put on the defensive for being domineering and emasculating, for being everything but beautiful and submissive, it is not surprising that the women of the National Welfare Rights Organization did not woo large-scale black support to its program.[55]

It should come as no surprise that it also did not woo the National Council of Negro Women.[56] The Council's records are virtually silent on welfare rights and it is not difficult to discern why. Nothing in its history or orientation had prepared its members to accept the idea that welfare was a right. Its initial program flowed from the black woman's tradition of work, work that had always been understood to provide a level of security for black women and their families. The Council had always aimed to integrate black women and black people into mainstream America as independent, not dependent, citizens. Its 1970s projects were not hell-raising direct-action campaigns against city, state, and national agencies, but, like earlier projects of the Association, were educational programs aimed at helping the poor manage their own lives. In 1968, for example, the Council began a program of home ownership for poor families called Operation Turnkey.[57] The program was described as "combining the work ethic with home ownership opportunity." Operation Turnkey, it boasted, *would not* be seen as part of the "endless 'hand-outs'" that "contributes little to giving the recipient control of their [sic] destinies." It would allow "low income people to own their own homes, to begin to make their own decisions about their own and their family's lives."[58] The terms "work ethic" and "low income" signified that this project, and many others the Council launched during this period, was in support of the working poor, not of women who did not work. Like the domestic workers who Tillmon overheard complaining about welfare women and their babies, the Council was uncomfortable with welfare mothers and the image they projected.[59]

This concern with babies is instructive. Babies resurrected images of black female sexuality, a topic the Council, just like the Association, perennially avoided. One hundred years after slavery's end, black women were still haunted by stereotypes that cast them as sensual. Correlations between their supposed promiscuity and their high birthrate were still being drawn. This was made painfully clear in 1968 when Senator Russell Long called female welfare rights leaders "brood mares," and refused to allow them to testify before his Senate Finance Committee.[60] Black middle-class women had always managed to have few children, and had spent most of the century trying to be models of asexual womanhood and respectability. However, lower-class black women still had one of the highest birthrates in the nation, a fact that was connected in the national consciousness with lax morals.[61] The Council program could support the welfare rights campaign for adequate aid for children, but it could not go as far as the National Welfare Rights Organization in support of single-parent female-headed households. Despite their century-long advocacy of self-reliant womanhood, and despite their greater tolerance for illegitimacy, black middle-class women's organizations still counseled a strict morality that championed motherhood within marriage, and child raising within a traditional nuclear setting. In light of this, it should come as no surprise that the NCNW did not launch a rebuttal to Senator Long's remarks.

The National Welfare Rights Organization did, however. Like the reaction of turn-of-the-century clubwomen to James Jacks's slanderous remarks, women of the NWRO picked up Senator Long's remarks and threw them back at him. In February 1968, they launched what Johnnie Tillmon called a "brood mare stampede" in response to Congress's enactment of a series of amendments to the Social Security Act in late 1967. Intended to slow the rise of the number of recipients, the federal government, among other things, required states to force recipients into work training and referral programs, and froze federal money so that states could not take on new recipients, regardless of how poor the women and children were.[62] In protest against this legislation, which welfare rights leaders saw as the government's way to take control of their children, the National Welfare Rights Organization kicked off a campaign that began on Mother's Day in 1968, and lasted through the summer. Across the country, welfare recipients lobbied black church groups to denounce the legislation. With their children, they picketed and protested in front of welfare centers, seats of government, and homes of congressmen.[63] "The welfare officials want to break up our families," they shouted as they reiterated their right to their children. "We refuse to be separated from our children one by one like puppys [sic] being separated from their mothers."[64]

Of course, the more apt comparison would have been to slave mothers on the auction block. It was during slavery times that black women had had their children torn from them, and were called, and treated like, "brood mares." It was during the pre–Civil War years that black women were worked like animals, while white men drew profit from black female fecundity. To erase the legacy of this painful past, middle-class women subsequently designed extensive programs to enhance the black woman's respectability. Now, despite their century-long labor, the term "brood mares" was being worn unself-consciously by poor black women who refused to internalize negative perceptions.

This refusal was manifested not only in their "stampede of brood mares" campaign but in their public advocacy of other issues that dealt with their sexuality. For example, welfare laws denied support if an able-bodied man made financial contributions to the household. Welfare recipients publicly demanded the right to male companionship outside of marriage and launched a court challenge to the constitutionality of midnight raids.[65] They also vigorously supported women's rights to reproductive freedom, which to them meant their right to have children. The stereotype of a welfare mother whose libido and fertility were out of control had potentially severe consequences for poor black women during these years when the Pill and other devices revolutionized birth control. In the nineteenth century, when white men controlled black fecundity, they manipulated the enslaved women's childbearing to maximize their profits. Now, there were many who thought it would better profit the nation if they could limit the number of children poor black women had.[66] Welfare rights women fought this. Affirming her right to choose, Mrs. Doris Bland of the Mothers for Adequate Welfare in Boston, proclaimed, "Ain't no white man going to tell me how many babies I can have, 'cause if I want a million of them, and I can have them, I'm going to have them. And ain't nobody in the world going to tell me what to do with my body, 'cause this is mine, and I treasure it."[67]

With the help of women like Bland, welfare mothers defended their right to have as many children as they wanted, and also protested surgical and chemical sterilization. They were particularly concerned over the drug Depo-Provera, which they claimed was approved by the Food and Drug Administration specifically for use on women in institutions and on women who "refuse or are unable to accept the responsibility demanded by other oral contraceptives."[68] In 1973 they joined with the Center for Law and Social Policy, and the Association for Voluntary Sterilization, in protest against the use of this drug and the forced sterilization of welfare recipients.[69]

By the time they did this, though, the organization was on the decline. It started to fall apart in 1969 when welfare mothers demanded not just voluntary leadership positions but salaried decision-making positions. An anonymously issued internal memo announced the new direction: "Recipients Must Be: Executive

Director, Associate Director, Administrative Director, Director of Field Operations, Director of Any Major Project. Power To The People/ End Professional Control, Begin Recipient Control/ Middle-class Professionals Should: Not be Executive Director, Not hold any other Important staff position, Give Technical Assistance only, Stop Treating recipients like Children, Reflect the racial constituency of NWRO members . . . ."[70] The last page, which read, "The NWRO Might as Well Be Dead, Without a Recipient As Head," marked the beginning of a bitter internal struggle that saw Johnnie Tillmon and others take over staff positions that had been held mostly by whites and men, and that eventually led to Tillmon becoming executive director.

In and of itself, this development did not hurt the organization. By 1969, and certainly by 1973 when Tillmon became executive director, she and other recipients had become welfare experts. Their organizational, speaking, and lobbying skills had been honed, and they knew what they wanted—jobs and training for women, child care centers, and a guaranteed annual income—and how they wanted to get it—through efforts by recipients at the local and national levels. As time passed and their confidence grew, they relied less on formally educated policy experts and more on themselves. In fact, many local welfare organizations dismissed nonrecipient organizers and ran fine-tuned programs under the direction and control of welfare mothers.[71] Annie Smart's experience as the Southern Regional Representative was similar to that of others. "The leadership role . . . has given me humility and strength. . . . In helping others . . . I have been able to help myself."[72]

Recipient control, however, brought black mothers into direct conflict with the black and white men who in the early years ran the organization. On the local level this meant that the mostly salaried male organizers had their places taken by welfare mothers who believed that more was gained when they helped women like themselves deal with welfare agencies and organize job campaigns. The emphasis was on "women helping women," with men providing technical assistance only.[73] On the national level it resulted in a showdown between George Wiley, a black man with an Ivy-League Ph.D., and Johnnie Tillmon, an articulate and increasingly feminist, poor black woman and welfare recipient.

While presenting some rather unique features, the clash between Wiley and Tillmon reflected the century-long conflict between black men and women. As in earlier times, black women were demanding their right to lead, to be in control of their organization, and to set an agenda for the race and for women. Wiley had different ideas. A former official at CORE, he believed in grass-roots organizing, but he put more confidence in men than women. When he first organized the National Welfare Rights Organization, he chose mostly white males to advise him. When female volunteer leaders resisted male leadership, he replaced the women with black men.[74] While welfare mothers increasingly advocated jobs and training for women, and a supporting system of child care, Wiley and his advisors clung to traditional patriarchal gender roles that put women in the home as child rearers and men in the labor force as breadwinners.[75] His testimony against recipient employment before the Senate Finance Committee in 1967 illustrated his position: "For the government to try to force them [welfare mothers] into the job market when there are not enough jobs for the men in the ghetto, is to add insult to absurdity."[76] Not only did he give priority to men in the job market, but he believed that the National Welfare Rights Organization could only survive by including "low paid male workers" and strategies that called for wage supplements for men. Wage supplements would help men support their families and also broaden the base of the welfare movement to include the working poor. Concerned about the welfare recipient's negative public image, Wiley believed that if the working poor joined the movement, especially poor working men, the movement would gain strength. Without these two constituencies, the stigma of welfare made the NWRO easy to isolate and destroy.[77]

Tillmon also sought the support of other groups, including the working poor. More than Wiley, Tillmon reached out to women, especially the National Organization of Women. In the early seventies, it, like the National Welfare Rights Organization, searched for a base broader than the largely urban middle-class white female following. The Women's Action Alliance, on which both Tillmon and Wiley served as executive board members, was one attempt to broaden the woman's movement. Although it was a disappointment to Jane Galvin-Lewis, Tillmon saw the Alliance as a "means of telling middle-class America what welfare is all about," a way "to show them that welfare mothers are not shiftless, lazy kind of folk."[78] One of the first joint programs was a welfare education project conducted in Baltimore. The purpose was to educate upper-, middle-, and working-class women on welfare recipient problems.[79]

Tillmon also got an education. Her association with the National Organization of Women deepened her understanding of the gendered nature of welfare and the part played by institutionalized sexism in stigmatizing welfare mothers and keeping them dependent. In a 1972 article in *Ms* magazine titled "Welfare Is a Women's Issue," she laid out her ideas. "Welfare," she said, "is a super-sexist marriage," an institution "invented mostly for women." In welfare "you trade in *a* man for *the* man." "You can't divorce him if he treats you bad. He can divorce you, of course, cut you off anytime he wants." After giving a short history of the contemporary welfare system, Tillmon explained the connection she saw among sexism, dependency, women, and welfare. Women, she argued, are supposed to please men, they aren't "supposed to work. They're supposed to be married." Men are supposed to take care of them while they spend their time sitting on their man's prosperity. "But if you don't have a man to pay for everything, particularly if you have kids, then everything changes. You've 'failed' as a woman, because you've failed to attract and keep a man. There's something wrong with you. It can't possibly be the man's fault, his lack of responsibility. It must be yours." The stigma associated with welfare and the myth of immorality, she argued, was invented by men as a way of punishing women. "Having babies for profit is a lie that only men could make up, and only men could believe. Men, who never have to bear the babies or have to raise them and maybe send them to war." In Tillmon's view, people believed the lies about welfare mothers because they believed certain myths about all women. They believed welfare mothers were lazy because they needed a way to rationalize the male policy of keeping women as domestic slaves; they believed welfare mothers were immoral because they believed that all women were likely to become whores unless they were kept under control by men and marriage. They believed welfare mothers misused their welfare checks because they believed all women had no head for money. And they believed recipients were the cause of slums and high taxes because they believed in Eve, the woman who brought all sin into the world. In an appeal to all women, Tillmon asked them to "Stop for a minute and think what would happen to you and your kids if you suddenly had no husband and no savings."[80] Every woman, she would later say, "is one man away from welfare,"[81] and welfare existed, was demeaned, and kept visible so that every woman would know what would happen to her if she failed to please a man, or tried to go it alone.

Go it alone was what the recipient leaders of the National Welfare Rights Organization tried to do, but without success. Association with the woman's movement was a mixed blessing. Welfare mothers got a new philosophical basis for their campaign for welfare rights, and new support.[82] However, the black woman's customary suspicion of white women was not quelled, and the programmatic differences between the two groups made for a shaky alliance. There were differences, for example, over their approaches to reproductive freedom. Welfare mothers fought for antisterilization rights, while the women of NOW put priority on abortion rights. Welfare recipients put greater emphasis on child care, while NOW put more emphasis on equal rights, especially in the job market. Understandably, welfare mothers were fearful that they would be denied child care, and that work incentive programs would force them to work in quality child care centers at low wages for the very professional women they were in alliance with.[83] Besides these differences, the National Organization of Women had its own image problems. Already saddled with stigmas, welfare mothers could ill afford to become associated with a group advocating nontraditional women's roles and sexual freedom. What the welfare movement needed most from the National Organization of Woman was money, something NOW did not have and could not give.

In any case, the alliance was short-lived because the National Welfare Rights Organization folded shortly after welfare mothers took control. When Johnnie Tillmon became executive director, the private foundations and church groups that had donated money and resources withdrew their aid. They were more comfortable with a male, Ivy-League, Ph.D. at the helm than they were with grass-roots leadership.[84] Tillmon's leave of absence from the executive directorship of the organization to study at the Massachusetts Institute of Technology did not make them more sanguine.[85] For all of his male chauvinism, Wiley was an effective fundraiser and he inspired confidence. Tillmon, by now a feminist welfare mother, did not. Wiley's departure, and the organization's inability to broaden its base beyond stigmatized poor black women, doomed it. By 1975 it barely existed.

Regrettably, it was not the only black women's organization of the period that was short-lived. By 1975 the National Black Feminist Organization had also come and gone. Organized when New Yorker Doris Wright held a meeting of thirty New York women in 1973, the New York chapter survived only a year and a half.[86] Like the National Welfare Rights Organization it forced black and white Americans to consider the varied sources of black female identity, and, like it, the National Black Feminist Organization was stigmatized to the point of extinction.

More than any organization in the century, the National Black Feminist Organization launched a frontal assault on sexism and racism. Its statement of purpose criticized America for stereotyping African-American women, for showing more concern about black men than black women, for persecuting them for being survivors, and for imposing on them standards of beauty that were unattainable. Members also criticized black nationalists. The black community, they insisted, had to stop using its women "only in terms of domestic or servile needs," had to remember that "there can't be liberation for half the race." The black liberation struggle had to continue to fight against racism, but, they warned, it would not be successful as long as sexism was crippling the black community from within. Black women could be leaders, they argued, only if the black community encouraged "*all* of the talents and creativities of Black women to emerge, strong and beautiful . . . and assume positions of leadership and honor. . . ."[87]

The principal goals of the black feminists were to defend black women and raise their consciousness about their needs and rights. In order to do this they pledged to work on specific issues like child care centers, unemployment, job training, domestic worker rights, black female addiction, abortion rights, welfare rights, and black female health care. They also supported ratification of the Equal Rights Amendment, the rights of black lesbians, and an end to sterilization.[88] Like the National Organization of Women, their principal organizing tool was consciousness-raising sessions. Small groups of women met in comfortable private settings and talked about problems relating to their identity as black females. They thought that as black women raised their level of awareness about their problems, and their understanding that many of their individual problems were in fact group concerns, competitiveness would decline, and black women would unite and organize around common issues.

While consciousness-raising was a technique that white feminists were using, the issues black feminists talked about were quite different. Brenda Eichelberger, the chairperson of the Chicago chapter of the National Black Feminist Organization, was quite clear on this point. For example, when asked to talk about the subjects raised in "cr" sessions, the first topic she mentioned was the black man/white woman phenomenon: "This problem is a thorn in the side of black

BRENDA EICHELBERGER WAS THE GUIDING SPIRIT BEHIND THE ORGANIZATION OF CHICAGO'S BLACK FEMINISTS. *Photo courtesy of National Park Service—Mary McLeod Bethune Council House NHS, Washington, D.C.*

women, the fact that some black men date and marry white women, especially when there are so many fewer black men than black women to begin with." Another unique issue she listed was that of self-image: "There's an in-group racism where light complexions, keen features, straight hair seem to be more desirable. Very dark women speak about being discriminated against by other black women." LeVerne Bennett, a member of the Chicago group, added "we as black women grew up feeling we weren't quite pretty. It's nothing explicitly stated, but something you feel." Other topics included the greater mobility of white women compared to black women, the lack of housing, and the prevalence of rape and crime in black communities. Morality and matriarchy were also issues. "Many persons think black women are more promiscuous than white," noted Eichelberger, "this misconception upsets many of us. . . ."Also upsetting was the myth of matriarchy. On this topic Eichelberger noted that "the 1970 United States Census shows most black families are headed by black men. The term 'matriarchy' connotes power. What power do black women have except to scrub Miss Ann's floors?"[89]

Acting on their concerns about matriarchy the Atlanta chapter of the National Black Feminist Organization campaigned vigorously against a popular television show called *That's My Mama* that featured a heavyset black woman as a domineering mother. In the fall of 1974, its chairperson, Sandra Flowers, held a news conference where she lambasted the show for portraying black women as "castrating matriarchs." Flowers claimed that the show "re-popularized the concept of the devious . . . black woman . . . not by implication, and not indirectly, but actively and by design." Black men needed to protest the show as much as black women, she argued, because as the emasculated counterparts of matriarchs, they were equally humiliated. In keeping with the NBFO's "responsibility to be sensitive to, attack, and attempt to halt any actions or attitudes which would hinder [the black woman's] progress," Flowers pledged the efforts of Atlanta's black feminists to get the show off the air.[90]

This stance against black female stereotypes touched the hearts and lives of countless black women. Like responses to Betty Friedan's *Feminine Mystique,* in which white women found that there was an unnamable problem with being female in America, many black women responded to black feminism with a gnawing feeling that something was wrong that black feminists might be able to fix. "I would like to get in the movement to see if I can fine [sic] my self," wrote one African-American mother of six, after viewing a Spring 1975 *Phil Donahue Show*. Alone since her seventeen-year-old was five, this woman was moved by black feminists to seek companionship and help.[91] Other women sought out black feminists because white feminist groups did not address their needs. "I have been working with the Flint chapter of NOW for the past 2 years. One problem that I have encountered is that not many blacks are involved. . . ." This woman was in her final year at the General Motors Institute in Michigan, and had problems that the predominantly white NOW did not address. "I am tired," she wrote. "Being in what is typically termed a 'man's field,' I get it from all sides, especially black men."[92]

Letters to black feminists revealed that this woman was not alone. Of all the problems addressed, male-female relationships and sexism elicited the most passionate responses. It was as if a dam had broken and feelings were finally allowed to flow. "I am sure many other women feel the . . . frustration, anger, and pain which sexist discrimination causes," wrote a Florida woman. Excited by the opportunity provided by black feminists to share ideas with other women "who are just beginning to experience an 'awakening,'" this woman thought the biggest step was to begin to change things "if no where else except in their own homes."[93] Sharing this belief, a Chicago woman thought it a shame that "Black men try to maintain chauvinistic ideas which have been perpetuated for hundreds of years against Black people." Expressing the sentiment voiced at the turn of the century by Anna J. Cooper and Fannie Williams, this woman saw no logical reason for black men to "expect the Black woman to have her place" because "both Black men and women have been discriminated against."[94]

The exalted position black men aspired to was also problematic for a Kansas woman, whose viewing of a *Phil Donahue Show* on black feminism literally changed her life. Painfully, she related how she had watched her mother manipulate her father so that he thought he had absolute authority. "She was a master at giving him ideas and allowing him to express them as if they were his own," she wrote to Chicago black feminists. She felt her mother should have been able to express her opinions and share authority with her father, but she understood the perils of doing so. On the one hand, she feared "robbing her husband of his manhood"; on the other, she risked "losing her husband when she knows there are so few marriageable black men, depriving her children of their father and the image they have of a man, and ultimately destroying the family structure." This, she claimed, "was too much responsibility for any woman." In a heartrending plea for comfort, she asked Chicago feminists to help her find answers to some nagging questions:

> When, oh when do black women have their day? When do black women stop accepting physical and emotional abuse from black men in the interest of [preserving] their manhood? When do black men become strong enough to handle white society like black women? Or is this a crutch we give our black men in our gaming to maintain control?

Ultimately, she found answers. Seven months after her original letter, she wrote proclaiming her divorce, a move that she credited to seeing black feminists on television. "I have found a new me," she proclaimed. "I . . . tried awfully hard to fill all of those roles but decided to give it up for something better."[95]

The responses the NBFO prompted suggest that all over the country black women were, and had been, searching for something. They did not all rush to join the National Black Feminist Organization, which would have been longer lived if they had, but they did make it clear that the silence imposed on them by black liberation movements and black misogyny had been broken. For example, black feminism prompted a Chicago lesbian to come out of the closet. "I am a lesbian," she wrote, "and since I have accepted my homosexuality, I am a much happier person."[96] A Florida lesbian wanted to join because of a deep need to join an organization "that backs its members."[97] A Michigan mother of two, who used a wheelchair, and who had recently been abandoned by her husband, wanted support to help her deal with her anxiety.[98] A Phoenix, Arizona, mother of a thirteen-year-old, who realized she had "become sort of a household ornament" and had used her "home as a sanctuary of protection" against "prejudice and ignorance," decided she wanted information that would help her improve herself, "not just as a woman, but as a black woman . . . ."[99] And a Los Angeles woman wrote just to tell the organization about her new resolution to date only white men. "Let the Black man take his traitorship to the witches," she wrote sharing her newfound wisdom. "We can forget that love thing and grow in grace."[100]

Certainly if all black women had been as unconflicted as these, the National Black Feminist Organization would have flourished; feminism, though, presented problems. Despite the black feminist claim that black woman's liberation was an essential part of black liberation, many black women felt that they weakened the race struggle when they emphasized their needs and rights. This was apparent in a letter from a black woman who claimed that "I do not believe in the concept (theory) of 'Women's Liberation. . . . I believe in NATIONAL LIBERATION.'" Unlike Anna Cooper, who had proclaimed that black people would be free only when the black woman was free, this woman maintained that "Black women cannot and will not be liberated until Black people, African people are liberated." This same woman, however, was ambivalent, for she also proclaimed "I am a feminist. I have been a feminist for 21 years." She was requesting information so that she could reassure herself that "in no way does being a feminist contradict being an agitator for national liberation."[101] A young engineer from Springfield, Illinois, was similarly irresolute. She saw a television talk show featuring black feminists and was "excited . . . to see and hear . . . and know that our plight as Black women has not been overlooked."Yet, she was terribly undecided. Her letter was addressed to "Ms. Eichelberger," the chairperson of the Chicago feminist group, but in it she purposely noted that she had used the title "Ms.," "not because I was trying to exemplify 'Liberation' as a point," but because "I did not know if it should be Miss or Mrs." "Black women," she maintained, "have been liberated in the sense that our counterparts have not throughout our existence." She nevertheless thought she would like to join a feminist alliance, and, signing off with the title "Miss," she again exclaimed her appreciation for feminists whose "astuteness and knowledge is closely parentaged with my own."[102]

This woman's response suggests that much of the ambivalence black women experienced had less to do with their understanding of who they were and what they wanted, and more to do with the relationship between their goals and those of white women and black men. As noted, black women had no abiding trust in white women; their history was different, white women's organizations had seldom reached out to black women, and many white women had recently been a part of, and even led, mobs against integration. Few African-American women thought black and white women had anything in common. And yet, many black women felt the limitations and repressiveness of black nationalism. They did not know how to reconcile their feelings with a racial ideology that prioritized black male autonomy and subordinated women. Never before had black women's decisions been so difficult to make because never before had there been any real possibility for an integrated woman's movement, nor so much public pressure for black unity at any cost.

To chisel a middle ground, black feminists reached back and claimed as their own one of the clubwomen's ideas, the notion that the African-American woman's needs were race needs, that the race was served when she was. Stopping short of claiming that "a race can rise no higher than its women," black feminists argued that their feminism was not opposed to black nationalism but part and parcel of it. Jane Galvin-Lewis reiterated this position: the woman's movement and the black movement were both concerned with human freedom. "A Black feminist movement," she asserted, "is just another arm of the overall Black struggle." Dorothy Pitman Hughes, a former member of the Congress of Racial Equality, a public housing advocate, and a founder of day care centers, thought that the whole race would benefit from the drive for job training for women. She cautioned against confusing black and white feminism. "You can't really base your understanding of black feminism in the context of what feminism has meant for white women. Our struggles are different, and our movement is not merely a sex struggle, it's a deeper political drive that will ultimately help Black men as well." Eleanor Holmes Norton, then a New York City Human Rights commissioner, added that Black feminism was another stage in the development of the Civil Rights movement. Many black women headed families alone, yet they were demeaned as strong powerful matriarchs. This lowered their self-esteem. Holmes felt this hurt the whole race. "I'm convinced," she said, "that by raising the level of esteem that Black women in general feel is one way of affecting other problems we have in the Black community."[103]

Besides indicating the congruity of the black and black feminist movements, feminists applauded their organization's inclusiveness and celebrated its links to the tradition of black protest. Margaret Sloan, president of the New York chapter, thought it a mark of progress that students, housewives, doctors, domestics workers, lawyers, secretaries, and welfare mothers were joined together in the fight against racism and sexism. She celebrated the fact that the organization had women of all ages and sexual orientations.[104] Doreen McGill, an executive board member of the New York chapter, thought it an improvement over other black women's groups. "All of the Negro women's organizations expressed interest mainly in middle-class Black women," she explained, "if ever a place I was excluded, that was it."[105] Feminists also traced their history from Sojourner Truth, through Frederick Douglass, W. E. B. Du Bois, Amy Jacques Garvey, and Mary McLeod Bethune. For those who scorned black female aggressiveness, they resurrected the sentiment expressed by W. E. B. Du Bois in his book *Darkwater*. He had warned black people to shun the white man's habit of petting, coddling, mystifying, and dehumanizing half of their population.[106]

Despite these efforts to put black feminism in the mainstream, the NBFO hit a wall of resistance. Black feminists were accused of separating from the black movement and dividing the race. They were charged with aligning with white women against black men. Their acceptance of homosexuality and the visibility of lesbian members fed man-hating charges, and their militant defense and support of black women revived images of matriarchy. One woman claimed that when she tried to discuss her thoughts on feminism she was "called everything from crazy to 'that one that's acting like a white woman.'"[107] Some of the most vicious criticism came from black women who objected to all aspects of feminism, but were most obdurate on the subject of white feminism. Said Brenda Verner, a teacher at the University of Massachusetts and a columnist for *Encore* magazine, black feminists were "all too willing to yield our cultural and political unity as an ethnic segment within the American electorate for some vague, emulative form of White feminism."[108] Verner and others wanted black women to be more original:

Why do we have to use White feminist terms to describe ourselves? . . . What about *womanhood?* We used to use it instead of "feminism." Why can't we call ourselves something other than what some White girls are calling themselves? And they're imitating us in the first place! Why do we have to use the White feminist emblem? Aren't we more creative than this? We don't have to come together to imitate a distorted imitation of ourselves!

The criticism that they were "acting like white women" and "imitating white feminists" had its corollary in the charge that black feminists were acting like men. This charge piggybacked on the feeling that feminists were antimale, which in turn fed homophobia. Verner and others were openly antigay, and were not at all impressed by the inclusiveness of the National Black Feminist Organization. Disparaging in her description of a meeting she attended, she deliberately described only those she found masculine. Like Frazier's attack on the physical appearance of middle-class women, Verner was derisive in her description of a woman who was "approximately six feet tall," who "wore a man's tan corduroy suit with a black turtle neck," and another woman who was "wearing a full Afro, mustache, man's sweater, pants, and ankle boots."[109]

The accusation that its members acted like white women, or like men, hurt the National Black Feminist Organization. It not only tapped some of the deepest fears and anxieties of black America, but it made the organization appear to be opposed to black liberation. To withstand the attacks, the organization needed a clear and concise definition of black feminism that all of its members and sympathizers could agree on. Black feminists themselves needed to be totally accepting of lesbianism, and the organization needed to raise enough money to disseminate its ideas and to initiate its programs.

On all counts they fell short. Personalities clashed over the issue of lesbianism with insinuations about member's personal relationships that were mean and hurtful.[110] Personality issues could probably have been overcome if there had been enough money to get the organization off the ground, but finances were never adequate, and the organization never had time to initiate programs that would have helped it work out theoretical issues of feminism. As it was, personality clashes and philosophical disagreement over feminism, fueled in part by intense criticism, weakened the organization before it really got started.[111]

Take the dispute over the use of the term "feminist" in the group's name, which arose at the first meeting of the Chicago chapter of the National Black Feminist Organization in June 1974. Those who wanted the term argued that it was pro-female, not antimale; those opposed thought correctly that the organization would be constantly on the defensive about its name. The pros countered that failure to use the name meant a break from the mother organization in New York, while those against thought it best for their group to go it alone and "become a completely autonomous unit working in conjunction *with*, not *against* Black men."[112]

Whether or not this last sentiment was a reaction against the close working alliance between the New York chapter and the predominantly white National Organization of Women, leaders in the New York NBFO, the so-called mother organization, maintained close ties with white feminists, and this caused problems. For example, many in the New York group did not want to work with the Women's Action Alliance because they thought it made them look dependent on white women. The use of the Alliance office space made some black feminists as uncomfortable as Galvin-Lewis thought it made the white women. Not only did they not want to be seen as close associates of white women, but many in the New York group felt that the NBFO needed to maintain distance in order to demonstrate the philosophical differences between white and black feminism.[113] Disagreement over these matters led to conflict, which in turn led to the resignation of its president, Margaret Sloan, and most of its executive board in July 1974. This wholesale resignation left the New York group in disarray, from which it never recovered. By 1975 it was almost defunct, and by the end of that year it had disappeared.[114]

The end of the New York chapter did not, however, mark the end of black feminism or even the end of black feminist organizations. The New York chapter was the pivotal organization, but there were chapters in Atlanta, Chicago, Washington, D.C., and Detroit. These organizations had formed with the intent of affiliating with New York, but the group dissolved before a national relationship could be established. While these groups called themselves "chapters" of the National Black Feminist Organization, they decided on their own programs and their own philosophy of black feminism. Thus they did not immediately dissolve when the New York group did.[115] The Chicago chapter, for example, changed its name to the National Black Feminist Alliance, and although beset by financial and personnel problems, it survived into 1981. It served primarily as a consciousness-raising vehicle for its members and for black women across the nation.[116]

With the demise of the feminists and welfare activists the only national secular black woman's organization with open membership to survive the tumultuous 1960s and 1970s successfully was the National Council of Negro Women. The National Association of Colored Women still met but was only a shadow of its former self. It still gave out scholarships, sponsored adult education projects, and provided services for the elderly, but its membership had shrunk, and it was having problems recruiting women under age thirty-five.[117] The Council had these problems, too, but it was a much more formidable organization. During the seventies and eighties it launched a variety of community projects. Among the most significant was the home ownership program noted earlier, a fact-finding project on hunger in black communities, a program called Operation COPE, aimed at teaching single female parents communication and computation skills, and a project called Sisters United, aimed at counseling female juvenile delinquents.[118] The Council also explored the business opportunities available for black entrepreneurs in the nation's school lunch program, reported on discrimination against women in housing, and contracted with the National Medical Association to help it with its outreach and community service programs.[119] While these projects demonstrated concern for black females, they also underscored the Council's continued approach to women's needs in the context of race work. In 1980, as in 1965, the Council operated from the position that black women could rise no higher than the race. Black women in 1980 were a part of, but not the center or pivot of, the Council's interest. No doubt this was a function of the ideological perspective of Dorothy Height as well as the ambivalence and hostility that surrounded black feminism. Interestingly enough, an independent evaluation of the Council's Sisters United project criticized it for its lack of inclusiveness. Financed by the Law Enforcement Assistance Administration and United Way, Sisters United was praised for its efforts with female juvenile delinquents but was chided for not allowing input from the parents and youth involved in the project. The evaluation also found fault with the background of the volunteers: "It has been found that most of those who contribute their services to the program come from professional and technical service or training . . . fields. It is recommended that Operation SU make special efforts to involve a broader cross-section of volunteers—with special reference to education, occupation and socio-economic status—into its operations."[120]

This evaluation says a lot. First, it suggests that the class makeup of the Council had not changed significantly from the 1940s when Helena Wilson and Rosina Tucker made similar observations. It also indicates that, despite the 1969 structural and ideological changes, young women were still not allowed to define the programs offered by the Council. And yet the Council's survival suggests that this was the kind of black woman's organization that mainstream black America was comfortable with. The Council was solidly middle class and traditional on issues of sexuality and social propriety. It made the time-honored practice of community service and race work the center of its program. Unlike the feminists and welfare mothers, it did not challenge accepted attitudes toward issues like monogamy, patriarchy, or heterosexuality. Its causes were not perceived to be divisive or in any way denigrating. The same could not be said of the National Welfare Rights Organization or the National Black Feminist Organization.

The survival of the Council and the demise of the national feminist and welfare organizations are indicative of the kind of women black people wanted as national representatives. Assertive welfare mothers seemed to confirm Moynihan's idea that single-parent female-headed households were destroying black communities, and his idea that "a fundamental fact of Negro American family life is the often reversed roles of husband and wife."[121] Likewise, feminists also seemed to confirm Moynihan's theory and the worst fears of some black nationalists. Militant in their demand for jobs and equal pay for equal work, here were the women who Moynihan claimed achieved more than men in the workplace, upset proper gender relations, and threatened black patriarchy. Spurned and judged unfeminine because they wanted a national voice, a national platform, and power, feminists stood in stark contrast to married, benign, middle-aged, middle-class Council women who had long since muted their militant advocacy of professional jobs for black women.[122]

Despite their demise, the importance of the National Welfare Rights Organization and the National Black Feminist Organization cannot be overstated. Both organizations presented to the nation and to black people the diverse identities of black women on terms set by their respective black female members. To paraphrase historian Darlene Clark Hine, women in these organizations "lifted the veil and broke the silence" on a variety of black women's issues. Because of them the country was more likely to see black women openly tackling issues about sexual identity, struggles with poverty, abuse, self-hatred, and misogyny. The NBFO, for example, inspired the creation of a number of small, local, feminist organizations like the Combahee River Collective.[123] Although they had to surmount class and political differences, and differences in sexual preference, they took black feminism into black communities, encouraged communication among neighbors, and established, among other things, rape crisis centers and battered women support groups. In doing so, they broadened feminism's base. Both the feminist and welfare movements drew attention to the issue of domestic violence and made possible groups like the Women of Color Task Force of the National Coalition Against Domestic Violence.[124] Feminism and welfare activism also further legitimized the various activities of community women who fought for better housing and community services. And, of course, the black feminist movement stimulated the creation of black women's studies—a black woman's movement to insert black women into the nation's consciousness and scholarship in a determined and systematic way; a movement that returned black women's advocacy to naming and defending themselves—principles established at the turn of the century.

Epilogue

❁

THE PAST AND FUTURE MEET

On the morning of January 13, 1994, more than two thousand black female scholars from all over the United States filed across the campus and into Massachusetts Institute of Technology's Kresge Auditorium, where a conference entitled "Black Women in the Academy: Defending Our Name" was about to begin. The conference had been called to highlight black women's scholarship, and the ways it had been undervalued or ignored in the academy. The scholars were there to account for the importance of their scholarship in the lives of all women of color, both within and outside the academy,[1] and to air their special problems with invisibility and isolation on campuses across the United States. But most of all, on that cold January morning, they thought about the way black women had recently been treated in the media. According to a conference organizer, M.I.T. professor Evelyn Hammonds, there was a need to deal with the negative stereotyping of black women by politicians and news organizations during recent debates over such issues as welfare reform. There

was also concern over the "public humiliation" of black female scholars Anita Hill and Lani Guinier, and the lack of an outcry in their
defense.[2] And so, just like the black women who met to form the
National Federation of Afro-American Women almost one hundred
years before in that very same area, these women now braved the icy
New England air to defend the character of black women.

It was fitting that Lani Guinier, Johnetta Cole, and Angela Davis
gave the keynote addresses. All were in the academy, Guinier and
Davis as professors, Cole as the president of Spelman College. All
had been victims of public character assassination. In 1970, Davis
was characterized as a "zealot," a "self-made martyr," and even a
"witch doctor," because of her membership in the Communist and
Black Panther parties. Despite her acquittal on murder charges
alleging that she supplied the weapons for a courtroom shoot-out in
which a judge was killed, she was nevertheless scorned because she
did not humble herself before the American judicial system.[3] Cole
was similarly spurned. Her opposition to the United States policy
toward Cuba came to the media's attention when she served on
President Bill Clinton's first transition team, and was mentioned as a
candidate for Secretary of Education. Ignoring her career as an
anthropologist, her presidency of Spelman, and her Coca-Cola
Enterprises board membership, Cole was dismissed as a "left-wing
sympathizer." By the time a flurry of spurious accusations settled,
she had been, as one comentator put it, "politically thrown to the
pavement."[4]

Of the three keynote speakers, law professor Lani Guinier had
been the most recent victim of public slander. When Clinton nomi-
nated her to the post of Assistant Attorney General for Civil Rights,
she was dragged through the press and misrepresented in a way that
insulted all black women. Specifically, Guinier's legal writings
explicitly opposed congressional districts that were all black or all
white. She argued that intragroup differences made it impossible for
a single black or white person to represent the varied interests of his
or her district. She also argued that it could not be assumed that

black people's interests were represented just because a black elected official had been sent to Congress. Altogether, Guinier's positions made her an opponent of electoral quotas, and a believer in the idea that black interests could be represented by whites. Guinier's real ideas, however, got lost in the myths created by her nomination, myths that had a historic ring to them. She was instantly labeled a "Quota Queen," and everything but a careful analysis of her legal scholarship made the headlines. She was called a "tart-tongued" law professor, a "leftist crazy," "a madwoman," "a crackpot." "You can't even pronounce her name," said one critic. "Strange name, strange hair, strange writing—she's history," began an article in *U.S. News & World Report*.[5]

In a way, Guinier really *was* history. She was one of a long string of black women who had been publicly maligned. As law professor Patricia Williams noted, as a quota queen, Guinier "evoked images of welfare queens and other mothers who rise to undeserved heights, complaining unwarrantably all the way." Guinier also "rekindled an examination of the power of stereotypical depiction—all those loony out-of-control black women, crazed by the repeated spurnings of men they just couldn't let go of." As the negative characterizations mounted against her, Guinier's own words were never heard because the White House had asked her, as was customary with executive branch nominations, not to give interviews before her confirmation hearing. When no one in the Clinton administration came to her defense, Americans were left to make up their own minds about who she was and what she stood for. In the process, she was depersonalized. As the public imagination ran wild, Guinier became, as Williams notes, "a visual aid reinforcing a stereotype."[6]

It was fitting, therefore, for Guinier to give the Conference's first keynote address, to be given the opportunity to speak candidly before many of the same women who had come to Anita Hill's defense in the November 1991 *New York Times* advertisement, "African American Women in Defense of Ourselves." These women certainly knew how difficult it was for black women to get a fair and objective hearing in America. Though different in substance, Guinier's and Hill's experiences were reminiscent of the public insult hurled at Ida B. Wells by James Jacks. At the turn of the century, it had been the morality of black women that was questioned; in 1994, as the nation took up the issue of sexual harassment, welfare reform, and "family values," the black woman's character was again held in disrepute. In 1895, the attack on Ida B. Wells resulted in organized resistance, and now, in 1994, the attack on Anita Hill, Lani Guinier, and other prominent black women had the same result. As a historian of the conference put it, there was a need for "a public forum of black women academics in order to address issues of research, survival in the academy, and the repressive political climate of the 1980s and 1990s, in which black people had been constructed as the domestic enemy and black women, in particular, vilified as welfare queens, whores, breeders and quota queens."[7] The black women who gathered at M.I.T. needed only to look at the recent experiences of some prominent black scholars to see and feel that they all were under attack.

Indeed, the conference had a "let's close ranks" atmosphere about it. Organizers expected only a few hundred participants; over two thousand showed up. An instant community was formed. Women accustomed to being the lone black scholar among mostly white and male colleagues were heartened by so many others who looked like them. Then and later there was testimony about the symbiosis that occurred. It was exciting to be around so many whose common experiences were so alike. As they gathered to hear the luminaries among them, as they went to sessions on every possible subject concerning the life and history of black women, they felt the rightness, even spiritualness, of what they were doing.

As a historian of organized black women I could have predicted this feeling, and some of the other conference developments. These women were doing not just what women in the 1890s did, but what black women had done throughout the century. Feeling the effects of both racism and sexism, concerned about issues affecting both women and blacks, unable to take sides against the self, black women throughout the twentieth century sought out each other as natural allies and organized on terms that made sense to them, but on terms often unacceptable to both black men and white women. From their associations they expected protection, support, friendship, and action on the causes they pursued. They expected relief from their alienation and marginalization. Sometimes they got all of what they craved, most of the time they got only some of it. As satisfying as it was to work together, personality clashes, regional allegiances, class, sexuality, and ideological differences made gender and race sameness no guarantee of a beloved sisterhood. Neither did it ensure a defense of black womanhood.

As it had been throughout the century, so it was at M.I.T. in the winter of 1994. After two days of panel discussions the natural differences that had been veiled by the initial euphoria slowly but surely materialized. In her evening keynote, Johnetta Cole, president of Spelman College, the largest predominately black female college in the country, put the issue of difference squarely—and ironically—before the conferees: "I know that at this conference when you say black women in the academy, you mean the women that work in the dining halls in colleges and universities across the U.S., the sisters that clean our offices, the clerical and technical workers, the black women that are not on the tenure track, as well as the professoriate."[8] There it was, that thorny issue of class. Cole could have been an alias for Katherine Macarthy, who raised a similar issue at the 1921 meeting of the National Association of Colored Women; for Rosina Tucker and Helena Wilson, who challenged the National Council of Negro Women to be more representative; for Johnnie Tillmon, who asked middle- and upper-class women to consider how close they were to a welfare check; or for feminist Doreen McGill, who felt left out of black women's middle-class organizations. Following in their footsteps, Cole challenged the female academics not just to be inclusive, but to grapple with difference, and to make it their mission to deal with it differently than other groups of

Americans. How could black women lay claim to their distinctive-
ness if, like other Americans, they organized along lines that were
exclusive and narrow?

This had been a challenge throughout the century and, following
in the tradition of black women's associations that preceded them,
M.I.T. conferees accepted the challenge. It was necessary, but predictably painful. Originally, they had addressed each other as "sister
professor." As they began to deal with their differences they were
forced to recognize that there were many there who were not professors, but graduate students, administrators, and independent
scholars. They had applauded black women who in identifying themselves revealed that they had "made it" at prestigious universities. On
reflection, they questioned their celebration, and wondered if they
were not endorsing an elitism they ordinarily scorned. The conference itself also came under closer scrutiny. Many had come expect-
ing a high-powered academic conference but were disappointed by
the polemical nature of some of the sessions. Others felt it was too
high powered, that there was too much theory. Many felt that the
conference was defined too narrowly. Wasn't there more to do than
just defend the black woman's name? And what about black women
in the Third World? Had American black women forgotten the larger
sisterhood? As they interrogated the meaning of their conference,
and looked self-consciously at themselves, they repeated a ritual that
had become common in black women's national organizing. As other
national gatherings of black women had demonstrated throughout
the century, they could not celebrate their community uncritically.
Indeed debate and dispute had occurred hand in hand with community. Identity neither guaranteed solidarity nor provided a shared
mission.[9]

In her closing address Angela Davis put this into perspective. She
reminded the black women of the support the then Surgeon General, Jocelyn Elders, needed as she fought for the decriminalization
of drugs. She applauded Toni Morrison who, as the first African-
American female Nobel Laureate and as Commander in the Arts and

Letters Order in France, had dramatically defended black women before the world. But then she gave a history lesson. She declared the black women who had gathered one hundred years ago admirable and courageous and their subsequent activism worthy of emulation. Yet, she noted that in defending their name they had imposed an orthodoxy that denied sexual agency to black women, an orthodoxy that denied freedom to their working-class sisters. In light of their foremothers' flaws and the problematic class relationships that accompanied the work of the National Association of Colored Women, Davis asked, "What about the ideological tradition of 'defending our name' do we wish to affirm and preserve? And what about it do we wish to break with?"[10]

Ironically, even though this question was new to this group of black women it was not new to the century. Each generation of black women had looked back and found the past ways of dealing with their issues inadequate for their present problems. Even more ironic was the fact that class and sexuality remained the perennial stumbling blocks of black women's national organizing. Therefore, even as Davis charted a new direction for black women she sounded some old themes. She noted, for example, that black women had to defend their names not just against the white establishment but "in those places we consider home as well." How often during the century had they confronted black men with their backward and stereotypical ideas about black women. Davis could have been Amy Jacques Garvey, who exhorted her sisters to fight the sexist policies of the UNIA. She could have been Rosina Tucker, who fought for Auxiliary autonomy; or Anita Hill, the most recent black woman to be publicly maligned as emasculating. She could have been any woman struggling against the masculinist and misogynist tendencies of black nationalism, or the race-focused programs of the National Council of Negro Women. Davis also cautioned against "reproducing the very forms of domination which we like to attribute to something or somebody else." Black women, she noted, were guilty of sentiments like: "She ain't Black. She don't even look Black. . . .

She's only interested in lesbians." Davis's caution had been heard before. It was a concern of Ida B. Wells, Katherine Macarthy, Helena Wilson, and numerous black feminists. Even when Davis said "we cannot afford to commit ourselves so fervently to defending our names that we end up poising ourselves against our Asian, Latina, Pacific Island and Native American sisters," she was not expressing a new concern. The women who founded the International Council of Women of the Darker Races of the World, who read and supported Jacques Garvey's "Woman's Page" of the *Negro World,* had sounded the same chord. So had Mary McLeod Bethune when she instructed black women to stay abreast of international issues, and so had Dorothy Height when she expanded the programs of the Deltas and the Council into the international arena.

The point is not that Davis was not forward looking, but that she understood that black women had to continue to be as tenacious as their problems had been, and would continue to be. Black women could look back and see how things had changed, and how they had helped things change, but Davis wanted to make sure that they did not rest on their laurels. The conference, thus, was a commentary on the problems of the past *and* the promise of the future. It was sad that one hundred years after the 1895 conference black women still had to meet to defend their name. On the other hand, that they were conscious of their class, political, and sexual differences proved they had come far in understanding themselves and the dynamics of race, class, and gender in American and African-American life. It was problematic that of the 940 professors at M.I.T. only three were black. The numbers revealed both the exclusivity of the academy and black women's marginality in it. They lacked opportunity at all economic levels in the labor force. On the other hand, in 1895, neither M.I.T. nor any white institution would have held such a conference. Racism and sexism would have prevented it as would the infinitesimally small number of black female collegiate academics. The promise of the 1994 conference was that there would be many more (the next one was scheduled to meet at Spelman), and that black women would continue the tradition of defending their name. Indeed, the promise was fulfilled when many black women organized to protest Clinton's subsequent dismissal of Jocelyn Elders, to protest African Americans' celebration of Mike Tyson after he served a prison term for raping a black female teen, to protest when black women were excluded from participation in the 1995 Million Man March. Then, as in a long past, black women told us—and continue to tell us—that although the weight of race, class, gender, and sexuality makes for a heavy load, it is one we can—and will—carry.

NOTES

LIST OF MANUSCRIPTS

Nettie Asberry Papers — University of Washington Manuscripts Collection, University of Washington Libraries, Seattle, Washington

Charlotte Hawkins Brown Papers — Arthur and Elizabeth Schlesinger Library at Radcliffe College, Cambridge, Massachusetts

Claude A. Barnett Papers — Chicago Historical Society, Chicago, Illinois

Brotherhood of Sleeping Car Porters Papers — Chicago Historical Society, Chicago, Illinois

John E. Bruce Papers — Schomburg Center for Research in Black Culture, New York City Public Library

Frederick Douglass Collection — Moorland-Spingarn Research Center, Howard University, Washington, D.C.

Eichelberger Collection	Chicago Historical Society, Chicago, Illinois
Fannie Lou Hamer Papers	Library of Congress, Washington, D.C.
The Papers of John and Lugenia Hope	Atlanta University Center, Woodruff Library, Atlanta, Georgia
National Black Feminist Alliance	Mary McLeod Bethune, Council House, National Historic Site, Washington, D.C.
National Black Feminist Organization	Manuscript Collection at University of Illinois at Chicago, Chicago, Illinois
National Council of Negro Women Papers	Mary McLeod Bethune Council House, National Historic Site, Washington, D.C.
National Welfare Rights Organization	Moorland-Spingarn Research Center, Howard University, Washington, D.C.
Josephine St. Pierre Ruffin Papers	Boston Public Library, Boston, Massachusetts
Mary Church Terrell Papers	Library of Congress, Washington, D.C.
Mary Church Terrell Papers	Moorland-Spingarn Research Center, Howard University, Washington, D.C.
Margaret Murray Washington Papers	Hollis Burke Frissell Library, Tuskegee University, Tuskegee, Alabama
Monroe Work Files	Hollis Burke Frissell Library, Tuskegee University, Tuskegee, Alabama

Introduction

DIVIDED AGAINST MYSELF

1. For a discussion of early sexual stereotypes of Africans see Winthrop Jordan, *White Over Black: American Attitudes Toward the Negro, 1550–1812* (Baltimore: Penguin Books, 1969), 236–237, 494–495.

2. For discussions of black sexuality and bestiality see ibid., 32–40, 150–154; George M. Fredrickson, *The Black Image in the White Mind: The Debate on Afro-American Character and Destiny, 1817–1914* (New York: Harper & Row, 1971), 256–282.

3. For an example of this sentiment see Eldridge Cleaver, *Soul On Ice* (New York: McGraw-Hill, 1968), 156–175; for a history of this sentiment see Nell Irvin Painter, "Hill, Thomas, and the Use of Racial Stereotypes," in Toni Morrison, ed., *Race-ing, Justice, En-gendering Power* (New York: Pantheon Books, 1992), 200–215.

4. Also in the *New York Times* on this date was an article on conflicts many black women experienced during the hearings. This article also put the conflicts in historical perspective. See Rosemary L. Bray, "Taking Sides Against Ourselves," *New York Times Magazine*, 17 November 1991.

Chapter 1
THE FIRST STEP IN NATION-MAKING

1. Mamie Garvin Fields with Karen Fields, *Lemon Swamp and Other Places: A Carolina Memoir* (New York: Free Press, 1983), 189–190.

2. Ibid., 191–203.

3. This letter was discussed in the Introduction. For a discussion of black women's service and club work before the 1890s see Stephanie J. Shaw, "Black Club Women and the Creation of the National Association of Colored Women," *Journal of Women's History*, 3(2):1–25 (Fall 1991).

4. Cooper, Anna Julia, *A Voice from the South: By a Black Woman of the South* (New York: Oxford University Press, 1988 [1892]), 122.

5. Some historians of women often note that black women have been traditionally more concerned with race than with women's issues. This book qualifies that view. It argues that black women never divided their identity into separate spheres. Even though one element may have been accentuated at a given time in history, black women always dealt with all parts of their identity at once.

6. W. Fitzhugh Brundage, *Lynching in the New South: Georgia and Virginia, 1880–1930* (Urbana: University of Illinois Press, 1993), 2.

7. Stewart E. Tolnay and E. M. Beck, *Festival of Violence: An Analysis of Southern Lynchings, 1882–1930* (Urbana: University of Illinois Press, 1995), 17.

8. Brundage, *Lynching in the New South*, 24–25.

9. August Meier and Elliott M. Rudwick, *From Plantation to Ghetto: An*

Interpretive History of American Negroes (New York: Hill and Wang, 1966), 174.

10. Floris Loretta Cash, "Womanhood and Protest: The Club Movement Among Black Women, 1892–1922" (Ph.D. dissertation: State University of New York at Stony Brook, 1986), 55–61; Dorothy Salem, *To Better Our World: Black Women in Organized Reform 1890–1920* (Brooklyn, N.Y.: Carlson, 1990), 12–21.

11. The practice of self-help was buttressed by an ideology of economic and social uplift that was as heartening as it was crippling. On the one hand, uplift stressed racial solidarity, where those with means helped those without it. As indicated in Terrell's Charleston speech, uplift marked the powerful ability of the powerless to triumph over the debilitating force of racism by achieving against the odds. It was a philosophy that taught black people to do for themselves, "to pick up their burdens in the heat of the day." However, as heroic as was this emphasis on self-reliance, uplift also marked a capitulation to racism. When black people picked up the burdens that white racism, violence, and negative stereotypes thrust upon them, they accommodated white exclusionary practices. They tacitly, and perhaps unwittingly, surrendered not only those basic civil and political rights enjoyed by white Americans but rights that were needed to maintain economic self-sufficiency. The ideology of uplift has been discussed by several authors. Two of the most recent scholars to examine uplift are Stephanie J. Shaw and Kevin Gaines. While Shaw emphasizes the self-reliant aspects of uplift, Gaines focuses on the more debilitating aspects of it. See Stephanie J. Shaw, *What a Woman Ought to Be and to Do: Black Professional Women Workers During the Jim Crow Era* (Chicago: University of Chicago Press, 1996), especially pages 1–2, 10; and Kevin K. Gaines, *Uplifting the Race: Black Leadership, Politics, and Culture in the Twentieth Century* (Chapel Hill: University of North Carolina Press, 1996), especially pages 1–17.

12. Cynthia Neverdon-Morton, *Afro-American Women of the South and the Advancement of the Race, 1895–1925* (Knoxville: University of Tennessee Press, 1989); Salem, *To Better Our World*, 89–90; Woman's Work 1913, Monroe Work Files; "The Tenth Annual Report of the Tuskegee Woman's Club" in Louis Harlen and Raymond Smock, eds., *The Booker T. Washington Papers*, vol. 8, 1904–1906 (Urbana: University of Illinois Press, 1979), 475–482.

13. "Fifth Annual Report of the Colored Woman's League of Washington, D.C." (Washington, D.C.: Smith Brothers, 1898), Reel 14, Mary Church Terrell Papers, Library of Congress.

14. *Savannah Tribune*, 29 July 1899, 6 May 1899, 24 February 1900, 13 October 1900; Black Women's Oral History Project, Arthur and Elizabeth Schlesinger Library at Radcliffe College (hereafter cited as Black Women's Oral History Project), interview with Christia Adair, 14.

15. Lillian S. Williams, "And Still I Rise: Black Women and Reform: Buffalo, New York, 1900–1940," *Afro-Americans in New York Life and History*, *14*(2):7–33 (1990).

16. The research for this book predates the publication of the NACW Papers. Research here reflects work in a variety of sources including convention proceedings and *National Association Notes*, the NACW newspaper. Letters reporting the activities of clubs can also be found in the private papers of NACW presidents and officers. On Texas, see *National Association Notes*, *17* (3):9–11; on the New Century Club see letter to Mrs. Washington from E. C. Carter, 22 July 1903, Box 132, Margaret Murray Washington Papers; see also Salem, *To Better Our World*, 65–100; W. E. Burghardt Du Bois, ed., *Efforts for Social Betterment Among Negro Americans* (Atlanta: Atlanta University Press, 1909), 47–64.

17. Adrienne Lash Jones, *Jane Edna Hunter: A Case Study of Black Leadership, 1910–1950*, in Darlene Clark Hine, ed., *Black Women in United States History*, vol. 12 (Brooklyn, N.Y: Carlson Publishing, 1990), 35–58.

18. Cash, "Womanhood and Protest," 142–175; Williams, "And Still I Rise," 533.

19. Salem, *To Better Our World*, 35, 37–38; Cash, "Womanhood and Protest," 76, 85, 95, 175; Neverdon-Morton, *Afro-American Women of the South*, 137–138, 197.

20. Ibid., 76, 95.

21. The term feminist was not used by clubwomen. It is being used here to make it easier for the contemporary reader to grasp the essence of the ideas about women held by early-twentieth-century black women.

22. Josephine Silone Yates, "Woman's Clubs," in Du Bois, ed., *Efforts for Social Betterment*, 47. Yates was NACW president from 1901–1906.

23. Miscellaneous, Reel 3, n.d., John E. Bruce Papers.

24. Fannie Barrier Williams, "The Club Movement Among Colored Women," *The Voice of the Negro*, *1*(3):102 (1904) (hereafter known as *Voice*).

25. Addie Hunton, "Negro Womanhood Defended," *Voice*, *1*(7):280 (1904).

26. *Woman's Era*, September 1894.

27. Ibid., June 1894.

28. Cooper, *A Voice from the South*, 139, 140.

29. Bert James Lowenberg and Ruth Bogin, eds., *Black Women in the Nineteenth Century, Their Words, Their Thoughts, Their Feelings* (University Park: University of Pennsylvania Press, 1976), 243–245.

30. Cooper, *A Voice from the South*, 143, 145.

31. Fannie Barrier Williams, "The Woman's Part in a Man's Business," *Voice*, 1(11):544 (1904).

32. Cooper, *A Voice from the South*, 138, 144.

33. For general overviews of black life with reference to this topic see Jacqueline Jones, *Labor of Love, Labor of Sorrow: Black Women, Work, and the Family from Slavery to the Present* (New York: Basic Books, 1985), 180–181; articles in vols. 1 and 2 of Hine, ed., *Black Women in United States History*; Julius Nimmons, "Social Reform and Moral Uplift in the Black Community 1890–1910: Social Settlements, Temperance, and Social Purity" (Ph.D. dissertation, Howard University, 1981); Meier and Rudwick, *From Plantation to Ghetto*, 177–212; Allan H. Spear, *Black Chicago: The Making of the Negro Ghetto, 1890–1920* (Chicago: University of Chicago Press, 1967).

34. Cash, "Womanhood and Protest," 8–11; Paula Giddings, *When and Where I Enter: The Impact of Black Women on Race and Sex in America* (New York: William Morrow, 1994), 96–100.

35. Karen Blair, *The Clubwoman as Feminist: True Womanhood Redefined, 1868–1914* (New York: Holmes and Meier, 1980), 93–115.

36. Salem, *To Better Our World*, 43.

37. Ibid., 39–41.

38. Alfreda Duster, ed., *Crusade for Justice: The Autobiography of Ida B. Wells* (Chicago: University of Chicago Press, 1970), 270–271.

39. See for example Ida B. Wells's reaction to the story, ibid., 271.

40. Yates, "Woman's Clubs," in Du Bois, ed., *Efforts for Social Betterment*. Yates was president from 1901–1906.

41. *National Association Notes*, 3(7):1 (January 1899).

42. Cooper, *A Voice from the South*, 29–31.

43. Monroe A. Majors, *Noted Negro Women: Their Triumphs and Activities* (Chicago: Donohue & Henneberry, 1893 [Reprint 1986]).

44. *National Association Notes*, 3(7):1 (January 1899).

45. Ibid., 7(11):18 (July 1904).

46. *Savannah Tribune*, 24 February 1900.

47. Mrs. Booker T. Washington, "Social Improvement of the Plantation Woman," *Voice*, 7(1):290 (1904). See also *National Association Notes*, 7(11):9–13 (July 1904); *Woman's Era*, 24 March 1894.

48. *National Association Notes,* n.d., in Booker T. Washington, Box 132 A, Convention Reports, Margaret Murray Washington Papers.

49. *Woman's Era*, November 1894.

50. *National Association Notes*, *XVII*(3):6−8.

51. Ibid.

52. *Woman's Era*, September 1894.

53. Cooper, *A Voice from the South*, 22−24, 68−69, 75, 78.

54. Washington's book *Up from Slavery* offers testimony to his ideas about the place of the community, home, and school in the uplift of the race, and gives Washington's version of how he came to his beliefs. See Booker T. Washington, *Up from Slavery* in *Three Negro Classics* (New York: Avon Books, 1965 [1901]), especially pages 122−123. See also Louis R. Harlan, "Booker T. Washington and the Politics of Accommodation," in John Hope Franklin and August Meier, eds., *Black Leaders in the Twentieth Century* (Urbana: University of Illinois Press, 1982), 3−4; William E. B. Du Bois, *The Souls of Black Folk* in *Three Negro Classics* [1903], 326, 280.

55. Yates to Washington, 16 May 1904; Yates to Washington, 28 February 1906, Box 132, Margaret Murray Washington Papers.

56. Cooper, *A Voice from the South*, 47.

57. Yates to Washington, 28 February 1906, Box 132, Margaret Murray Washington Papers.

58. *Woman's Era*, November 1894.

59. Mary Church Terrell, "The Progress of Colored Women," *Voice,* *1*(7):293 (1904).

60. Williams, "The Club Movement Among Colored Women," 99. See also *Woman's Era*, November 1894.

61. Synopsis of the lecture by Mrs. Booker T. Washington, "The Organizing of Woman's Clubs," Box 132A, Convention Reports, Margaret Murray Washington Papers.

62. Lowenberg and Bogin, eds., *Black Women in Nineteenth-Century American Life*, 274−275.

63. Ibid., 329.

64. Salem, *To Better Our World,* 26, 20−28; Neverdon-Morton, *Afro-American Women of the South,* 191−194; Giddings, *When and Where I Enter,* 85−118; Cash, "Womanhood and Protest," 55−76; Duster, ed., *Crusade for Justice,* 242.

65. These ideas are expressed in the writings of most of the leading clubwomen. See, for example, Josephine Bruce, "What Has Education Done for Colored Women," *Voice, 1*(7) (1904); Addie Hunton, "Negro

Womanhood Defended," *Voice*, *1*(7) (1904); Hunton, "The Southern Federation of Colored Women," *Voice*, *2*(12) (1905); Anna Jones, "The American Colored Woman," *Voice*, *2*(10) (1905); Mrs. Booker T. Washington, "Social Improvement of the Plantation Woman," *Voice*, *1*(7) (1904); Williams, "The Club Movement Among Colored Women," *Voice*, *1*(3) (1904); Williams, "The Woman's Part in a Man's Business," *Voice*, *1*(11) (1904); Williams, "The Colored Girl," *Voice*, *2*(6) (1905).

Chapter 2
THE DILEMMAS OF NATION-MAKING

1. John Hope Franklin and Alfred A. Moss, Jr., *From Slavery to Freedom: A History of Negro Americans*, 6th ed. (New York: Alfred A. Knopf, 1988 [1947]), 256; Ridgely Torrence, *The Story of John Hope* (New York: Arno Press, 1969 [1948]), 114–115.

2. Undated Speech, Reel 21, 0213, the Papers of John and Lugenia Hope.

3. Ibid.

4. Ibid.

5. *Woman's Era*, 2 December 1894.

6. *The Voice of the Negro*, *1*(7):310–311 (1904) (hereafter cited as *Voice*).

7. *New York Age*, 22 July 1922, in Woman's Work, 1922, Monroe Work Files.

8. *National Association Notes*, *29*(9):4 (1927). See also *29*(8):2 (1927).

9. Cooper, *A Voice from the South*, 135; *National Association Notes*, *17*(3):10 (n.d., probably 1914 or 1915).

10. Duster, ed., *Crusade for Justice*, 43–45.

11. William Hannibal Thomas, *The American Negro, What He Was, What He Is and What He May Become* (New York: MacMillan, 1901), 195; Hunton, "Negro Womanhood Defended," *Voice*, *1*(7):280 (1904).

12. Williams, "The Colored Girl," *Voice*, *2*(6):403 (1905).

13. *Savannah Tribune*, 13 April 1907; *Washington Bee*, 27 May 1893. Quoted in Nimmons, "Social Reform and Moral Uplift in the Black Community," 245, 258; *Savannah Tribune*, 10 June 1899; see also *Savannah Tribune*, 16 February 1895, 5 August 1899.

14. E. L. Park to Mary Church Terrell, 14 March 1925, Container 7, Mary Church Terrell Papers, Library of Congress.

15. See notes 7 and 8.

16. *Savannah Tribune*, 5 May 1900, 4 February 1899, 15 December 1900. See also 12 September 1896, 1 April 1899, 13 May 1899.

17. Bishop W. J. Gaines, *The Negro and the White Man* (New York: Negro Universities Press, 1969 [1897]), 144–145, 152–157.

18. Tulia Hamilton, "The National Association of Colored Women, 1896–1920" (Ph.D. dissertation, Emory University), 56–58; Dorothy Salem, *To Better Our World: Black Women in Organized Reform, 1890–1920,* in Darlene Hine, ed., *Black Women in American History,* vol. 14 (New York: Carlson Publishing, 1990), 32–34; Terrell's version of what happened has herself the victim of a plot hatched by Illinois delegates. See letter from Terrell to Frances, 5 September 1899. Wells's version can be found in Duster, ed., *Crusade for Justice,* 258–260.

19. *National Association Notes, 2(*12) (May 1899) and *3(*1) (June 1899).

20. Jacqueline Rouse, *Lugenia Burns Hope: Black Southern Reformer* (Athens: University of Georgia Press, 1989) 57–90, 54–55.

21. Rouse, *Lugenia Burns Hope,* 23–24, 36–37.

22. As to Du Bois's feminism, see David Levering Lewis, *W. E. B. Du Bois, Biography of a Race: 1868–1919* (New York: Henry Holt, 1993), 417–419. Most of Du Bois's writings reveal him to be more feminist than most of the men of his generation. See, for example, *Darkwater: Voices from Within the Veil,* especially chapter seven, "The Damnation of Women." He was, however, quite a Victorian husband and father. See Eric J. Sundquist, ed., *The Oxford W. E. B. Du Bois Reader* (New York: Oxford University Press, 1996), 481–623, and also David Levering Lewis, *W. E. B. Du Bois: Biography of a Race,* 417–419, 449–452.

23. W. E. B. Du Bois, "The Work of Negro Women in Society" in *Writings by W. E. B. Du Bois in Periodicals Edited by Others* (Millwood, N.Y.: Kraus-Thomas Organization, 1982), 140, 139–144.

24. See Note 8.

25. Hunton, "Negro Womanhood Defended," 280.

26. Sylvanie Francaz Williams, "The Social Status of the Negro Woman," *Voice,* 1(7):299 (1904).

27. Clubwomen often described this duty as a "burden." See, for instance, Lucy Laney, "The Burden of the Educated Colored Woman," in Lowenberg and Bogin, eds., *Black Women in Nineteenth-Century American Life,* 297–301.

28. Ibid.; Hunton, "Negro Womanhood Defended," 280.

29. Bart Landry, *The New Black Middle Class* (Berkeley: University of California Press, 1987), 18–66. The black middle class also conforms to what Max Weber called a status group. See Max Weber, *Essay in Sociology,* ed., H. H. Gerth and C. Wright Mills (New York: Oxford University

Press, 1946), 186, 194, 300–301. For studies that cite a transformation in the make-up of the black middle class around 1920 see Willard B. Gatewood, *Aristocrats of Color:The Black Elite, 1880–1920* (Bloomington: Indiana University Press, 1990), 332–348; Willard B. Gatewood, "Aristocrats of Color: South and North the Black Elite, 1880–1920," *Journal of Southern History, 54*(1) (February 1988); August Meier, "Negro Class Structure and Ideology in the Age of Booker T. Washington," *Phylon, 23*(3):258–266 (1962); August Meier and David Levering Lewis, "History of the Negro Upper Class in Atlanta, Georgia, 1890–1958," *Journal of Negro Education* 28:128-139 (Spring 1959).

30. Anna Jones, "The American Colored Woman," *Voice* 2(10):692 (1905); Jones, "How Can We as Women Advance the Standing of the Race?" *National Association Notes,* 7(11):9 (July 1904).

31. Adella Hunt Logan, "Why the National Association of Colored Women Should Become a Part of the National Council of Women of the United States," *National Association Notes, 3*(8):1 (September 1899).

32. There were few issues of *Woman's Era* or *National Association Notes* that did not carry some kind of advice for black women. There were also few articles or speeches about the club movement that did not rehearse the advice litany that was offered well into the 1920s and beyond. See, for instance, the Booker T. Washington Papers, September 1898, speech by Mrs. Booker T. Washington, 462–468; Josephine Silone Yates, "The Social Elements of Life," *National Association Notes, 2*(12):2–3 (May 1899); Bruce, "What Has Education Done for Colored Women," *Voice, 1*(7):294–298 (1904); Mrs. H. E. Thomas, "The Social Instinct—How I Meet It," *National Association Notes, 15*(4):1–5 (January 1912); Lena Harris, "Thrift in the Community," *National Association Notes, 19*(4):1–3 (January 1917); "Dr. Waring Wins N.A.C.W. Presidency in Spirited Campaign With Mrs. Charlotte Brown," Oklahoma City, Women's Work, 1933, Monroe Work Files.

33. Rouse, *Lugenia Burns Hope,* 70.

34. Gloria T. Hull, ed., *Give Us Each Day:The Diary of Alice Dunbar-Nelson* (New York: W. W. Norton, 1984), 179, 224. Nelson used the same language when describing meetings of the Daughter Elks and other black working-class functions. See 123, 187, 237.

35. Cooper, *Voice from the South,* 34; Mary Church Terrell, Diary Entry, 24 May 1936, Container 2, Mary Church Terrell Papers, Library of Congress.

36. Fannie Williams, "The Intellectual Progress of the Colored Women of the United States Since the Emancipation Proclamation," in Lowenberg and Bogin, ed., *Black Women in the Nineteenth Century,* 272.

37. Letter from Ida B. Wells to Booker T. Washington, 30 November 1890, in Louis Harlan, Stuart Kaufman, and Raymond Smock, eds., *The Booker T. Washington Papers,* vol. 3, 1889–1895 (Urbana: University of Illinois Press, 1974), 108.

38. Fannie Williams, "Religious Duty to the Negro," in Lowenberg and Bogin, ed., *Black Women in the Nineteenth Century,* 269.

39. Speech given by Mrs. Booker T. Washington in 1898 in Charleston, S.C. See Louis Harlan, Stuart Kaufman, Barbara Kraft, and Raymond Smock, eds., *The Booker T. Washington Papers,* vol. 4, 1895–1898 (Urbana: University of Illinois Press, 1975), 467.

40. Fields, *Lemon Swamp and Other Places,* 135–138.

41. Thomas, "The Social Instinct—How I Meet It," 1.

42. Charlotte Hawkins Brown, "The Quest of Culture," Series 1, Speeches, 1929, Charlotte Hawkins Brown Papers.

43. To get some idea of the number of "culture" clubs see Du Bois, ed., *Efforts for Social Betterment Among Negro Americans,* 47–64. See also 37–38.

44. Kansas City Federation of Colored Women's Clubs, Collection 28, Box 4, Folder 98, Frederick Douglass Collection.

45. Anne Meis Knupfer, *Toward a Tenderer Humanity and a Nobler Womanhood: African American Women's Clubs in Turn-of-the-Century Chicago* (New York: New York University Press, 1996), 35.

46. Hull, ed., *Give Us Each Day,* 365.

47. 8 January 1904, Box 132, Margaret Murray Washington Papers.

48. Mary Church Terrell, "Society Among the Colored People of Washington," *Voice,* 1(4):152 (1904).

49. Quoted in Sharon Harley, "Mary Church Terrell: Genteel Militant," in Leon Litwack and August Meier, eds., *Black Leaders in the Nineteenth Century* (Urbana: University of Illinois Press, 1988), 311.

50. Ursula Wade, "Importance of Mothers' Unions," *National Association Notes,* 7(11):18–19 (July, 1904); Addie Dickerson, "The Status of the Negro Woman in the Nation," in ibid., 17(3):7–8 (n.d., probably 1914); see also Victoria Earle Matthews's comment made in 1894: "In the absence of the best, the worst will prevail." *Woman's Era,* May 1894.

51. Gatewood, *Aristocrats of Color,* 149–181.

52. This issue is taken up in the next chapter.

53. Quoted in Salem, *To Better Our World,* 35.

54. Gatewood, *Aristocrats of Color,* 169–170; T. Thomas Fortune, "Who Are We? Afro-Americans, Colored People or Negroes?" *Voice,* 3(3):194–198 (1906); J. W. E. Bowen, "Who Are We? Africans, Afro-Ameri-

cans, Colored People, Negroes or American Negroes?" *Voice*, 3(1):30–36 (1906).

55. Gatewood, *Aristocrats of Color*, 244–245.

56. Hull, *Give Us This Day*, 187–188.

57. Fields, *Lemon Swamp*, 218–219.

58. Gatewood, *Aristocrats of Color*, 244.

59. Undated speech, Reel 21, 0213, the Papers of John and Lugenia Hope. The clubwoman's movement in Atlanta seems to have accomplished much more than Hope gave them credit for, see Neverdon-Morton, *Afro-American Women of the South*, 139–163. Although it never affiliated with the NACW, the Neighborhood Union utilized many of the talents of Atlanta clubwomen. See Rouse, *Lugenia Burns Hope*, 57–90. See also Jones, "The American Colored Woman," 693; Williams, "The Club Movement Among Colored Women," 100; Mrs. Morris White, "The Texas Federation of Colored Women's Clubs," in *National Association Notes*, 17(3):9.

60. Williams, "The Club Movement Among Colored Women," 101–102; see also a letter from Ursula Wade to Margaret Murray Washington complaining that the individual clubs worked at cross purposes and random projects, that the clubs had to work in harmony with each other if NACW was to accomplish anything. See 11 September 1903, Box 132, Margaret Murray Washington Papers.

61. Letter from Elizabeth Lindsay Davis to Margaret Murray Washington, 13 June 1905, Box 132, Margaret Murray Washington Papers; Women's Work Files, 1922, Monroe Work Files; "Women's Federation in Annual Meeting," *New York Age*, 22 July 1922; "A Citizenship Call Sounded to Race Women," *Norfolk Journal*, 4 October 1924; Woman's Work, 1924, Monroe Work Files. For other references to classism see Letter from Josephine Yates to Margaret Washington, 30 September 1906. Yates writes about black women who have difficulty relating to blacks. In a letter dated 16 May 1904, Yates complains of women who are members only for show and talk. In another letter sent to Washington, Ursula Wade expresses concern over clubs who act independently of the NACW and of the need to tie them to the organization in a consistent way. See Box 132 , Margaret Murray Washington Papers; see also Jessie Abbott's description of the way Tuskegee women faculty, most of whom were probably members of the Tuskegee Woman's Club (it was mandatory for female faculty), treated the student girls who worked in their homes for tuition fees. According to Abbott "they were not too nice to some of the student girls. They made too big a distinction with the workers and did not treat the girls as one of

the family." According to Abbott it was common to make the girls enter through the back door. Black Woman's Oral History Project, Arthur and Elizabeth Schlesinger Library at Radcliffe College, Interview with Jessie Abbott, p. 15. Additionally, on 7 July 1907, Mary Church Terrell received a letter from Agalia Martin, a poor, struggling young woman hoping to enter Fisk, who expressed contempt for "social queens," 1907 Folder, Container 4, Mary Church Terrell Papers, Library of Congress.

62. Katherine Macarthy, "The Club and the Community," *National Association Notes*, *23*(4, 5, 6):12 (Winter, 1923).

63. Letter from Heydell Campbell to Mary Church Terrell, 15 September 1905, Personal Correspondence, Container 5, Mary Church Terrell Papers, Library of Congress.

64. For examples of regionalism see letter from Margaret Murray Washington to Elizabeth Carter saying that women of the North could learn a lot from Southern women. See letters dated 22 July 1903 and 3 August 1903, Box 132, Margaret Murray Washington Papers.

65. See letter from M. C. Crosthwaith (registrar at Fisk) to Charlotte Hawkins Brown in which Brown says that Margaret Murray Washington blocked a position paper that supported suffrage. See also Margaret Murray Washington to Lucy Brown Johnston for a vague letter (21 May 1912) wherein Washington sidesteps the issue of suffrage, in Louis R. Harlan and Raymond W. Smock, eds., *The Booker T. Washington Papers*, vol. 11 (Chicago: University of Illinois Press, 1981), 539–540.

66. Josephine Yates to Margaret Murray Washington, 19 February 1906, Box 132, Margaret Murray Washington Papers.

67. Yates to Washington, 19 February 1906.

68. Yates to Washington, 16 May 1904, Box 132, Margaret Murray Washington Papers.

69. Josephine St. Pierre Ruffin to Mrs. Chiney, 24 March 1896, MS. A. 10.1 #87, Josephine St. Pierre Ruffin Papers.

70. Although Washington controlled the paper, she was not always listed as the editor, at least according to the masthead of *National Association Notes*. In November 1913 B. K. Bruce was listed as editor, and after that Hallie Q. Brown. Washington's name appears as editor from 1917–1922, but in 1923 the paper moved to Kansas City where Anna Jones is listed.

71. Hamilton, "The National Association of Colored Women," 62; Duster, ed., *Crusade for Justice,* 328–329.

72. Yates to Washington, 16 May 1904; 28 or 29 February 1906, Box 132, Margaret Murray Washington Papers.

73. Hamilton, "The National Association of Colored Women," 62; Salem, *To Better Our World*, 104–108.

74. Salem, *To Better Our World*, 104–105, 148–156.

Chapter 3
THEIR OWN BEST ARGUMENT

1. Mary Roberts Rauchart to Terrell, n.d. Box 102-2 #44. This comment was similar to those made by editors and publishers. See Mathilde Weil to Terrell, 19 November 1932, Box 102-2 #40; Herbert Jenkins to Terrell, 15 April 1927, 102-2 #29. All of the above are in the Terrell Papers at the Moorland-Spingarn Research Center, Howard University.

2. Mary Church Terrell, *A Colored Woman in a White World* (Washington, D.C.: Ransdell Inc. Pub., 1940).

3. Darlene Clark Hine, "Rape and the Inner Lives of Black Women in the Middle West: Preliminary Thoughts on the Culture of Dissemblance," *Signs, 14*:95 (Summer 1989).

4. "Charlotte Hawkins Brown," by William Pickens, Series 1, Speeches, Charlotte Hawkins Brown Papers.

5. Deborah Gray White, "Mining the Forgotten: Manuscript Sources for Black Women's History," *Journal of American History, 74*:237–242 (1987).

6. Linda Gordon, *Pitied But Not Entitled: Single Mothers and the History of Welfare 1890–1935* (Cambridge, Mass.: Harvard University Press, 1994), 121.

7. Hamilton, "The National Association of Colored Women," 39–53; Linda Gordon, "Black and White Visions of Welfare: Women's Welfare Activism, 1890–1945," *Journal of American History, 78* (2): 568–570 (Sept. 1991); Giddings, *When and Where I Enter,* 108; Gordon, *Pitied But Not Entitled,* 122.

8. For an overview of black women's lives during this period see Jones, *Labor of Love, Labor of Sorrow,* 79–195.

9. Letter from Margaret James Murray to Booker T. Washington, 26 October 1891 and 17 July 1892 in Louis R. Harlan, Stuart B. Kaufman, and Raymond W. Smock, eds., *The Booker T. Washington Papers,* vol. 3 (Urbana: University of Illinois Press, 1974), 175, 248, 249; Washington was twenty-seven years old when she admitted that she disliked children.

10. Hull, ed., *Give Us Each Day,* 26, 62, 73.

11. Ibid., 179; Dunbar-Nelson shared the responsibility of raising six children.

12. Ibid., 198; see also 224.

13. E. W. M. Lindon to Terrell, 13 June 1908, Container 4, Mary Church Terrell Papers, Library of Congress.

14. Mary Church Terrell to Robert Terrell, 16 January 1905, Container 3, Mary Church Terrell Papers, Library of Congress. See also Mary Church Terrell to Robert Terrell, 16 January 1905, Container 4, Mary Church Terrell Papers, Library of Congress.

15. Mary Church Terrell to Robert Terrell, 18 August 1900, Container 3, Mary Church Terrell Papers, Library of Congress.

16. Duster, ed., *Crusade for Justice*, 244–245.

17. Mary Church Terrell to Robert Terrell, 12 August 1900, Container 3, Mary Church Terrell Papers, Library of Congress.

18. Mary Church Terrell to Robert Terrell, n.d., Container 3, Mary Church Terrell Papers, Library of Congress.

19. Mary Church Terrell, Diary Entries, 20 November 1900, 29 November 1909, Container 1, Mary Church Terrell Papers, Library of Congress.

20. Duster, ed., *Crusade for Justice*, 250–255.

21. Ibid., 18–20.

22. Charlotte Hawkins Brown, "Some Incidents in the Life and Career of Charlotte Hawkins Brown growing out of racial situations, at the request of Dr. Ralph Bunch," 6, Series 1, #2, Charlotte Hawkins Brown Papers.

23. Terrell Diary Entries, 24 February 1905, 15 October 1905, 19 October 1905, 28 October 1905, and 5 April 1908, Container 1, Mary Church Terrell Papers, Library of Congress.

24. Terrell, *A Colored Woman in a White World*, 250–259.

25. Incidents of passing in Terrell's diaries: 28 January 1908, 9 April 1908, 26 July 1908, 9 February 1909, 4 April 1909, 10 June 1909, Container 1, Mary Church Terrell Papers, Library of Congress.

26. Hull, ed., *Give Us Each Day*, 69.

27. Terrell Diary Entry, 30 January 1908, Container 1, Mary Church Terrell Papers, Library of Congress.

28. Terrell Diary Entry, 8 April 1909, Container 1, Mary Church Terrell Papers, Library of Congress.

29. Hazel Carby's discussion of this concept in a literary framework has relevance for historians. See Hazel Carby, *Reconstructing Womanhood. The Emergence of the Afro-American Woman Novelist* (New York: Oxford University Press, 1987), 89–94.

30. The word "potentially" is used because black domestic workers also had a realistic view of white people and also functioned as mediators.

31. Black Woman's Oral History Project, Arthur and Elizabeth Schlesinger Library at Radcliffe College, Interview with Norma Boyd, 26.

32. Carby, *Reconstructing Womanhood*, 73, 187n.

33. See Chapter 1 for more information on Brown and her emphasis on culture.

34. Brown, "Some Incidents in the Life and Career of Charlotte Hawkins Brown"; Charlotte Hawkins Brown, "A Biography," Series 1, #1, 17, Charlotte Hawkins Brown Papers.

35. Adrienne Lasch Jones, *Jane Edna Hunter: A Case Study of Black Leadership*, in Hine, ed., *Black Women in the United States*, vol. 12, 25—31, 94.

36. Ibid., 50, 256. See also Tera Hunter, "The Correct Thing: Charlotte Hawkins Brown and the Palmer Institute," *Southern Exposure, XI*:37—43 (Sept./Oct. 1983).

37. Mary Church Terrell to Robert Terrell, 27 October 1912, Container 3, Mary Church Terrell Papers, Library of Congress.

38. Washington says she lived with white Quakers but there seems to be some question as to who she lived with as a child. See Harlan's explanation in Louis R. Harlan, Pete Daniel, Stuart B. Kaufman, Raymond W. Smock, and William M. Welty, eds., *The Booker T. Washington Papers,* vol. 2 (Urbana: University of Illinois Press, 1972), 515.

39. Letter from Margaret James Murray Washington to Emmett Scott, 31 January 1911, in Louis R. Harlan, Raymond W. Smock, Geraldine McTigue, Nan E. Woodruff, eds., *The Booker T. Washington Papers* , vol. 10 (Urbana: University of Illinois Press, 1981), 565—566.

40. Charlotte Hawkins Brown, "Some Incidents in the Life of Charlotte Hawkins Brown," Series I, #5, Charlotte Hawkins Brown Papers.

41. Ibid.

42. Mary Grinnell to Charlotte Hawkins Brown, 25 January 1910, 6 September 1912, 18 December 1912, 17 February 1913, 12 July 1911, Series II, Correspondence, Charlotte Hawkins Brown Papers.

43. Mary Grinnell to Charlotte Hawkins Brown, 21 September 1915, Series II, Correspondence, Charlotte Hawkins Brown Papers.

44. Mary Grinnell to Charlotte Hawkins Brown, 4 March 1910, Series II, Correspondence, Charlotte Hawkins Brown Papers.

45. Most of the correspondence in Brown's Papers, Series II, between 1911 and 1917, demonstrates this point. See for example the 1914 Easter Sunday letter from Annie Howe to Brown. See also Kimball's instructions

to Brown in letters dated 17 August 1909, 1 December 1906, 6 March 1907, 22 March 1902, 30 August 1909, Series II, Correspondence, Charlotte Hawkins Brown Papers.

46. Frances Guthrie to Charlotte Hawkins Brown, n.d., around 1907, Series II, Correspondence, Charlotte Hawkins Brown Papers.

47. Helen Kimball to Charlotte Hawkins Brown, 9 April 1908, Series II, Correspondence, Charlotte Hawkins Brown Papers.

48. Charlotte Hawkins Brown to Mrs. Macmahon, 14 October 1921, Series II, Correspondence, Charlotte Hawkins Brown Papers.

49. Letter fragment from Brown to Mr. Stone, 1921, Series II, Correspondence, Charlotte Hawkins Brown Papers.

50. Jones, *Jane Edna Hunter*, 35–58, 92–96.

51. Ibid., 201–212.

52. Salem, *To Better Our World*, 40. Carrie Chapman Catt to Mary Church Terrell, 20 January 1920, Container 6, Correspondence, Mary Church Terrell Papers, Library of Congress; Ida Husted Harper to Elizabeth Carter, 18 March 1919, Container 5, Correspondence, Mary Church Terrell Papers, Library of Congress; Walter White to Mary Church Terrell, n.d., 1919, Container 5, Correspondence, Mary Church Terrell Papers, Library of Congress; Nannie Burroughs, "The Negro Woman and Suffrage," Box 46, Nannie Helen Burroughs Papers, Library of Congress; Rosalyn Terborg-Penn, "Discontented Black Feminists: Prelude and Postscript to the Passage of the Nineteenth Amendment," in Lois Scharf and Joan Jensen, eds., *Decades of Discontent: The Woman's Movement, 1920–1940* (Westport, Conn.: Greenwood Press, 1983), 261–278.

53. Duster, ed., *Crusade for Justice*, 229–230.

54. Salem, *To Better Our World*, 126.

55. Louis R. Harlan, Stuart B. Kaufman, Barbara S. Kraft, and Raymond W. Smock, eds., *The Booker T. Washington Papers,* vol. 4 (Urbana: University of Illinois Press, 1975), 238; Louis R. Harlan, Raymond W. Smock, and Barbara S. Kraft, eds., *Booker T. Washington Papers,* vol. 5 (Urbana: University of Illinois Press, 1976), 560–561.

56. Both black men and women formed the NAACP, for example, Wells and Addie Hunton were founding members, and Christia Adair of Texas along with many others worked to make the NAACP an effective organization.

57. Cooper, *A Voice from the South,* 134.

58. Hull, ed., *Give Us Each Day,* 352–353; Charlotte Hawkins Brown to Margaret Murray Washington, 27 September 1916, Series II, Correspon-

dence, Charlotte Hawkins Brown Papers; Josephine Silone Yates to Margaret Murray Washington, 11 September 1908, Box 132, Margaret Murray Washington Papers; Jones, *Jane Edna Hunter*, 74.

59. Black Woman's Oral History Project, Arthur and Elizabeth Schlesinger Library at Radcliffe College, Interview with Adair, 44–45.

60. Individual biographies, Box 1, 1081, Location: B III A 16/1, Nettie Asberry Papers.

61. Kansas City Federation of Colored Women's Clubs, folder 92, Frederick Douglass Collection.

62. Minutes of the 19th Biennial Convention, July 1935, Container 23, Subject Files, Mary Church Terrell Papers, Library of Congress.

63. Duster, ed., *Crusade for Justice*, 329.

64. Ibid., 271–274; Salem, *To Better Our World*, 106.

65. Mary Church Terrell to Margaret Murray Washington, 13 November 1922, Terrell to Lampkins, 21 April 1925, Terrell to Burroughs, 14 April 1925, Terrell to Bethune, 16 February 1926, Terrell to Waring, 17 August 1935, 22 November 1934. All in Correspondence, Container 7, Mary Church Terrell Papers, Library of Congress.

66. Bethune to Terrell, October 1932, Mary Church Terrell Papers, Moorland-Spingarn Research Center, Howard University.

67. Louise Daniel Hutchinson, *Anna J. Cooper: A Voice from the South* (Washington, D.C.: Smithsonian Institution Press, 1982), 36; A 11 January 1908 diary entry seems to supply evidence of a vendetta Terrell carried on against Cooper, although the subject is referred to only as "Mrs. C." See Diary Entry, Container 1, Mary Church Terrell Papers, Library of Congress; Charles F. Weller to Mary Church Terrell, 15 October 1910, confirms the estrangement between Terrell and Cooper, Mary Church Terrell Papers, Moorland-Spingarn Research Center, Howard University; see Hutchinson pp. 66–83 on the M Street School controversy.

68. Mary Church Terrell to Frances, 5 September 1899, Container 3, Correspondence, Mary Church Terrell Papers, Library of Congress.

69. Duster, ed., *Crusade Against Justice*, 260; Josephine Silone Yates to Washington, 8 January 1904, 13 December 1903, Mary Church Terrell to Washington, May 1900. The article written by Cooper is mentioned in this letter. All in Box 132, Margaret Murray Washington Papers.

70. Letter from sister-in-law Laura to Mary Church Terrell, 15 October 1933, Container 3; on her problems in her elderly years see diary entry for 12 April 1935, 6 July 1935, Container 2; on problem with friends see letter from Janet Swift to Terrell, 13 March 1921, Container 6. All in

Mary Church Terrell Papers, Library of Congress. Dunbar-Nelson also complained of being friendless, see Hull, ed., *Give Us Each Day*, 130, 209, 283, 284, 309.

71. Mary Talbert to Charlotte Hawkins Brown, 10 January 1920, Series II, Charlotte Hawkins Brown Papers.

72. Laura to Terrell, 15 October 1933, Container 3, Mary Church Terrell Papers, Library of Congress. This convention was particularly contentious and was reported in several newspapers as such. See *Indianapolis Recorder*, 29 July 1933, *Baltimore Afro-American*, 5 August 1933. See Woman's Work, 1933, Monroe Work Files.

73. Eleventh Annual Convention, Washington State Federation of Colored Women's Organizations (1928), 1081, Location: B III A 16/1, Nettie Asberry Papers.

74. Hull, ed., *Give Us Each Day*, 250.

75. Terrell to Bethune, 16 February 1926, Container 7, Correspondence, Mary Church Terrell Papers, Library of Congress.

Chapter 4

A NEW ERA

1. E. David Cronon, *Black Moses: The Story of Marcus Garvey* (Madison, Wisc.: University of Wisconsin Press, 1955), 62–64; Theodore G. Vincent, *Black Power and the Garvey Movement* (New York: Ramparts Press, 1972), 113–114; Amy Jacques Garvey, *Garvey and Garveyism* (New York: Octagon Books, 1978), 48–49.

2. Cited in Vincent, *Black Power and the Garvey Movement*, 114.

3. This is a very simplistic explanation of Garveyism. For the full complexity of the ideas expressed at the convention see Vincent, *Black Power and the Garvey Movement*, 114–127.

4. Paul S. Boyer et. al., *The Enduring Vision: A History of the American People*, 3rd ed. (Lexington, Mass.: D. C. Heath and Company, 1996), 775–776; Frederick Lewis Allen, *Only Yesterday: An Informal History of the 1920's* (New York: Harper & Row, 1931), 73–101.

5. Burroughs's quote comes from Friday's session of the National League of Republican Colored Women, n.d., Box 309, Nannie Helen Burroughs Papers, Library of Congress.

6. For a general history of this period consult Nancy Cott, *The Grounding of Modern Feminism* (New Haven, Conn.: Yale University Press, 1987); J. Stanley Lemons, *The Woman Citizen: Social Feminism in the 1920's* (Char-

lottesville, Va.: University Press of Virginia, 1973); Anne Firor Scott, *Natural Allies: Women's Associations in American History* (Urbana: University of Illinois Press, 1991), 172–174; Nancy Woloch, *Women and the American Experience* (New York: Alfred Knopf, 1984), 381–418.

7. For a general history of this period consult Franklin and Moss, *From Slavery to Freedom,* 310–338; David Levering Lewis, *When Harlem Was in Vogue* (New York: Knopf, 1981); Nathan Huggins, *Harlem Renaissance* (New York: Oxford University Press, 1971).

8. William H. Chafe, *The Paradox of Change: American Women in the Twentieth Century* (New York: Oxford University Press, 1991), 26–28; Scott, *Natural Allies,* 171–172.

9. Claude McKay, "If We Must Die," in Arna Bontemps, ed., *American Negro Poetry* (New York: Hill and Wang, 1963), 31.

10. J. E. McCall, "The New Negro," *Opportunity: Journal of Negro Life,* V(7):211 (July 1927).

11. John R. Lynch, "Some Historical Errors of James Ford Rhodes," *Journal of Negro History* (JNH), *II* (4):345–368 (October 1917); Lynch, "More About the Historical Errors of James F. Rhodes," *JNH, III* (1):345–368 (April 1918); A. A. Taylor, "The Negro in South Carolina during the Reconstruction," *JNH, IX* (3,4):241–364, 381–569 (July, October 1924); A. A. Taylor, "The Negro in the Reconstruction of Virginia," *JNH, XI* (2, 3):243–415, 425–537 (April, July 1926); James Hugo Johnston, "The Participation of Negroes in the Government of Virginia from 1877–1888,"*JNH, XIV*(3):251–271 (July 1929). Blacks in Reconstruction governments was a major topic of discussion at the January 1925 and April 1926 meetings of the Association for the Study of Negro Life and History.

12. Speech by George Woodson, Miscellany, National League of Colored Republican Women, n.d., (but probably mid-twenties), Box 309, Nannie Helen Burroughs Papers, Library of Congress.

13. Speech, 28 May 1922, John Edward Bruce Papers, Reel 1, Schomburg Manuscripts, New York City Public Library.

14. Gloria Hull, *Color, Sex, and Poetry: Three Women Writers of the Harlem Renaissance* (Bloomington: Indiana University Press, 1987) 11, 10–13.

15. *The Negro World,* 23 June 1923. Cited in Barbara Bair, "True Women, Real Men: Gender, Ideology, and Social Roles in the Garvey Movement," in Dorothy O. Helly and Susan M. Reverby, *Gendered Domains: Rethinking Public and Private in Woman's History* (Ithaca, New York: Cornell University Press, 1992), 156.

16. Bair, "True Women, Real Men," 158.

17. Ibid.

18. Williams, "The Colored Girl," *Voice,* 2(6):403 (1905).

19. *The Negro World,* 30 June 1923. Cited in Bair, "True Women, Real Men," 158.

20. *The Negro World,* 9 June 1923. Cited in Bair, "True Women, Real Men," 156.

21. Garvey as cited in Cronon, *Black Moses,* 191–192.

22. Garvey's vendetta against these organizations and leaders is documented in Cronon, *Black Moses,* 190–193; Vincent, *Black Power and the Garvey Movement,* 70–71, 168.

23. Garvey as cited in Cronon, *Black Moses,* 192–193.

24. As quoted in Rupert Lewis and Patrick Bryan, eds., *Garvey: His Work an Impact* (Trenton, N.J., 1991), 75.

25. Woloch, *Women and the American Experience,* 401–402.

26. Quoted in Daphne Duval Harrison, *Black Pearls: Blues Queens of the 1920's* (New Brunswick, N.J.: Rutgers University Press, 1988), 111.

27. Harrison, *Black Pearls,* 63–111.

28. Ibid., 79–80, 90.

29. Hazel Carby, "It Jus Be's Dat Way Sometime: The Sexual Politics of Women's Blues," *Radical America,* 20(4):22 (1986).

30. Harrison, *Black Pearls,* 102.

31. Carby, "It Jus Be's Dat Way Sometime," 18, 21.

32. Ibid., 21.

33. Woloch, *Women and the American Experience,* 381–382, 401–402.

34. John D'Emilio and Estelle B. Freedman, *Intimate Matters: A History of Sexuality in America* (New York: Harper and Row, 1988), 241.

35. Gertrude E. Rush, "Forces Contributing to the Delinquency of Our Girls," *National Association Notes,* 26 (11):11 (July 1924).

36. It is possible that Stewart institutionalized this direction when she reorganized the NACW's structure so that its thirty-eight departments were consolidated into only two—first, Mother, Home, and Child, and second, Negro Women in Industry. Stewart's structure left little room for black women's work in politics. See Darlene Clark Hine, *When the Truth is Told: A History of Black Women's Culture and Community in Indiana, 1875–1950* (Indianapolis, Indiana: The National Council of Negro Women Indianapolis Section, 1981), 62.

37. "Negro Womanhood's Greatest Needs, A Symposium," *The Messenger,* June 1927.

38. Ibid.

39. John Hope died February 20, 1936.

40. See also *National Association Notes*, *31*(6):12 (March 1929).

41. National Association Notes, *31*(6):12 (March 1929).

42. Quoted in Elizabeth Clark-Lewis, "'This Work Had a End': African-American Domestic Workers in Washington, D.C., 1910–1940," in Carol Groneman and Mary Beth Norton, eds., *"To Toil the Livelong Day": American Women at Work, 1780–1980* (Ithaca, N.Y.: Cornell University Press, 1987), 201; for a history of the migration experience see Elizabeth Clark-Lewis, *Living In, Living Out: African American Domestics in Washington, D.C., 1910–1940* (Washington, D.C.: Smithsonian Institution, 1994), 51–95.

43. For general information on the reality of domestic workers see ibid., 196–212; Susan Tucker, *Telling Memories Among Southern Women: Domestic Workers and Their Employers in the Segregated South* (Baton Rouge: Louisiana State University Press, 1988); Judith Rollins, *Between Women: Domestics and Their Employers* (Philadelphia: Temple University Press, 1985); Elizabeth Clark-Lewis, *Living In, Living Out.*

44. See for instance, Katherine D. Tilman, "Paying Professions for Colored Girls," *The Voice of the Negro*, 4: 55–56 (1907); Fannie Barrier Williams, "An Extension of the Conference Spirit," *Voice*, *1*(7):302 (1904). Open letter from Nannie Burroughs, 20 October 1921, explaining the purpose and nature of the National Association of Wage Earners, Box 308, Miscellaneous Folder, Nannie Helen Burroughs Papers; see also article written in *Chicago Defender* by Nannie Burroughs, 18 June 1938.

45. See for example *Black Dispatch*, Oklahoma City, Oklahoma, 3 August 1933. This article was syndicated by the Associated Negro Press.

46. Quoted in Elizabeth Clark-Lewis, "'This Work Had a End,'" 205.

47. See Clark-Lewis, "'This Work Had a End'"; Gerda Lerner, ed., *Black Women in White America. A Documentary History* (New York: Random House), 219–238; Rollins, *Between Women*, 63–88; Tucker, *Telling Memories.*

48. "Some Facts for Colored Women to Think About," pamphlet written by Mary Church Terrell, Box 102-5, Folder 150, Mary Church Terrell Papers, Moorland-Spingarn Research Center, Howard University. For the official position taken by the NACW on the Mammy Statue see the letter to the American Press written by then-president Hallie Q. Brown entitled "The Black Mammy," *National Association Notes*, *23*(4, 5, 6)(1923); Brown's response was not forceful enough for Neval Thomas. Terrell wrote a protest in the *Boston Herald* and Thomas wrote Terrell congratulating her for taking a strong position. See his letter, 10 February 1923, to Mary

Church Terrell complaining that the NACW posture in relation to the statue was weak and ineffectual, Mary Church Terrell Papers, Library of Congress.

49. Minutes of the Temporary Organization of the National League of Republican Colored Women, Box 309, Nannie Helen Burroughs Papers, Library of Congress; Minutes of the National League of Republican Colored Women, 9 August 1924, Box 309, Nannie Helen Burroughs Papers, Library of Congress; Meeting of the Executive Committee of the National League of Republican Colored Women, Oakland, Calif., 6 August 1926, Box 309, Nannie Helen Burroughs Papers, Library of Congress; see also "Colored Women in Politics," a questionnaire for the purpose of "collecting information with a view to using it in the most effective way to help our women become a factor in the body politic," NLRCW folder 308, Nannie Helen Burroughs Papers, Library of Congress. In the same folder are the results of the questionnaire.

50. Clubwomen in Chicago had already demonstrated their resolve to become active in politics when, in 1915, they lobbied and rallied support and votes for Oscar Stanton DePriest, Chicago's first black alderman. See Wanda A. Hendricks, "'Vote for the advantage of ourselves and our race'; The Election of the First Black Alderman in Chicago," *Illinois Historical Journal,* 87:171–184 (Autumn 1994).

51. Minutes of the International Council of Women of the Darker Races, 1924, Constitution of the International Council, "International Council of Women of the Darker Races of the World," unknown author, Container 21, Subject Files, Mary Church Terrell Papers, Library of Congress.

52. As cited in Bair, "True Women, Real Men," 160–161.

53. As cited in Bair, "True Women, Real Men," 161.

54. As cited in Bair, "True Women, Real Men," 162; Vincent, *Black Power and the Garvey Movement,* 130–131.

55. As cited in Tera Hunter, "Feminist Consciousness and Black Nationalism: Amy Jacques-Garvey and Women in the Universal Negro Improvement Association," unpublished paper, 1983, 22.

56. Ibid., 22–23.

57. Ibid., 23.

58. Hunter, "Feminist Consciousness and Black Nationalism," 5.

59. As cited in Hunter, "Feminist Consciousness and Black Nationalism," 1.

60. Hunter, "Feminist Consciousness and Black Nationalism," 1–2.

61. Ibid., 9.

62. As cited in ibid.

63. As cited in ibid., 12.

64. Ibid.

65. According to Beryl Satter, to UNIA men, marriage, motherhood, and childcare had special significance. To them it meant that while they were to uplift the race through aggressive engagement in business and commerce, Garveyite women were literally to produce a "better and stronger race" through the quality of their child care. *Negro World* columnists repeatedly heralded this more biological form of race-building as "the greatest privilege that can come to any woman in this age, and to the Negro woman in particular." It was a privilege that Du Bois had once extended to Spelman College women and, like them, UNIA women declined. See Beryl Satter, "Marcus Garvey, Father Divine and the Gender Politics of Race Difference and Race Neutrality," *American Quarterly, 48*(1):57–53 (March 1996).

66. As cited in Lerner, ed., *Black Women in White America,* 579.

67. Satter, "Marcus Garvey, Father Divine and the Gender Politics of Race Difference and Race Neutrality," 52.

Chapter 5
RETHINKING PLACE

1. Pinkie Pilcher to President Roosevelt, 23 December 1936. As cited in Lerner, ed., *Black Women in White America,* 401–402.

2. Lutensia Dillard to President Roosevelt, 23 April 1941. Cited in Lerner, ed., *Black Women in White America,* 405.

3. From Louise Mitchell, "Slave Markets Typify Exploitation of Domestics," *The Daily Worker,* 5 May 1940. As cited in ibid., 229–231.

4. Lerner, ed., *Black Women in White America,* 226.

5. Black Women's Oral History Project, Arthur and Elizabeth Schlesinger Library at Radcliffe College, interview with Arline Yarbrough, 15.

6. See Karen Tucker Anderson, "Last Hired, First Fired: Black Women Workers during World War II," *The Journal of American History, 69*(1):82–97 (June 1982).

7. Salem, *To Better Our World,* 103–144.

8. NACW women helped sororities in their formative years, serving as role models and sometimes as speakers at annual events. Anna Julia

Cooper was an inspiration to sorors whose aim was to excel in higher education. Cooper, an AKA soror, who received her Ph.D. from the Sorbonne in France, was celebrated at the AKA's 1925 national Boule. Mary Church Terrell wrote the Delta Sigma Theta oath, and Tuskegee Institute's Delta chapter held their chapter meetings in the home of Margaret Murray Washington. See Marjorie Parker, *Alpha Kappa Alpha: In the Eye of the Beholder* (Washington, D.C., 1978), 33; Mary Elizabeth Vroman, *Shaped to Its Purpose: Delta Sigma Theta—The First Fifty Years* (New York: Random House, 1965), 7, 14; Paula Giddings, *In Search of Sisterhood: Delta Sigma Theta and the Challenge of the Black Sorority Movement* (New York: William Morrow, 1988), 92.

9. Cott, *The Grounding of Modern Feminism*, 96

10. Franklin and Moss, *From Slavery to Freedom,* 390–393. For a general overview of the period see Patricia Sullivan, *Days of Hope: Race in the New Deal Era* (Chapel Hill: University of North Carolina Press, 1996).

11. Minutes, 5 December 1935, Series 2, Box 1, Folder 1, National Council of Negro Women (hereafter cited as NCNW) Papers.

12. NCNW brochure, Folder 330-5, Claude A. Barnett Papers; Minutes, 5 December 1935, Series 2, Box 1, Folder 1, NCNW Papers.

13. See Series 2 and 4 comprising the minutes and reports of the NCNW, NCNW Papers.

14. Findings of the 1944 Annual Workshop of the NCNW Inc., Series 2, Box 2, Folder 22, NCNW Papers.

15. "Report of the Executive Secretary, NCNW 1939–1940," Series 2, Box 1, Folder 8, NCNW Papers.

16. "Metropolitan Council Reports for 1943" Series 2, Box 1, Reports, 1943, NCNW Papers.

17. Findings of the Conference on the participation of Negro Women in Federal Welfare Programs, Series 4, Box 1, Folder 6, NCNW Papers.

18. Copies of the *Aframerican* can be found in Series 13, Box 2 of the NCNW Papers.

19. See Elaine Smith, "Bethune, Mary McLeod, 1875–1955," in Darlene Clark Hine, ed., *Black Women in America. An Historical Encyclopedia* (Brooklyn, N.Y.: Carlson Pub. Inc., 1993), 113–127; Giddings, *When and Where I Enter,* 199–215; Rackham Holt, *Mary McLeod Bethune* (New York: Doubleday, 1964).

20. Leslie H. Fishel, "A Case Study: The Negro and the New Deal," in Alonzo L. Hamby, ed., *The New Deal: Analysis and Interpretation* (New York: Welbright and Talley, 1969), 225. For an overview of this period see

Nancy Weiss, *Farewell to the Party of Lincoln: Black Politics in the Age of FDR* (Princeton, N.J.: Princeton University Press, 1983).

21. Smith, "Mary McLeod Bethune," 114.

22. B. Joyce Ross, "Mary McLeod Bethune and the National Youth Administration: A Case Study of Power Relationships in the Black Cabinet of Franklin D. Roosevelt," in Franklin and Meier, *Black Leaders of the Twentieth Century,* 199, 201.

23. The history of these problems is briefly as follows. In 1916, eleven years after the death of Frederick Douglass's second wife, Helen, the NACW valiantly assumed the mortgage of Frederick Douglass's home. Club leaders felt that Douglass, an abolitionist, feminist, and civil rights advocate ought to be immortalized by having his home transformed into a National Shrine, and in fact they referred to the home as the Douglass Shrine. After two years of intense fundraising, representatives from clubs across the nation celebrated the purchase of the home in a mortgage-burning ritual at the 1918 biennial meeting. Clubs still were asked to contribute to the upkeep of the home, however, something they were willing to do until they were also asked to pay for the National Headquarters building that was purchased under the leadership of Mary McLeod Bethune when she became president in 1924. Since many clubwomen felt that the Douglass Shrine could, and should have, served as both a monument and headquarters, they not only were miserly about contributing, resulting in several missed mortgage payments, but debated the wisdom of the purchases bitterly.

Besides giving club leaders yet another reason to tear into each other, the dispute over the Headquarters and Douglass Shrine exposed a critical weakness in the NACW structure. Closer to the community, local clubs had always spearheaded projects that conformed to the direction set by Association leaders. When money was needed for work such as antilynching, the Association called on local clubs, which in turn raised money that they sent to the NACW. Similarly, when the Association undertook the Douglass Shrine project, clubs dutifully conducted fundraisers and sent the money along. Local clubs, though, were by and large autonomous, setting their own membership criteria, dues, and programs. Therefore, when the NACW asked for money to finance what most clubs considered an unnecessary headquarters building, many just quietly severed their connection with the National Association of Colored Women and continued to function as a local club, connected maybe to a city, state, or regional federation but not to the national group. The headquarters' mortgage was eventually paid off, but controversy over the purchase exacerbated a problem that many had complained about for years, namely the ever-increasing distance between the local clubs and the NACW. Ironically, the very structure built to physically institutionalize the Association actually proved to be one of a series of blows that permanently weakened it. See Salem, *To Better Our World,* 116–117, 125. For the resulting bitterness see letter from Julia West Hamilton to Mary Waring, 22 November 1934, Container 10, Mary Church Terrell Papers, Library of Congress. On dispute over caretaker expenses of Douglass Shrine see Mary Church Terrell to Mary Waring, 17 August 1935, Container 10 Correspondence, Mary Church Terrell Papers, Library of Congress; Minutes of the June 1924, June 1926, January 1948, annual conventions (the seventh, ninth and thirty-first respectively) of the Washington State Federation of Colored Women's Clubs, Box 1, 1081, Location: B III A 16/1, Nettie Asberry Papers; letter from Margaret Barnes to Claude Barnett, Barnett Papers, 11 April 1937, Folder 329-7; and Margaret Barnes, "Prominent Ohio Club Woman Flays Leadership of National Association of Colored Women," *Associated Negro Press*, 1037, Folder 329-7, Claude A. Barnett Papers.

24. See for example manuscript article by Margaret E. Barnes, "Prominent Ohio Club Woman Flays Leadership of National Association of Colored Women," Folder 329-7, Claude A. Barnett Papers.

25. Women's Work, Monroe Work Files, 1935.

26. Folder 329-7, Claude A. Barnett Papers.

27. See, for example, letter from Addie Hunton to M. Jacob Anderson, 20 December 1935, Folder 329-7, Claude A. Barnett Papers.

28. Women's Work, 1946, Monroe Work Files.

29. For the service work of the Deltas see Giddings, *In Search of Sisterhood,* especially 124–198. For AKA see Parker, *Alpha Kappa Alpha*; on AKA lobbying for Mississippi Health Project, see Ida Jackson to Claude Barnett, 7 January 1936, Folder 331-1, Claude A. Barnett Papers.

30. Giddings, *In Search of Sisterhood,* 144.

31. The "brown bag" test refers to using a brown paper bag as the standard of lightness one's skin had to be to "pass" the test; on color in sororities see Giddings, *In Search of Sisterhood,* 104–105.

32. Ida Jackson to Claude Barnett, September 1936, Folder 331-1, Claude A. Barnett Papers.

33. Giddings, *In Search of Sisterhood,* 144.

34. Jones, *Labor of Love, Labor of Sorrow,* 196–231, especially 205.

35. Ibid., 209.

36. Helena Wilson to Rosina Tucker, 4 November 1942, Folder 28-2, Brotherhood of Sleeping Car Porters (hereafter cited as BSCP) Papers.

37. Helena Wilson to Jeanetta Welsh Brown, 29 September 1943, Folder 29-2, BSCP Papers.

38. Ibid.

39. Jeanetta Welsh Brown to Helena Wilson, 16 October 1943, Folder 29-2, BSCP Papers.

40. Ibid. See also letter from Jeanetta Welsh Brown to Helena Wilson, 24 September 1943, Folder 29-2, BSCP Papers.

41. Mary McLeod Bethune to Helena Wilson, 4 October 1943, Folder 29-2, BSCP Papers.

42. Rosina Tucker to Helena Wilson, 9 November 1942, Folder 29-2, BSCP Papers.

43. Natalie Moorman to Helena Wilson, 16 October 1944, Folder 29-5, BSCP Papers.

44. Helena Wilson to Natalie Moorman, 23 October 1944, Folder 29-5, BSCP Papers.

45. William H. Harris, *The Harder We Run: Black Workers Since the Civil War* (New York: Oxford University Press, 1982), 83–84; see also William Harris, *Keeping the Faith: A. Phillip Randolph, Milton P. Webster, and the Brotherhood of Sleeping Car Porters, 1925–37* (Urbana: University of Illinois Press, 1977).

46. Harris, *The Harder We Run*, 77.

47. Positions taken by the Auxiliary can be found in their convention reports scattered throughout their papers.

48. Information on individual auxiliaries are located in folders devoted to particular cities as well as in convention reports.

49. Helena Wilson and Alice Ward, "Open letter to members," 2 December 1941, Folder 34-3, BSCP Papers.

50. Darlene Clark Hine, "Housewives' League of Detroit," in Hine, ed., *Black Women in America,* 584–585; see also Darlene Clark Hine, "The Housewives' League of Detroit: Black Women and Economic Nationalism," in Suzanne Lebsock and Nancy Hewitt, eds., *Invincible Women* (Urbana: University of Illinois Press, 1993); Jones, *Labor of Love, Labor of Sorrow,* 215.

51. Helena Wilson to Lucile Jones, 26 January 1942, Folder 27-5, BSCP Papers.

52. Helena Wilson to S. W. Austin, 26 November 1941, Folder 27-4, BSCP Papers.

53. Open letter from Wilson, 19 January 1940, Folder 27-3, BSCP Papers. For similar sentiments of white women trade unionists see Convention address of Mary E. Ryder, President Emeritus of the Missouri State Federation of Women's Auxiliary, 1956, Folder 34-2, BSCP Papers; Mrs. Kelsey's address to the 1959 convention, Conventions Folder, BSCP Papers.

54. Helena Wilson to C. L. Dellums, 30 July 1943, Folder 29-2, BSCP Papers; Rosina Tucker's Speech before the 1942 Convention, Folder 28-1, BSCP Papers; Helena Wilson to Velmer Coward, 11 December 1942, Folder 28-2, BSCP Papers; "Why Is Women's Part Important in the Cooperative Movement?", Folder 34-3, BSCP Papers; Wilson to Membership, 19 January 1940, Folder 27-3, BSCP Papers; Helena Wilson to S. W. Austin, 26 November 1941, Folder 27-4, BSCP Papers; Chicago Ladies Auxiliary debate on "Who is the Better Union Member, Man or Woman?" Folder 33-3, BSCP Papers.

55. Hine, "The Housewives' League of Detroit: Black Women and Economic Nationalism," 231.

56. Jones, *Labor of Love, Labor of Sorrow*, 215.

57. Mary McLeod Bethune to Helena Wilson, 22 December 1944, Folder 29-5, BSCP Papers; Helena Wilson to Mary McLeod Bethune, 4 January 1945, Folder 29-5, and 16 January 1945, Folder 29-6, BSCP Papers.

58. Helena Wilson to Elizabeth Craig, 3 May 1945, Folder 34-4, BSCP Papers; Helena Wilson to Elizabeth Craig, 6 March 1945, Folder 29-6, BSCP Papers.

59. Mary McLeod Bethune to Helena Wilson, 6 August 1948, Folder 31-4, BSCP Papers.

60. Fannie Caviness to Helena Wilson, 30 October 1942, Folder 28-2, BSCP Papers.

61. Estelle Harris Blanks to Helena Wilson, 19 May 1950, Folder 36-12, BSCP Papers; Helena Wilson to Estelle Harris Blanks, 8 June 1950, Folder 36-12, BSCP Papers.

62. See also Mabel Brown to Beenie Smith, 18 March 1943, Folder 29-1, BSCP Papers; B. F. McLaurin to Helena Wilson, 3 December 1952, Folder 33-4, BSCP Papers; Helen Williams to Helena Wilson, 26 April 1943, Folder 29-1, BSCP Papers; Helena Wilson to C. L. Dellums, 11 August 1943, Folder 29-2, BSCP Papers.

63. 1956 news release: "Rock-n-Roll Music," Folder 34-2, BSCP Papers.

64. This determination is made from applications to their labor schools.

65. This information can be gleaned from local auxiliary reports and from the applications for labor scholarships.

66. Constitution of New York Economic Council, 1926, Folder 27-2, BSCP Papers; 1940 Convention speech of Rosina Tucker, Folder 27-3, BSCP Papers.

67. Jeanetta Brown to Helena Wilson, 24 September 1943, Folder 29-2, BSCP Papers; Elizabeth Craig to Helena Wilson, 25 April 1945, Folder 29-6, BSCP Papers.

68. Report of Rosina Tucker, 1955 "The International Secretary Treasurers Report" (Re: Special Assignment of Nation-Wide Tour), Folder 34-1, BSCP Papers.

69. Ibid.

70. Wilson's Convention Address before the 7th Biennial, 1950, Folder 33-1, BSCP Papers.

71. Letter to Height from Vivian Mason 8 July 1954, reveals that local council people complain that the local Deltas do not cooperate with local Council, see Series 18, Box 1; letter to Eleanor Dailey from Jeanetta Welsh Brown complains that women of Chicago affiliates do not know why the local Chicago Council exists, see Dailey to Brown, 3 September 1944, Series 18, Box 1. All in NCNW Papers.

Chapter 6

THE SACRIFICES OF UNITY

1. Black Women's Oral History Project, Arthur and Elizabeth Schlesinger Library at Radcliffe College, Interview with Dorothy Height, 149–150.

2. Ibid., 135.

3. Ibid., 139.

4. Ibid., 135.

5. Ibid., 147.

6. Though it is impossible to prove, careful reading of the NCNW records of the 1960s suggest that Height came to this conclusion in hindsight.

7. James Oliver Horton, *Free People of Color: Inside the African American Community* (Washington: Smithsonian Institution Press, 1993), 90.

8. Giddings, *When and Where I Enter,* 314.

9. On the imperfections of Executive Order 8802 see Franklin and Moss, *From Slavery to Freedom,* 389.

10. Franklin and Moss, *From Slavery to Freedom,* 411–419; Ronald Takaki, *A Different Mirror: A History of Multicultural America* (Boston: Little, Brown and Company, 1993), 395–404; August Meier, Elliot Rudwick, and Francis Broderick, *Black Protest Thought in the Twentieth Century* (Indianapolis: Bobbs-Merrill Educational Publishing, 1971), 220–287.

11. Helena Wilson 1950 Convention Address, Folder 33-1, Brotherhood of Sleeping Car Porters (BSCP) Papers.

12. "The International Secretary-Treasurer's Report," 1955, Folder 34-1, BSCP Papers.

13. Harris, *Keeping the Faith,* 225.

14. See for instance Clayborn Carson, *In Struggle. SNCC and the Black Awakening of the 1960's* (Cambridge, Mass.: Harvard University Press, 1981), 217; William Q. Wilson, *The Declining Significance of Race* (Chicago: University of Chicago Press, 1978), 134–137.

15. 1956 Convention Reports, Folder 34-2, BSCP Papers.

16. Ibid.

17. 1968, Convention Folder, BSCP Papers.

18. On NCNW's financial situation see Mrs. Gertrude Alexander to Mrs. Vivian Mason, 13 October 1955, Series 12, Box 1, Folder 8, National Council of Negro Women (hereafter cited as NCNW) Papers.

19. Louisiana Folder, Series 17, Box 1953; Membership Report, Series 12, Box 2, Regular Membership Folder, 1964–1965, NCNW Papers.

20. NCNW, "Annual Report of the Director of Junior Councils," Series 2, Box 7, Folder 73, NCNW Papers.

21. Ibid.

22. NCNW Memo on Life Membership Guild, November 11, 1954, Series 12, Box 1, NCNW Papers.

23. Dollie Alexander to Mrs. Mason, 14 November 1955, Series 12, Box 1, NCNW Papers.

24. Vivian Mason to Mrs. Alexander, 5 December 1955, Series 12, Box 1, NCNW Papers.

25. Claude Barnett to Mrs. Nancy Woolridge, 24 January 1951, Folder 332-3, Claude A. Barnett Papers.

26. Claude A. Barnett to Mrs. Marion H. Bluitt, 24 April 1951, Folder 331-8, Claude A. Barnett Papers.

27. Claude Barnett to Mrs. Gresham, 5 December 1953, Folder 332-3. Claude A. Barnett Papers.

28. E. Franklin Frazier, *Black Bourgeosie: The Rise of a New Middle Class in the United States* (London: Coller-MacMillan, Ltd., 1957), 84, 169, 183.

29. Ibid., 183.

30. Interview with Dorothy Height, 1–6, 16, 34.

31. Height, 51–54.

32. Height, 8–10, 21–22.

33. Height, 48.

34. Height, 47–48; Giddings, *In Search of Sisterhood,* 218, 204–206.

35. Giddings, *In Search of Sisterhood*, 218–221.

36. Dorothy Ferebee served as president from 1949 to 1953. She was a former Supreme Basilei (president) of Alpha Kappa Alpha (AKA). Her successor, Vivian Carter Mason, was a former North Atlantic Regional Director for AKA.

37. Series 18, NCNW, Box 1, Vivian Mason to Height, 8 July 1954, reveals that local council people complain that the local Deltas do not cooperate with local Council; letter to Eleanor Dailey from Jeanetta Welsh Brown complains that women of Chicago affiliates do not know why the local Chicago Council exists, see Eleanor Dailey to Jeanetta Welsh Brown, 3 September 1944, Series 18, Box 1, NCNW Papers.

38. Giddings, *In Search of Sisterhood,* 221–224, gives explanation of their activities. See also "American Council on Human Rights Womanpower Talent Search," Folder 330-7, Claude A. Barnett Papers.

39. Giddings, *In Search of Sisterhood,* 233–236.

40. Open letter from Helen Edmonds to Dorothy Height, 8 January 1957, Series 18, Box 1, Delta Folder, NCNW Papers.

41. Height, 56.

42. See NCNW Press Release, 19 December 1966, Series 12, Box 1, 1966 Folder, NCNW Papers; Gladys Zales serves as co-chairman with Lena Horne of 1965 Life Membership Drive. See Height to Gwen Higginbotham, 2 December 1965, Series 12, Box 1, Folder 12, NCNW Papers; Mary Rockefeller became a life member in 1967. See Life Membership List for January 1967, Series 12, Box 1, 1967 Folder, NCNW Papers; Mrs. Franklin D. Roosevelt was made Honorary Chairman of a benefit held in order to raise money to erect a monument to Bethune. See "Open Letter to Women Leaders," August 1960, Folder 330-3, Claude A. Barnett Papers; for all of the events and people Height involved in NCNW activities see Series 12, Box 1, NCNW Papers.

43. Life Membership Files 1970, Series 12, Box 1, 1970 Folder, NCNW Papers.

44. "Bare Sexual Abuse of Negro, White Women Arrested in Dixie Civil

Rights Demonstration," New York, Associated Negro Press, Folder 330-4, Claude A. Barnett Papers.

45. Height, 144–146

46. See Series 19, Box 1, NCNW Papers; Height, 146–154; Polly Cowan Oral History, Moorland-Spingarn Research Center, Howard University, 13–32.

47. See Fannie Lou Hamer Papers, Box 29, Folders 1, 2, 6, 7, Library of Congress; Hamer to Friend, 16 December 1969, Series 9, Box 16, Folder 112, NCNW Papers.

48. Height, 166–169.

49. Height, 170.

50. Height, 170–171.

51. For instance, Height wanted the NCNW's 1965 Life Membership campaign to compare favorably with the NAACP's Life Membership campaign. See Height to Gwen Higginbotham, 2 December 1965, Series 12, Box 1, Folder 12, NCNW Papers.

52. Height, 130–133.

53. Lee Rainwater and William L. Yancey, *The Moynihan Report and the Politics of Controversy* (Cambridge, Mass.: M.I.T. Press, 1967), 17–37.

54. Daniel Patrick Moynihan, *The Negro Family: The Case for National Action* (Washington, D.C.: Office of Policy Planning and Research United States Department of Labor, 1965); see also Rainwater and Yancey, *The Moynihan Report and the Politics of Controversy*, 29–31.

55. Ibid., 29.

56. Ibid.

57. Ibid., 30.

58. Ibid., 30–45.

59. Ibid., 34.

60. Ibid., 42. Moynihan's council came at the very moment the United States increased its troops in Vietnam and escalated the war.

61. See for example K. Sue Sewall, *From Mammy to Miss America and Beyond: Cultural Images and the Shaping of US Social Policy* (London: Routledge, 1993), 24, 37–44, 45, 48, 94, 131, 183–184, 189, 195.

62. Ibid., 29.

63. Michele Wallace, *Black Macho and the Myth of the Superwoman* (London: Verso, 1990 [1978]), 12, 31.

64. Jones, *Labor of Love, Labor of Sorrow*, 302–305.

65. Wallace, *Black Macho*, 12.

66. Moynihan, *The Negro Family*, 34; Lerner, *Black Women in White America*, 589.

67. Rainwater and Yancey, ed., *The Moynihan Report*, 20, 29.

68. From Pauli Murray, "The Negro Woman in the Quest for Equality," *The Acorn* (publication of Lambda Kappa Mu Sorority, Inc.), June 1964. Cited in Lerner, *Black Women in White America*, 592–599.

69. See Lerner, *Black Women in White America*, 607. Lerner cites Mary Reinholz, "Storming the All Electric Doll House," *West Magazine, Los Angeles Times*, 7 June 1970.

70. *Washington Post*, 3 October 1970. Cited in Lerner, *Black Women in White America*, 589.

71. This position will be addressed more fully in the next chapter when black women's attitudes about white women are discussed.

72. NCNW Press Release, 19 December 1966, Series 12, Box 1, 1966 Folder, NCNW Papers.

73. Height, 162

74. Ann Moody, *Coming of Age in Mississippi* (New York: The Dial Press, Inc., 1968), 298.

75. Ibid., 275.

76. Ibid., 286.

77. Ibid., 333.

78. Guida West, *The National Welfare Rights Movement: The Social Protest of Poor Women* (New York: Praeger Publishers, 1981), 223.

79. Pat Robinson and Group, "Poor Black Women's Study Papers by Poor Black Women of Mount Vernon, New York," in Toni Cade, ed., *The Black Woman: An Anthology* (New York: New American Library, 1970), 190, 194, 189–197.

80. Goodman to Height, 17 July 1969, Series 9, Box 15, Folder 105, NCNW Papers.

81. Press release from NCNW, 15 July 1969, Series 9, Box 5, Folder 105, NCNW Papers.

82. Ibid.

83. Ibid. NCNW "resolutions" Series 9, Box 14, Folder 97, NCNW Papers.

84. Ibid.

85. NCNW "resolutions" Series 9, Box 14, Folder 97, NCNW Papers.

86. Ibid.

87. Mary McLeod Bethune to Helena Wilson, 6 August 1948, Folder 31-4, BSCP Papers.

88. Goodman to Height, 17 July 1969, Series 9, Box 15, Folder 105, NCNW Papers.

89. This subject is taken up in the next chapter.

90. Jan Douglass to Lynn Littman, 10 June 1968, Series 9, Box 14, Folder 94, NCNW Papers; Mrs. Anna Lois Jones to Mrs. Jewell Shipperd, Series 9, Box 14, Folder 94, NCNW Papers; Ruth A. Sykes to Dorothy Height, 4 October 1968, Series 9, Box 14, Folder 98, NCNW Papers.

91. National Council of Negro Women, "Resolutions" Series 9, Box 14, Folder 97, NCNW Papers.

92. Ibid.

93. Goodman to Height, 17 July 1969, Series 9, Box 15, Folder 105, NCNW Papers; Memo, "Proposal For Action On Direct Membership," July 1969, Series 12, Box 2, NCNW Papers; Open letter from Height, 6 August 1969, Series 17, Box 2, NCNW Papers.

94. Height to Jean Crowther, 11 October 1968, Series 9, Box 14, Folder 98, NCNW Papers.

95. See Carson, *In Struggle:* SNCC's opposition to hierarchy is one of the themes of Carson's excellent study.

96. Ibid.

Chapter 7

MAKING A WAY OUT OF NO WAY

1. "Proposal: Women's Action Alliance, Inc.," Woman's Action Folder, Box 2210, National Welfare Rights Organization (hereafter cited as NWRO) Papers.

2. "Statement of Grievance," Woman's Action Folder, Box 2210, NWRO Papers.

3. Ibid.

4. Ibid.

5. Ibid., 252.

6. Ibid., 249.

7. Manning Marable, *Race, Reform and Rebellion: The Second Reconstruction in Black America, 1945–1982* (Jackson: University of Mississippi Press, 1984), 128–155.

8. Calvin C. Hernton, *Sex and Racism in America* (New York: Doubleday, 1965), 139–140.

9. William H. Grier and Price M. Cobbs, *Black Rage* (New York: Basic Books, 1968), 41, 47.

10. Cleaver, *Soul On Ice,* 168.

11. Frantz Fanon, *Black Skin, White Masks*, Trans. Lam Markman (New York: Grove Press, 1967), 49.

12. Hernton, *Sex and Racism*, 154–155.

13. Grier and Cobbs, *Black Rage*, 96–101.

14. Ibid., 52.

15. From Murray, "The Negro Woman in the Quest for Equality." Cited in Lerner, ed., *Black Women in White America*, 592–599; Giddings, *When and Where I Enter*, 311–314.

16. Giddings, *When and Where I Enter*, 317–324.

17. Elaine Brown, *A Taste of Power: A Black Woman's Story* (New York: Pantheon Books, 1992), 108–109, 357.

18. As of 1997 Dorothy Height was still president.

19. Black women feminists include Shirley Chisholm and Pauli Murray. See Shirley Chisholm, *Unbought and Unbossed* (Boston: Houghton Mifflin Co., 1970) and Pauli Murray, *The Autobiography of a Black Activist, Feminist, Lawyer, Priest and Poet* (Knoxville: University of Tennessee Press).

20. Lerner, ed., *Black Women in White America*, 589. Ibid., 590. Quoted in 1963 in Moynihan, *The Negro Family*, 30–31. Moynihan took the quote from the Report of Consultation of Problems of Negro Women, President's Commission on the Status of Women, 19 April 1963, 35. Height was again quoted saying the same thing in 1969, *New York Magazine*, 10 March 1969, 36.

21. Giddings, *When and Where I Enter*, 305–311.

22. Toni Morrison, "What the Black Woman Thinks About Women's Lib," *New York Times Magazine*, 22 August 1971.

23. The forces that made the first NWRO convention possible were many. The Civil Rights Movement had already mobilized Americans to fight for the rights of excluded groups, and had trained students and local people to organize purposely for community and individual empowerment. Similarly, the Black Power Movement had mobilized African Americans to fight forcefully and demandingly. While the nation's consciousness had been raised by President Johnson's War on Poverty, and private foundations such as the Ford Foundation had begun making sizable contributions toward solving the problems of the underprivileged, position papers and best-selling books had helped fix bureaucratic and political attention on the paradox of poverty amid plenty. West, *The National Welfare Rights Movement*, 19–22; Frances Fox Piven and Richard A. Cloward, *Poor People's Movement: Why They Succeed, How They Fail* (New York: Vintage Books, 1977), 266–274.

24. Larry Jackson and William Johnson, *Protest by the Poor* (Lexington, Mass.: Lexington Books, 1974), 31.

25. Nick Kotz and Mary Lynn Kotz, *A Passion for Equality: George A.Wiley and the Movement* (W. W. Norton & Company, 1977), 220.

26. Speakers Bureau Folder, Box 2209, "Heading Welfare Hardly a Hand-Out," by Patricia Burstein, *Miami News*, 5 July 1972, Section B, Speakers Bureau Folder, Box 2209, NWRO Papers.

27. Johnnie Tillmon, "Welfare Is a Woman's Issue," *Ms. Magazine,* Spring 1972. Reprinted in Francine Klagsbrun, *The First Ms. Reader* (New York: Warner Books, 1973), 51.

28. Kotz and Kotz, *A Passion for Equality*, 220.

29. Kotz and Kotz, *A Passion for Equality,* 221.

30. Ibid.

31. Jackson and Johnson, *Protest by the Poor,* 63; Kotz and Kotz, *A Passion for Equality*, 221–222.

32. Lawrence Neil Ballis, *Bread or Justice: Grassroots Organizing in the Welfare Rights Movement* (Lexington, Mass.: D.C. Heath, 1974), 4.

33. Ballis, *Bread or Justice,* 11; Jackson and Johnson, *Protest by the Poor*, 39.

34. Jackson and Johnson, *Protest by the Poor*, 35.

35. *NOW News,* 7 November 1968, 17 November 1968.

36. Box 2086, NWRO Papers.

37. Carol McEldowney, *Welfare Rights:WIN Training for What* (Cleveland, Ohio: Legal Aid Society, 1969); *Your Rights in WIN TALMADGE* (Washington, D.C.: National Welfare Rights Organization, 1972).

38. West, *The National Welfare Rights Movement,* 86–89, Tillmon, "Welfare Is A Woman's Issue," 57.

39. Gordon, *Pitied But Not Entitled,* 293–299.

40. This proposal was quite different from the flat grant proposals instituted by cities and states. Flat grants replaced special needs and minimum standards provisions that had allowed recipients to apply and fight for such extras as clothing, furniture, food, and health care. Across-the-board flat grants were inadequate, and both local groups and the National Welfare Rights Organization strongly condemned and bitterly fought against them with limited success. They also fought President Nixon's Family Assistance Plan, which in 1972 was supposed to provide an income floor of $2,400, and which paid single mothers less than unemployed men, the blind, disabled, and aged. Since most states at this time paid recipients more than this amount, Nixon's plan was given the same treatment as flat grants. The

National Welfare Rights Organization lobbied, protested, and—unlike in the case of state and city flat grants—defeated the measure. Jackson and Johnson, *Protests by the Poor,* 37–38, 123–126; Tillmon, "Welfare Is a Woman's Issue," 57–58; Piven and Cloward, *Poor People's Movements,* 335–338.

41. One obvious similarity was the decentralized structure of both organizations. Even though direct membership in the Council was possible after 1969, it functioned fairly independently with input from autonomous local organizations and Metropolitan Councils. Similarly, local welfare groups only received assistance from the National Welfare Rights Organization when they asked for it. For example, when the Nevada State Welfare Department summarily terminated 3,000 recipients and simultaneously reduced the grants of another 4,500, the National Welfare Rights Organization provided staff and legal assistance to the local Clark County WRO. Together the local and national groups helped rescind the state's actions. See Jackson and Johnson, *Protests by the Poor,* 40.

42. Tillmon, "Welfare Is a Woman's Issue, " 51–52; West, *The National Welfare Rights Movement,* 89–90.

43. Kotz and Kotz, *A Passion for Equality,* 224–225.

44. Tillmon, "Welfare Is a Woman's Issue," 51–52.

45. Interview with Espanola Jackson Oral History, Moorland-Spingarn Research Center, Howard University, 8.

46. *Welfare Fighter,* 3(3):12 (March 1972).

47. Convention Folder, Box 2193, NWRO Papers.

48. Gordon, *Pitied But Not Entitled,* 17, 27, 33.

49. The history of the modern welfare system is complex. A review of it would take this chapter beyond its intended scope. Gordon's book is an excellent and lucid account of this subject. I am indebted to it for helping me formulate some of the questions I asked of my sources. See Gordon, *Pitied But Not Entitled,* 15-35.

50. West, *The National Welfare Rights Movement,* 210–232; Piven and Cloward, *Poor People's Movements,* 320–321.

51. Kotz and Kotz, *A Passion for Equality,* 253.

52. Ella Baker Oral History, Moorland-Spingarn Research Center, Howard University, 35–37.

53. West, *The National Welfare Rights Movement,* 231.

54. Tillmon, "Welfare Is a Woman's Issue," 51.

55. Sociologist and social policy experts attribute the decline and failure of the NWRO to the tactics they either adopted or did not adopt. Some

believe the organization was doomed from the minute it went national since the needs of the constituents were immediate and more tangible than some of the goals of the national group. It is argued that once local members received the additional clothing, furniture, and money they needed they abandoned the organization. Others cite the tactics used by local organizations, claiming that even the locals could not maintain themselves once the immediate needs of their recipient members were met. See Ballis, *Bread or Justice*, 3. Still others look at the broader picture and maintain that the Welfare Rights Movement was doomed because in order to get the backing it needed to launch and sustain its national movement it had to make its goals consistent with the white church and civic groups that supported it. When it did this, it lost touch with its own constituency, the welfare mothers. When it refused to follow the lead of the supporters, it lost their financial backing. It is also argued that the National Welfare Rights Organization compromised its radicalism when it chose to work within the traditional political and legislative processes to effect change. See Piven and Cloward, *Poor People's Movements*, 264–359. The purpose of this discussion is not to locate the reason for NWRO's demise but to analyze its significance in the history of black women's organizations and defense of themselves.

56. West, *The National Welfare Rights Movement*, 238–239.

57. Series 20, Folder 19, NCNW Papers.

58. Series 20, Box 2, Folder 23, NCNW Papers.

59. Patricia Burstein, "Heading Welfare Hardly a Hand-Out."

60. *NOW News,* 7 February 1968.

61. See for example Drake and Clayton, *Black Metropolis,* 589–590, 658–660.

62. For details of the bill see Piven and Cloward, *Poor People's Movements*, 318–319.

63. *NOW News,* 7 February 1968.

64. *NOW News,* 7 February 1968; see also *NOW, 2*(8), (1968).

65. See for example speech by Beulah Sanders, October 1971, Equal Rights Folder 2210, NWRO Papers; interview with Johnnie Tillmon in *Washington Post,* 13 May 1968, reprinted in *NOW, 2*(8), (1968).

66. Jessie M. Rodrique, "The Black Community and the Birth-Control Movement," in Ellen Carol DuBois and Vicki L. Ruiz, eds., *Unequal Sisters: A Multicultural Reader in U. S. Women's History,* 1st ed. (New York: Routledge, 1990), 337–338; Linda Gordon, *Woman's Body, Woman's Right: Birth Control in America* (New York: Penguin Books, 1976), 400–401.

67. *NOW News,* 2 February 1968.

68. Memo, "Notes from National," 1973, Box 2208, 1973 File, NWRO Papers; "Forced Sterilization a Threat to the Poor," *The Welfare Fighter*, 4(1), (February 1974).

69. Ibid. Flyer 1973, Box 2193, NWRO Papers.

70. Flyers, n.d., Box 2122, NWRO Papers.

71. West, *The National Welfare Rights Movement*, 103–104.

72. Mrs. Annie Smart to Mrs. Beulah Sanders, 9 January 1972, Box 2193, NWRO Papers.

73. West, *The National Welfare Rights Movement*, 102.

74. West, *The National Welfare Rights Movement*, 113–123; "Rift Erupts at Welfare Rights," *Washington Afro-American*, 19 August 1969.

75. West, *The National Welfare Rights Movement*, 93.

76. Testimony of Dr. George A. Wiley, Director, Poverty/Rights Action Center, Washington, D.C., 22 September 1967, Box 1967, NWRO Papers.

77. West, *The National Welfare Rights Movement*, 93, 134.

78. Newspaper clippings, Woman's Action Folder, Box 2210, National Black Feminist Organization (hereafter cited as NBFO) Papers.

79. See correspondence and proposals in the Women's Action Folder, Box 2210, NWRO Papers.

80. Tillmon, "Welfare Is a Woman's Issue," 52–56.

81. West, *The National Welfare Rights Movement*, 260.

82. West, *The National Welfare Rights Movement*, 251–254, 256–261.

83. Tillmon, "Welfare Is a Woman's Issue," 54–55.

84. West, *The National Welfare Rights Movement*, 121–123.

85. Tillmon Personal Folder, Box 2209, NWRO Papers.

86. The life of the National Black Feminists Organization is usually dated through the founding and demise of the New York chapter. There were, however, other National Black Feminist Organizations founded throughout the country. The organizations in Chicago, Detroit, Atlanta, and Washington organized and hoped to affiliate with the NBFO. The New York chapter never established the methods and rules for affiliation, however. This discussion of the National Black Feminist Organization is based primarily on the files of the Chicago NBFO.

87. "Statement of Purpose," Box 74-56, Folder 1-12, NBFO Papers.

88. Ibid.

89. Carol Kleiman, "When Black Women Rap, The Talk Sure Is Different," *Chicago Tribune*, 1 June 1975.

90. Sandra Flowers to NBFO Sisters, 6 October 1974, Box 74-56, Folder 1-7, NBFO Papers.

91. Juanita Hill to Chicago NBFO, 29 May 1975, Folder H-1975, #20, Eichelberger Collection.

92. Ivy Anderson to Chicago Black Feminists, 19 December 1978, Box 3, Folder 25, Eichelberger Collection. See also Antoinette Smith to Chicago Black Feminists, January 1979, Box 3, Folder S-1979, #44, Eichelberger Collection; Dorothy Savage, February 1979, Box 3, Folder S-1979, #44, Eichelberger Collection; Diana Momon, 7 January 1974, Box 2, Folder 1974, Eichelberger Collection.

93. M. Weusi to Chicago Black Feminists, 18 October 1978, Box 3, Folder W-1979, #48, Eichelberger Collection.

94. Brenda Smith to Chicago Black Feminists, 3 December 1974, Box 2, Folder 1974-RS, #93, Eichelberger Collection.

95. Theda Woodson Scroggins to National Alliance for Black Women, 10 November 1976, Box 2, Folder S-1976, #51, Eichelberger Collection; Theda Woodson to Brenda Eichelberger, 25 April 1977, Box 3, Folder B-1977, #2, Eichelberger Collection.

96. Betty Rowland to Chicago Black Feminists, n.d., Box 2, Folder R-1975, #28, Eichelberger Collection.

97. Marie Cain to Chicago Black Feminists, July 1975, Box 2, Folder 1975-C, #15, Eichelberger Collection.

98. Doris Russell to Chicago Black Feminists, 5 May 1975, Box 2, Folder R-1975, #28, Eichelberger Collection.

99. Glenda Frierson to Chicago Black Feminists, 8 November 1976, Box 2, Folder F-1976, #38, Eichelberger Collection.

100. Ester Sykes to Brenda Eichelberger, 9 December 1974, Box 2, Folder 9, 1974-RS, Eichelberger Collection.

101. Faye L. Williams, November 1976, Box 2, Folder W-1976, #55, Eichelberger Collection.

102. Dorothy Jones to Brenda Eichelberger, 3 August 1976, Box 2, J-1976, #43, Eichelberger Collection.

103. Bernette Golden, "Black Women's Liberation," *Essence Magazine*, February 1974, Box 74-56, Folder 1-12, NBFO Papers.

104. Margo Jefferson and Margaret Sloan, "In Defense of Black Feminism," *Encore*, July 1974 in Box 74-56, Folder 1-12, NBFO Papers.

105. Candidate Position Statement, Box 74-56, Folder 1-4, NBFO Papers.

106. Margo Jefferson and Margaret Sloan refer to Darkwater in their *Encore* article. See, "In Defense of Black Feminism," *Encore*, and W. E. B. Du Bois, *Darkwater: Voices from Within the Veil*, in Eric J. Sundquist, ed., *The Oxford*

W. E. Du Bois Reader (New York: Oxford University Press 1996 [1920]), 564–580.

107. Deborah Austin to Brenda Eichelberger, 31 October 1978, Box 3, Folder A-1979, #26, Eichelberger Collection; See also Pyle Center to Brenda Eichelberger, 23 April 1975, Box 17, Folder 17, Eichelberger Collection.

108. Brenda Verner, "Brenda Verner Examines 'Liberated Sisters,'" *Encore,* April 1974, Box 74-56, Folder 1-12, NBFO Papers.

109. Ibid.

110. See for example letter from Jackie Johnson to Brenda Eichelberger, 20 May 1975, Box 17, Folder NBFO Correspondence from Membership, Eichelberger Collection

111. See for example Michelle Wallace's description of NBFO conflict: Michelle Wallace, "Anger In Isolation: A Black Feminist's Search for Sisterhood," in *Words of Fire: An Anthology of African-American Feminist Thought* (New York: The New Press, 1995), 226–227. Wallace's article first appeared in the *Village Voice* in 1975.

112. Minutes of the First Meeting of the National Black Feminists Organization, Chicago Chapter, Box 74-56, Folder 1-2, NBFO Papers.

113. Letter from Executive Board to Sister, 18 September 1974, Box 74-56, Folder 1-4, NBFO Papers. One can only imagine what a difficult situation Galvin-Lewis was in as she tried to mediate between black and white women who were truly uncomfortable in each other's presence.

114. Letter from Diane Lacey, Deborah Singletary, Elizabeth Bell, Jane Galvin-Lewis, Chris Walton, Doreen McGill to Sister, 18 September 1974, Box 74-76, Folder 1-4, NBFO Papers; Minutes of the Third Meeting, National Black Feminist Organization, Chicago Chapter, 3 July 1974, Box 74-56, Folder 1-2, NBFO Papers. This scenario has been pieced together from correspondence and minutes. It is by no means meant to be a complete picture of the turmoil that beset the NBFO in 1974.

115. Sandra Flowers to NBFO Sisters, 6 October 1974, Box 74-56, Folder 1-7, NBFO Paper; Sandra Hollin Flowers to Brenda Eichelberger, 15 August 1974, Box 74-56, Folder 1-3, NBFO Papers; Sandra Hollin Flowers to Jane Galvin-Lewis, 9 September 1974, Box 74-56, Folder 1-7, NBFO Papers.

116. For information on the finances and membership of this organization see Box 9, National Black Feminist Alliance Papers

117. Marilyn Marshall, "Alaska Summit," *Ebony*, October 1982. See also Karen De Witt, "For Black Clubwomen, a New Era Dawns," *New York Times*,

4 August 1996. Both articles speak of the contemporary problems the organization was having recruiting women under 35.

118. On home ownership see Series 13, Box 3, Folder 52; Series 20, Box 2, Folder 23; Series 20, Box 5, Folder 4; on Operation COPE see Series 22, Box 15, Folders 19, 22, and Series 22, Box 16, Folder 10; on the Hunger Program see Series 26, Box 7, Folder 6. All in NCNW Papers.

119. On entrepreneurs in school lunch programs see Series 22, Box 7, Folder 9; on women in housing see Series 34, Box 6, Folder 15; Series 34, Box 3, Folder 8; the contract with the National Medical Association can be found in Series 27, Box 9, Folder 8. All in the NCNW Papers.

120. On Sisters United see Series 23, Boxes 1, 2, NCNW Papers.

121. Moynihan, *The Negro Family,* 30.

122. In her excellent article, Wahneema Lubiano explores this analysis at length. See "Black Ladies, Welfare Queens, and State Minstrels: Ideological War by Narrative Means," in Morrison, ed., *Race-ing, Justice, En-gendering Power,* 323–363.

123. The Combahee River Collective, "A Black Feminist Statement," in *Words of Fire: An Anthology of African-American Feminist Thought* (New York: The New Press, 1995), 232–240.

124. See for example Beth E. Richie, "Battered Black Women: A Challenge for the Black Community," in ibid., 398–404.

Epilogue
THE PAST AND FUTURE MEET

1. Courtney Leatherman, "Black Women in Academe," *The Chronicle of Higher Education*, 26 January 1994, A17, A19.

2. Ibid., A17.

3. See *Knickerbocker News, Union Star,* 27 August 1970. The articles on Davis are just too numerous to cite. Davis was accused in August 1970 and acquitted in June 1972.

4. See Derrick Z. Jackson, "Once Again, Clinton Allows a Dangerous Silencing of Views," *Boston Globe,* 6 June 1993, 73; see also Thomas D. Boston, "A Testament to the American Dream," *The Atlantal Journal/The Atlanta Constitution,* 17 December 1992; Michael Kelly, "Ideology Seems to Doom Cabinet Contender," *New York Times,* 17 December 1992, 23.

5. "Hillary's Choice On Civil Rights: Back to the Future," *Wall Street Journal,* 7 May 1993. See Patricia J. Williams, "Lani, We Hardly Knew Ye:

How the Right Wing Created a Monster Out of a Civil Rights Advocate and Bill Clinton Ran in Terror," *Village Voice*, 15 June 1993, 27.

6. Williams, "Lani, We Hardly Knew Ye," 28.

7. Saidiya Hartman, "The Territory Between Us: A Report on 'Black Women in the Academy: Defending Our Name: 1894–1994," in *Callaloo, 17*(2):440 (1994).

8. Hartman, "The Territory Between Us," 446.

9. Ibid., 445.

10. Angela Davis, "Black Women and the Academy," *Callaloo, 17(*2):426 (1994).

INDEX

Page numbers in *italics* refer to illustrations.